THE

MOTHER'S BOOK;

EXEMPLIFYING

PESTALOZZI'S PLAN

OF

AWAKENING THE UNDERSTANDING OF CHILDREN
IN LANGUAGE, DRAWING, GEOMETRY,
GEOGRAPHY, AND NUMBERS.

BY P. H. PULLEN.

London:

PRINTED FOR THE AUTHOR;
AND SOLD BY
ALEXANDER BLACK, FOREIGN LIBRARY, 18, PALL-MALL.

1820.

Entered at Stationers' Hall.

LONDON:
PRINTED BY WILLIAM CLOWES,
Northumberland court.

PREFACE.

———

THE education of Youth aims at nothing
less than to produce by a series of intuitive
exercises the cultivation of all the reasoning
faculties and dispositions of children; to
awaken the understanding, fix the attention,
and implant in the soul perfect and correct
ideas of religion, virtue, and happiness :—
these are the most important and principal
objects which are marked out to us by nature
and by the great Creator of the Universe.
Religion and Science must go hand in hand.
Mothers and teachers who have any influence
on the education of youth are bound to exert
themselves to that end, and as early as possible
to lay the foundation on a solid basis in the

mind of children; they should make it the first and chief object of their exertions, and proceed by an intellectual and persuasive mode of reasoning, so that this threefold aim may be attained by them in the surest manner.

The following pages are designed to shew mothers and teachers how to open " THE BOOK OF NATURE" to children, so as to give them power and comprehension: it is not to make the head a magazine of confused and undigested ideas, but to enlighten the understanding, and give to all the senses such clear and demonstrative proofs, that they may learn to contemplate with accuracy, to examine all the objects of nature, and to class, arrange and compare them in their own minds and apply them properly in the search of TRUTH.

The most efficient mode of instruction will always be found that which is produced by INTUITION, and this may be arranged under the following heads :

I. The intuition of the outward senses;

namely, of the sight, hearing, feeling, smelling, and tasting, in all the objects of nature and art or their representations.

II. Of the imagination, in rendering as present, objects that are absent in recollection, narration, and description.

III. Intuitions of the inward sense, by which we perceive within ourselves, the ideas, thoughts, feelings and dispositions of the soul.

IV. Mathematical intuitions, notwithstanding they are internal, have a peculiar distinguished character; by them we view the proportions of *numbers, forms, extents*, which are externally represented by ciphers or figures, and are at the same time so recognised within ourselves, that we immediately acknowledge their truth and incontestable certainty. As for example, nothing can be more certain than that *two* and *two* are equal to four, or that a triangle can have neither more nor less than three sides and three angles.

V. Religious intuitions by which Religion
and Morality are unfolded to the child, particularly his dependance on GOD, his duty to
his Creator and Redeemer, with the essential
principles of Love, Gratitude, and Confidence.
Of these the first buds naturally open and
expand on the lap of the mother—they are
instilled by the close relation of the child to
her, and produce in the juvenile heart a full
conviction of the difference between right and
wrong, good and evil. Hence they are led to
the first emotions of the sense of the *sublime*,
which addresses the soul of the child in a direct
and positive manner, and are the subjects of its
immediate perception; consequently, include
a direct recognizance of that which is sublime
and pleasant, hideous and unpleasant.

To this end in the following introduction
to Language, Drawing, Geometry, Geography,
and Numbers, a few preparatory lessons are
given for the purpose of disclosing to Mothers
and Teachers the plan of teaching children

intuitively, gradually unfolding the united faculties of the mind, and exercising them progressively, so that the preceding is always the foundation of that which immediately succeeds it; and the child is thereby imperceptibly led to the augmentation of all its powers, and perceives its progress in every branch of knowledge, without having experienced the least degree of lassitude or exertion; consequently the child rejoices at its improvement, feels encouraged and stimulated to proceed to a further increase of knowledge, and thus the formation of the faculties, becomes the free self-activity of the mind of the child.

In English Grammar we have selected from the best and most approved writers on that subject clear demonstrations of the several parts of speech; and it was our intention to have represented them by allegorical figures similar to the plan mentioned in "THE BATTLE OF THE ALPHABET" supposed to have been written by the Princess of Hesse Homburg, but at the request of several friends we gave it up. The interrogatories, at the end of each section, will, it is presumed, prove useful.

The Parsing exercises are arranged nearly upon the plan given in Murray's Grammar, and they will be found truly beneficial to such parents and teachers as have not a correct knowledge of their native tongue—which at present is much neglected both in families and schools owing to the desire for foreign languages : this is certainly very injudicious, and parents and teachers will find it of considerable advantage were they to unite such languages as the children may have to learn with that of their own ; as for example, the following exercise in French may be given with the English lesson page 13, and vice versâ :

Qu'est-ce que je tiens dans la main ?

Vous tenez une orange.

Prononcez le mot orange.

En épelant le mot, prononcez chaque lettre, à mesure que je les écrirai sur l'ardoise, et en suite écrivez sur vos ardoises le nom de la chose que je viens de présenter à votre vue.

Quelle est la *forme* de cette orange ?

Elle est ronde.

Ecrivez le mot ronde en prononçant chaque lettre distinctement.

Nous avons à present deux mots écrits sur les ardoises; savoir, " *orange*" et " *ronde*," est-ce que le mot ronde signifie l'orange ?

Non, c'est la forme de l'orange.

Outre la forme de l'orange, pouvez-vous y découvrir autre chose ?

Oui, la couleur.

Quelle est la couleur de l'orange ?

Elle est jaune.

Ecrivez le mot jaune, de la même manière que je vous ai fait écrire le mot orange.

Quand vous dites jaune, est-ce que vous voulez parler de l'orange ?

Non, c'est de la couleur, &c. &c.

Those who may have neglected to cultivate

a knowledge of their mother tongue, may by teaching a class agreeably to the rules given in the following pages, perfect themselves in the English language in a very short period; the frequent repetition of the rules for parsing, which must be done at every step, may probably appear tedious at first, but it will not prove so, and this exercise will supersede the still more difficult plan of learning them by heart, because the constant recurrence of the several rules will give the children as well as the teacher a perfect knowledge of them. As all nouns are of the third person, it would be superfluous to repeat it through all the exercises; it has therefore been generally omitted, neither has the gender of nouns been mentioned except in particular cases, questions for that purpose should be proposed to the pupils.

The rules for composition given in the last section will it is hoped prove advantageous, the children should be repeatedly questioned until they perfectly comprehend them. In exercises on composition the parent or teacher must render their pupils every assistance, and by a series of interrogatories develop such ideas or trains of ideas as they may wish to become the object of inquiry, and thus lead them on step by step from simple narrative or stories, themes, orations, &c., to the most sublime and elevated subjects. Here, as in every other exercise, it may be essential to caution parents and teachers from expecting too much to be done at once ; never hurry them, let every proposed subject be perfectly understood, revise and re-revise until precision and accuracy are acquired, or until they can

> " give to airy nothing
> A local habitation and a name."

We have to acknowledge our obligation to many writers on similar subjects, from whom we have made such selections or taken such extracts as suited our purpose: and we are fully persuaded that they as well as ourselves

will derive great pleasure in having con-
tributed to a work designed to give children
and adults a perfect knowledge of their native
tongue.

London, August 30, 1820.

Mr. Pullen *gives private Lessons to Ladies and*
Gentlemen on Pestalozzi's plan in Mental Cal-
culations, Geometry, Geography, Drawing, En-
glish, Grammar, Writing, &c. &c. &c.

ENGLISH GRAMMAR AND PARSING.

PART I.

AN ADDRESS TO MOTHERS AND TEACHERS.

---

§ 1. OF LANGUAGE.

IN an age of refinement and taste, when the British Empire teems with books on Education, it may be considered presumptuous to add one more to the catalogue; nor would I do so were I not confident that the utility of PESLALOZZI's plan will silence every objection, and prompt mothers and teachers to adopt his system

OF INTELLECTUAL INSTRUCTION.

Children, naturally curious and observing, wish to see, to know, and to analyze every thing. We ought then as much as possible to assist this spirit of observation, to awaken the dormant faculties, and to bring all their sensitive and intellectual powers into action, the development of which is the chief object of education.

Mothers cannot begin to instruct their children at too early an age; and I earnestly recommend them to have the children seated at a black painted table, or a table inlaid with slate; with a large slate, or board painted black, placed immediately opposite the children, on which they should communicate the

B

first principles of grammar beginning with the alphabet, distinguishing the vowels from the consonants by writing the former with a *red crayon* and the latter with *chalk*. The children must be taught the correct sound of each letter, and be accustomed to pronounce them distinctly altogether as one voice, proceeding letter by letter; and write them on their slates with red crayons or French chalk, agreeably to their copy; nor should they be permitted to leave any letter until they can pronounce it according to the following table :

Roman.	Italic.	Old English.	Name.
A a	*A a*	𝕬 𝖆	a
B b	*B b*	𝕭 𝖇	bee
C c	*C c*	𝕮 𝖈	see
D d	*D d*	𝕯 𝖉	dee
E e	*E e*	𝕰 𝖊	e
F f	*F f*	𝕱 𝖋	ef
G g	*G g*	𝕲 𝖌	jee
H h	*H h*	𝕳 𝖍	aitch
I i	*I i*	𝕴 𝖎	i *or* eye
J j	*J j*	𝕵 𝖏	ja
K k	*K k*	𝕶 𝖐	kay
L l	*L l*	𝕷 𝖑	el
M m	*M m*	𝕸 𝖒	em
N n	*N n*	𝕹 𝖓	en
O o	*O o*	𝕺 𝖔	o
P p	*P p*	𝕻 𝖕	pee
Q q	*Q q*	𝕼 𝖖	kue
R r	*R r*	𝕽 𝖗	ar
S s	*S s*	𝕾 𝖘	ess
T t	*T t*	𝕿 𝖙	tee
U u	*U u*	𝖀 𝖚	u *or* you
V v	*V v*	𝖁 𝖇	vee
W w	*W w*	𝖂 𝖜	double u
X x	*X x*	𝖃 𝖝	eks
Y y	*Y y*	𝖄 𝖞	wy
Z z	*Z z*	𝖅 𝖟	zed

In considering the sounds of these first principles of language, we find that some are so simple and unmixed, that there is nothing required but the opening of the mouth to make them understood, and to form different sounds; whence they have the names of VOWELS, from *vox*, a voice, or vocal sound. On the contrary, we find that there are others, whose pronunciation depends on the particular application and use of every part of the mouth, as the teeth, the lips, the tongue, the palate, &c., which yet cannot make one perfect sound but by their union with the vowels or vocal sounds; and these are called CONSONANTS, from *consono*, to sound together, *i. e.,* letters sounding with other letters.

Vowels are generally said to be five in number; namely, *a, e, i, o, u;*—*y* and *w* are called vowels when they end a syllable or word, and consonants when they begin one.

Each of the vowels has at least three distinct sounds; the *narrow* or *slender*, the *middle* or *intermediate*, and the *broad* or *full;* as in the following table:

	Narrow	*middle*	*broad*
A,	glass	far	wall
E,	men	her	them
I,	fin	bird	bind
O,	not	ton	tom
U,	dull	use	us
Y,	bully	physic	by

Two vowels forming but one syllable are generally called a diphthong; and three a triphthong; a few of which are given in the following table:

DIPHTHONGS.

aa	Isaac	*ia*	poniard
ae	Cæsar	*ie*	friend
ai	praise	*oa*	coat

ao	gaol	*oe*	potatoe
au	taught	*oi*	voice
aw	law	*oo*	moon
ay	say	*ou*	found
ea	clean	*ow*	now
ee	reed	*oy*	decoy
ei	vein	*ua*	guard
eo	people	*ue*	pursue
eu	feud	*ui*	guide
ew	jewel	*uy*	buy
ey	they		

TRIPHTHONGS.

eau	beau	*oeu*	manœuvre
eye	eye	*uai*	quaint
ieu	lieu	*uea*	queasy
iew	view	*uee*	queen

The consonants are divisible into *mutes, semi-vowels,* and *liquids.*

The mutes are such as emit no sound without a vowel, as, *b, p, t, d, k,* and *c* and *g* hard.

The semi-vowels are such as emit a sound without the concurrence of a vowel, as, *f, v, s, z, x,* g soft or *j.*

The liquids are such as flow into, or unite easily with, the mutes, as, *l, m, n, r.*

But, besides these, there is another classification of the consonants, of great importance to a just idea of the nature of the letters; and that is, into such as are *sharp* or *flat,* and *simple* or *aspirated.*

The *sharp* consonants are, *p, f, t, s, k, c,* hard.

The *flat* consonants are, *b, v, d, z, g,* hard.

The *simple* consonants are those which have always the sound of one letter unmixed with others, as, *b, p, f, v, k, g* hard, and *g* soft, or *j.*

The *mixed* or *aspirated* consonants are those which have sometimes a hiss or aspiration joined with them, which mingles with the letter, and alters its sound, as, *t* in mo*t*ion, *d* in sol*d*ier, *s* in mi*ss*ion, and *z* in a*z*ure.

There is another distinction of consonants, arising either from the seat of their formation, or from those organs which are chiefly employed in forming them. The best distinction of this kind seems to be that which divides them into *labials, dentals, gutturals*, and *nasals*.

The labials are *b, p, f, v*. The dentals are *t, d, s, z*, and soft *g*, or *j*. The gutturals are *k, q, c* hard, and *g* hard. The nasals are *m, n*, and *ng*.

As soon as children have acquired a perfect knowledge of the alphabet, the mother or teacher should make the external parts of the body the first objects of observation, and class them under the grand divisions of *head, trunk*, and *limbs*.

Beginning with the *head*, each child should be called upon to name a particular part of the head, which must be written on the large slate, and by the children on their table or slates; and when the parts of the head have been named, proceed in a similar manner with those of the *body* and *limbs*.

The exercise should then be varied, and children led by simple questions to declare the situation of the several parts of the head, &c. as for example:— " Where is your mouth situated?"—" Above my chin, between my cheeks, and below my nose." When questions of this kind have been answered relative to all the parts of the head, they may be varied in the following manner:—" In what part of your body is your mouth?"—" In my head." " Why?"—Because my mouth is a part of my face, and my face is a part of my head."

They may then be called upon to name all the

parts of their head that are two-fold, such as two eyes, two ears, two lips, &c.

Next the properties or the qualities of these parts should be named; as for example, of the lips, they are red, moveable, elastic, soft, smooth, &c.

In the first commencement with words, the children should be led, by simple questions, to explain all the letters of which each word is composed; as for example, in the word *face*; " How many vowels are there in the word *face?*—" Two." " What are they?"—*A* is the first and *e* the second." " What consonant precedes the vowel *a?*"—"*f.*" " What consonant follows it?"—" *c.*" What is the situation of the vowel *e?*"—" It follows the consonant *c.*"

To what class of consonants does the letter *f* belong?—" *F* is a semi-vowel." " How is the consonant *c* classed?—" *C* is a mute, as well as a sharp, consonant."

In this manner examine the children in every word they spell, until they have a perfect knowledge of all the letters used in the English language.

As soon as the children have been fully exercised in the functions of the several parts of the body, the parent or teacher should ask them simple questions relative to such familiar objects as they may be acquainted with, and which ought at all times to be presented to their notice; and the NAME of every thing thus brought to their view must be written on the large slate or board, and then by the children on their table; but if a table, as before directed, cannot be readily procured, each child may have a small slate placed before him.

By this mode of proceeding, the *eyes* and the *hands* of the children are fixed and occupied. The mother or teacher must always pronounce the name of the *thing*, of which the *word* traced on the slate is the *sign;* and the children invariably repeat the sound of the word altogether as one voice, before they write it on their table or slates.

Here they exercise at the same time, independently of the *eye* and *hand,* the sense of *hearing,* the organ of the *voice,* and above all, the *force of attention,* which it is so important to create and cultivate in children.

This mode of conveying instruction unites the advantages of occupying and exercising *four* organs at the same time.

I. The *eye* being fixed on the large slate or painted board, observes and retains the forms of the letters, ciphers, or other signs of the science which is the object of study.

II. The *ear* gathers and retains the sounds resulting from the pronunciation of the characters, or expression of the written word.

III. The *mouth* repeats the sounds which the ear has caught.

IV. The *hand* traces the forms of alphabetical characters, ciphers, and other sounds which the eye has distinguished.

This mode of instruction satisfies four conditions, so essential to the complete success of education.

I. Of *instruction given by the senses,* or intuitive.

II. Of *instruction active and animated,* or practical.

III. Of *mutual instruction.*

IV. Of *instruction common* to *all the children* of the same family circle, or class.

At the commencement of this exercise, the children should be directed to name every thing they can eat and drink; all the articles of their dress; the games at which they can play, and all the playthings they make use of; every thing they can see in the streets, in the garden, in the fields, and on the water; such articles of furniture as they are acquainted with; every part of the house; all the implements used in the garden, &c.

After they have named one article, the mother or teacher must pronounce it correctly, and make the children do the same; then write it on the large slate or board, and direct them to write it on their table or small slates.

The FIVE SENSES should be the next inquiry, and as soon as they have discovered them by developing questions, similar to the following,

How do you know the large slate is there?

Yes, you *see* it; then SEEING is one of the senses.

But supposing it was quite dark, how would you know it was there?

True, by *feeling* it; FEELING then is another sense; and so on with the sense of HEARING, SMELLING, and TASTING.

We should direct each child to name an article that he can discover by *seeing;* let such things as can be produced be shewn to the children; the name properly pronounced, as before directed, and written on the large slate or board; and when they have written the word on their table or slates, let another article be given, until they have named every thing they can discover by the sense of seeing. Proceed in a similar manner with all the articles they can discover by the senses of *feeling, hearing, smelling,* and *tasting.*

The works of the CREATION may next be introduced, under the following heads, *animal, vegetable, fossil,* and *fluid.*

Here the children should be informed, that every thing which breathes and moves, from the smallest insect to the elephant, is an ANINAL SUBSTANCE; and present them with an assortment of animals in miniature, which may easily be procured at a toy shop, in what is called a " *Noah's Ark,*" and arrange them properly in pairs, so as to shew the children how they are divided into classes; such as *men, beasts* and *cattle, birds, insects* and *reptiles, fishes,* and *amphibious animals.*

The names of all the animals in each class should be pronounced to, and repeated by the children; then written on the large slate, and on the table or small slates.

When they have been well instructed in the names, &c., of all the animal substances; then tell them that every thing which grows in the earth, from a blade of grass to the loftiest tree, is called a VEGETABLE SUBSTANCE. Here also such a variety of specimens should be produced, as may be sufficient to prove to their understanding, the classification of vegetables in the following order:—I. TREES, under the names of *forest trees, fruit trees, shrubs,* and *brambles.* II. HERBS, under the heads of *garden vegetables, garden flowers, weeds, grasses, grain, moss,* and *funguses.*

Then explain to them and write the names of all the forest trees, fruit trees, shrubs, and brambles; also those of the vegetables, flowers, weeds, grasses, grain, &c.

Next inform them that every thing which is dug out of the earth is called a FOSSIL or MINERAL SUBSTANCE, and are generally classed under the following heads: *metals, crystals, stones, earths, sands,* and *salts;* to this class mineralogists also add *petrifactions.* Here a few specimens of each class should be produced, and the names of every article written on the large slate, and by the children on their slates, until they are well acquainted with this exercise.

The mother or teacher will afterwards instruc them in the nature of FLUID SUBSTANCES, by informing them that liquids of every description belong to this class:—A few specimens of animal, vegetable, and fossil fluids should be introduced and the names explained and written, as before directed*.

When the children have acquired a clear and comprehensive knowledge of all the SUBSTANCES in the animal, vegetable, fossil, and fluid *kingdoms*, they must be led to the discovery of every part of their dress, and describe the SUBSTANCE from whence they were made. The same with all the furniture they have seen; also their play-things; every thing they can eat, drink, &c.

To awaken the attention and exercise the thinking faculties of children, an inquiry should be made into all the trades with which they are acquainted, and the substances used by each, also of the tools employed, and the substances of which they are composed; as for example,

Who makes bread?

From what does the baker make it?

What does the flour come from?

From whence do we get the wheat?

What substance then is wheat?

True it is a vegetable substance, but why is wheat a vegetable substance?

Right, it grew or vegetated in the earth, and therefore it is a vegetable substance.

Proceed in a similar manner with other trades.

---

* The following verses may be committed to memory by the children, to assist them in the discovery of substances.

> In earth the VEGETABLES grow,
>   Fast rooted in the soil;
> And MINERALS lie deep below,
>   Dug thence with care and toil.
>
> But ANIMALS have power and motion,
>   For life to them is given;
> On earth, or in the air, or ocean,
>   Each kind's preserved by Heaven.

It will now be proper to direct the children to keep a daily account of all their exercises; and to make a vocabulary of the *words* they have discovered as the *sign* or representative of *things:* and then call upon them to write a given number of the articles that are made chiefly of animal substances; and, in every exercise of this kind, direct them to begin alphabetically.

They may next be directed to write all the articles they are acquainted with that are made chiefly of vegetable substances, also of fossil and fluid substances, with the names of the tradesmen by whom they are made.

Then combine the substances, and call upon them to name such things as are made of animal and vegetable substances; animal and fossil substances; and lastly, unite all the substances. Exercises of this kind should never exceed half an hour.

It will be essential to inform the children, that every SUBSTANCE which they have named is called in grammar, a NOUN SUBSTANTIVE; that the word NOUN is taken from the Latin word *nomen,* which signifies the NAME of the thing; and the word SUBSTANTIVE denotes the substance; as for example, a *boy* is a noun substantive; the *noun* or *name* is BOY, but the *substance* or *substantive* is ANIMAL.

Now produce them a *quill,* or any other substance, and question them in the following manner.

What is that?

It is a quill.

What do you call it in grammar?

It is a noun substantive.

What is the name or noun?

The noun or name is quill.

What is the substantive or substance?

The substantive or substance is animal

Why is it an animal substance?

Because it was taken from an animal

What is the name of the animal from which the quill was taken?

It was taken from a goose.

Then take a pen.

What do I hold in my hand?

You hold a pen in your hand.

What was it before it was formed into a pen?

It was a quill.

Recollect that a quill, as taken from a goose, is called a *natural substance*, or *natural product;* but a pen, having been cut and made of a quill, is called an *artificial substance,* or *artificial product.* Tell me then the difference between a *quill* and a *pen?*

Developing questions should be proposed, until the children have discovered that the *quill* is a *thing,* and not a *person;* also that every *thing* has a *name,* a sign, a mark, a mode of being, that it is a reality, that it has an existence, an extended, passive, visible substance, that it has a part, a member, a half, &c. Also that things have their cause, nature, beginning, end, order, time, number, place, space; that every thing has a body, and every body has form, figure, &c.

The parent or teacher may now exercise the understanding of the children, and call upon them to name a given number of *natural objects* in each kingdom; also some *artificial objects,* which should be written by the children on their slates.

They should then be led to the parts of natural and artificial objects, by familiar questions.

The names of all the parts of speech used in the English grammar should be the next exercise; for this purpose, a few questions may be proposed by the parent or teacher.

The most simple that can be asked are those arising from the functions of eating; the answers to the question " What do you eat?" will be sub-

STANTIVES; as, *bread, meat, fruit,* &c. The question "What sort of bread do you eat?" produces ADJECTIVES; as, *brown, white,* &c. The questions, *how, where, when,* &c. give ADVERBS, PREPOSITIONS, and CONJUNCTIONS, in the answers, "I eat *out of* a basin *with* a spoon," "I eat *quickly, slowly, much, little, here, there, now, then,*" &c. And the action of eating is a VERB.

In this manner all the parts of speech may be rendered perfectly familiar and distinguishable by their attributes and position with respect to each other, during these exercises; and their *names**, forms, terminations,* rules of agreement, *&c.* afterwards discovered by experience, and added.

As soon as the children have been exercised in the preceding manner, the following mode of questioning the class may be adopted; first, presenting an orange to their view, say,

What do I hold in my hand?

You hold an orange in your hand.

Pronounce the name, write it on the large slate, and direct the children to write it on theirs.

What is the shape or *form* of this orange?

It is round.

Write that word on the slates.

We have now two words written; namely, "*orange*" and "*round.*" Does the word round signify the orange?

---

* 1 Nouns—see part II. section 2.
  2 Articles—see part II. section 3.
  3 Adjectives—see part II. section 4.
  4 Pronouns—see part II. section 5.
  5 Verbs—see part II. section 6.
  6 Adverbs—see part II. section 7.
  7 Prepositions—see part II. section 8.
  8 Conjunctions—see part II. section 9.
  9 Interjections—see part II. section 10.
  10 Participles—see part II. section 6.

No, it is the form of the orange.

Can you discover any thing about the orange besides the form of it?

Yes, the colour.

What is the colour of the orange?

It is yellow.   Write that word also*.

Apply the same remark with regard to the *colour*, as to the *form* of the orange.

Then, by developing questions, inquire to how many of the senses the orange is perceptible. And let some other object be presented to them; for instance, a book.

What do I hold in my hand?

You hold a book in your hand.

Where shall I write the word book, under orange, round, or yellow?

Under the word orange.

Why?

Because it is the name of it.

How will you describe the shape of this book?

It is oblong.

Where shall I write the word oblong?

Under the word round.

Why?

Because it declares the form of the book, as round does that of the orange.

Can you point out any other quality belonging to the book?

Yes, it is green.

Where shall I write the word green?

Under yellow.

Why?

Because the word green describes the colour†.

---

* *Orange.   Round.   Yellow.*
† These words will stand thus on the slates,

| ORANGE. | ROUND. | YELLOW. |
| BOOK. | OBLONG. | GREEN. |

Proceed in this manner with a few other articles; question them about the name, form, and colour of each as before, and write them on the slates; then question them with regard to the parts of speech to which each word belongs.

Is the orange an animal, vegetable, or fossil substance?

Why is it a vegetable?

Is it a natural or an artificial product?

Why is it a natural product?

What substance did you say the orange was?

If a vegetable substance, what part of speech is it?

You are right, it is a noun substantive.

What is the noun or name?

And what is the substance or substantive?

We have two words written in a line with that of orange, namely, *round* and *yellow*; do these represent the orange?

No; the word *round* describes the form, and *yellow* the colour of the orange.

Do you consider these words as belonging to the noun substantive orange?

Most assuredly.

One of them, you say, describes the *form*, and the other the *colour* of the orange; these words are therefore qualities belonging to that noun, and are called ADJECTIVES. Tell me then for what purpose adjectives are used?

In a similar manner lead them on to explain all the words written on the slate. Then take the *orange*, and give it to one of the children, saying,

" I GIVE YOU THE ORANGE."

Write the sentence on the large slate, and direct the children to write it on theirs. And, by questions, enable them to discover the several parts of speech used in the sentence.

To whom did I give the orange?

You gave it to Mary.

Then, pointing to the pronoun " 1," ask them if they know what it means? Is it a person or a thing? Does it represent the person who gave, or the person who received the orange? Is a person a noun substantive? What kind of substanee is a person?

You are right, a person is an animal substance; then "I" is used as the sign or representative of a person, instead of a NOUN. In grammar this is called a PRONOUN; *pro* signifies *for*, therefore the word *pronoun* and *for a noun* have both the same meaning. What part of speech then is I?

Does the word " YOU" mean a person or a thing?

Does it mean the person to whom the orange was given?

What part of speech is YOU?

Right, it is a pronoun.

Now, as "I" gave and "YOU" received the orange, must I give before you can receive?

Then, which of the two was first employed?

Yes, I was the first; then which is the first personal pronoun, *I* or *you*?

True *I* is a personal pronoun, and the sign of the first person. What person is *you*?

Yes, you is a personal pronoun, and the sign of the second person.

Give me the orange again. Now, can I give you, or you give me the orange, without moving some part of the body?

You are right. Recollect the *word* expressing any action performed, and every thing that can be done, is called a VERB.

In giving the orange, was any action performed by the person who gave, or the person who received it?

What part of speech is the word give?

You informed me that the arm was put in motion, and an action performed, both in giving and receiving the orange; therefore " GIVE" is an *active verb*.

Can you inform me to what part of speech the word " THE" belongs?

To what does it refer?

Does it qualify the noun orange?

Then it cannot be an adjective. Does it describe an action?

Then you are certain it is not a verb.

Does it represent a person or thing?

You see the word " THE" is neither a *noun*, an *adjective*, *pronoun*, nor *verb*. Did I give Mary the orange or the book?

Does the word " THE" refer to the orange or the book?

Yes, to the orange the *article* given to Mary; then " THE" is the particular article to the noun orange.

There are only two articles in the English language, namely, *the general article A*, and *particular article THE:* when the article *a* is used before a word beginning with a vowel, as orange, we add *n* after the *a*, and say *an* orange.

What part of speech is the word THE?

Right, it is a particular article, because it specifies a particular thing.

What part of speech is orange?

This mode of etymological parsing should be entered on the large slate, and copied by the children on their slates, thus,

I—a personal pronoun, the sign of the first person singular.

Give—a verb active

You—a personal pronoun, the sign of the second person singular.

The—the particular article

Orange—a noun substantive.

Now direct Mary to put the orange on the table, and write the sentence thus,

" PUT THE ORANGE UPON THE TABLE."

Here make the children explain every word as before, and by developing questions lead them to discover what the preposition UPON is used for; you may therefore question them in the following manner:

Would it be proper to say *" put the orange table?"*

Does it not require another word to make the sentence complete?

Are you acquainted with any part of speech used for this purpose?

Right, to connect nouns and parts of sentences together, we use PREPOSITIONS.

What part of speech is the word " UPON?"

After the preceding sentences are perfectly comprehended by the children, and the etymological parsing entered on their slates, give them any other sentence, and introduce a conjunction and an adverb, as,

" JANE AND CHARLES HAVE WRITTEN THEIR EXERCISES VERY WELL."

Here lead the children to inquire, by developing questions, what the word " AND" does; whether it connects Jane *and* Charles together, until they discover it to be a CONJUNCTION.

Every word in this sentence must be etymologically parsed, and written as before directed.

In explaining the verb " *have written,*" interrogatories must be used until they discover, by the questions, that the action of writing has been performed; and, consequently, " *have written*," is a verb.

The pronoun " *their*," will require a few questions; as, who or what do you mean by the word *their?* Do you know Jane and Charles? If Jane and Charles were to stand out by themselves, and I were to point to them, and say, " *They have written their exercise very well*," to whom would the word " *they*" allude? Do the words " *they*" and " *their*" mean the same persons? What part of speech is the word " *their?*"

THEIR is a possessive pronoun; and " EXERCISES" is a noun.

In leading them to discover the meaning and use of " VERY WELL," questions like the following may be asked.

What does an adjective do?

For what purpose are adjectives employed?

As adjectives qualify nouns, so adverbs are sometimes used to qualify verbs; and these are readily discovered by asking the questions " *how*" or " *what;*" as, how have Jane and Charles written?

Do the words " *very well*" qualify Jane and Charles?—or exercises?—or have written? Do they declare how they have written? Then what do the words " *very well*" qualify?

Right, they qualify the verb " *have written*." What is " *very well*" called in grammar?

Another sentence may be given when the last has been completely parsed, and perfectly understood, containing a PARTICIPLE and an INTERJECTION.

AH! I SEE SUSAN TAKES PLEASURE IN TEACHING HER BROTHER JAMES.

Developing questions must be introduced, enabling the children to discover that the word *Ah!* might have been omitted without altering the sense and prove to them, that words of this kind are a sudden exclamation of the speaker, expressive of joy, anger, grief, approbation, &c., and are called in grammar INTERJECTIONS.

In a similar manner, lead them to see the nature of the PARTICIPLE " *teaching;*" and, by familiar questions, enable them to discover how it is derived from the verb " *to teach.*"

Proceed thus with the children until they are well acquainted with etymological parsing.

They may now be amused with the classification of colours; and a box containing pieces of stained glass of a circular form, about two inches diameter, should be produced. Colours that form the most striking contrast are generally selected at first by children, but their attention may easily be awakened to a chaste gradation of colours; and a few exercises will enable them to compare, sort, and judge, even those that do not suit well together. The powers of observation should be carefully directed to this purpose. The above exercise, however, will ultimately prove more essential to them in drawing than in language.

As soon as they have acquired a general knowledge of colours, and are well acquainted with the name of each, direct them to write such natural or artificial products as they can think of, and qualify each noun-substantive with the adjective that describes the colour of the noun. Together with such substances as are round, square, oval, hollow, solid, triangular*, &c.

---

* NOTE.—A similar plan for teaching French, Latin, Italian, &c., should be pursued; refraining on all occasions from explaining the meaning of any part of speech, word or thing; but, by a variety of simple questions, enable the children to discover it themselves.

§ 2. OF DRAWING.

As soon as children are capable of taking a pencil in their hands, they appear desirous of drawing lines or figures; we are therefore assured that the exercise of drawing will be cheerfully embraced by every child. Consequently it behoves parents and teachers to cultivate this instructive and amusing science to the utmost of their power.

The art of drawing is not exclusively designed for instructing painters, but as a general introduction to the polite arts, it has, in conjunction with the mathematics, received an important place in the field of education, as a means to cultivate the whole of man, and to bring all his intellectual powers into action.

The fingers must be rendered very pliable, and accustomed to hold the crayon or pencil perfectly free; the more light and easy the crayon is held, the greater will be the command and execution.

The HAND having been properly taught how to handle the pencil in drawing, the next exercise is that of the EYE; which must be attentively led to examine, not only the most minute, but also the most sublime objects in nature. This is a very essential exercise, and must be done at an early age; that they may be enabled to judge and determine the size and relative proportion of every object, from the loftiest mountain to the minutest particle. They should therefore frequently be directed to measure distances, so as to give them a correct idea of height and distance, and compare one with another.

If we attentively mark the actions of children in a state of nature, we shall invariably find them anxious to imitate the various forms of nature, and shew a predilection for certain objects. Many preceptors are of opinion that this ought to be considered as a primitive basis for drawing; which, on the one hand, may be true, but, on the other, a false principle. Drawing natural objects has its school, as the primitive of the family circle; the first exercises, therefore, can be practised at a very early period, by making the children imitate all the objects that present themselves to their view within the sphere in which they move.

As there exists a pure development in numbers as well as in the elementary forms of geometry, so is there also in the forms of drawing; which appears hitherto to have been neglected by many teachers.

In drawing exercises, the reasoning faculties of children should be strengthened until they are capable of reproducing all the different objects with which they are acquainted.

The first exercises in drawing must be of the most simple form, namely, lines in all the variety possible, long lines, short lines, thick lines, thin lines, &c., quickly and slowly, until they draw them firmly and ably. They must not be confined too long at straight lines, let them draw regular and irregular, curved or crooked lines, so as to avoid monotony: they must have liberty, as well as adroitness.

Whatever the exercise may be, the mother or teacher must first draw the line on the large slate or black board; and while drawing the line, they should declare what kind of line they are drawing; thus, if drawing a horizontal line, they should say, " *I am drawing a horizontal line from the left to the right;*" and when the line is drawn, say, " *I have drawn a horizontal line from left to right.*" All the children in the class should repeat the same words. No line whatever should be drawn without a similar declaration.

Horizontal lines must also be drawn from right to left. Slanting lines may be drawn downwards to the right, or to the left; also upwards to the right, or to the left. Upright lines are drawn either upwards or downwards.

Curved lines are drawn as a regular exercise, at first towards the right or left, bending upwards or downwards; also drawn upwards or downwards, and bending to the right or to the left.

By a curved line is meant the fourth part of a circle.

This exercise, as well as the former and subsequent lessons, must not be passed over until the children can draw any line from dictation with accuracy and precision.

These lines are now to be applied to figures, *natural objects,* such as windows, doors, tombs, monuments, houses, &c., which the mother or teacher will first draw on the large slate or board, declaring the name of each line, until the children are well acquainted with lines of every description.

With the exercise of drawing, children should be accustomed to geometrical exercises every day, so as to make them acquainted with the application of lines in the formation of angles, triangles, squares, parallelograms, &c., and employ them as drawing exercises, by giving certain lines to form figures, containing a given number of right, acute, or obtuse angles, triangles, squares, &c., to keep the imagination on the stretch, and to improve the taste of children in ornamental designs, as urns, vases, monuments, &c.

After straight lines have been applied to various figures, and the taste of the children displayed in the execution, curved lines should be introduced in the most simple yet pleasing variety, by drawing parts of the face, as the eye, mouth, nose—the head, ear, &c., in various positions.

Lastly, the arm, hand, leg, foot, &c,. may be given. Also natural objects, such as geometrical solids, trees, leaves, fruits, flowers, birds, beasts, insects, &c.; and then let them copy from the works of the most approved masters.

§ 3. OF GEOMETRY.

The first geometrical exercise should consist of horizontal lines. Make two points on the large slate or board, and draw a horizontal line from one point to the other, directing the children to do the same; then inform them that the beginning and ending of every line is a point. Now let them see what you can do with a line; namely, *" that you can draw a horizontal line between two points from right to left, or from left to right—that you can lengthen the line at one, or at both ends;"* and shew them how to do it; *that you can shorten it at one, or at both ends,"* and rub out a part of the line at each end. Next inform them, *" that you can divide the line into any number of parts,"* and shew them how to do it: and, lastly, *that you can rub the line out,* and do so. Then inquire what they can do with a line; and let them all declare what they can do with a horizontal, upright, inclined, or slanting line, and make them prove the truth of it on their slates, until they perfectly comprehend what can be done with a line.

Draw on the large slate two short horizontal lines, one after the other, about an inch asunder, and ask the children whether these lines can be joined together so as to represent one line; then prove it can be done, and lead them to discover that lines of this kind are called *" lines in the same direction,"* because either of them can be lengthened so as to form but one line.

Then draw two horizontal lines of equal length, one above another, and preserve a uniform distance between them. Here also questions must be asked, until the children are led to see that these lines are equally distant from each other; and, though produced or lengthened at the greatest possible extent, can never meet, and are called PARALLEL LINES.

Draw also two lines that are not parallel, one horizontal, and one slanting, in such a manner that when produced or lengthened, they will either touch or pass through each other, and question them until they are satisfied that these *lines are not parallel.*

From these exercises a useful combination of lines may be produced, by directing the children to draw on their slates a given number, agreeable to the preceding form, namely, lines in the same direction, parallel, and not parallel to each other, in the greatest possible variety. For example, give them five lines, and draw them on the large slate in four directions.

I. Draw three lines parallel, one not parallel, and one line in the same direction with the parallel lines.

II. Two lines parallel, two not parallel, and one in the same direction with the line that is not parallel.

III. Two lines parallel, two not parallel, and one in the same direction with the line that is not parallel.

IV. Two lines parallel, two not parallel, and one in the same direction with the parallel line.

Extend this exercise to 6, 7, 8, 9, or 10 lines, and have each number drawn and described as above, by the children on their slates, but not to give them a copy; yet if they cannot carry on the series, question them as to such as may be omitted.

The next step should be the re-union and intersection of a given number of lines from the least to the greatest number of points of re-union and intersection, also the least to the greatest number of ends of lines not united.

When two lines meet in one point, the one horizontal and the other upright, they form a *right angle*. When a line is added to a right line, or two inclined or slanting lines meet and form an angle less than a right angle, it is called *an acute angle ;* but if larger than a right angle, they form *an obtuse angle.*

When a horizontal line has an upright line passing through it, they form *four right angles ;* but when a slanting line passes through an upright or a horizontal line, they form *two acute* and two *obtuse angles.*

Four angles produced by the intersection of two lines, contain 360 degrees. If they are right angles, each will contain 90 degrees. An acute angle contains less, and an obtuse angle more than 90 degrees.

Here an interesting exercise for cultivating the reasoning powers of children may be introduced, by directing them, with a given number of lines, to form from the least to the greatest number of points of re-union and intersection. In exercises of this kind, one or two figures should be drawn on the large slate, and copied by the children; then by interrogation, lead them to discover the rest.

When figures of this kind are drawn, the children must not only declare the number of points and ends of lines, but the interior and exterior angles in each figure must be mentioned, describing them as right, acute, or obtuse angles.

From the re-union of lines, we pass on to geometrical figures or regular bodies; namely, the triangles, square or quadrilateral, parallelogram, pentagon, hexagon, heptagon, octagon, nonagon, decagon, and duodecagon.

When drawn on the large slate, and copied by the children, the angles in each figure should be numbered and described, the whole of which will be interior angles.

Then draw a quadrilateral, pentagon, and hexagon, with one exterior angle; a hexagon and a pentagon, with two exterior angles in each figure; heptagons, with one, two, three, exterior angles; octagons, with one, two, three, four, five, exterior angles, &c.

Now lead them on to the nature and application of lines in the formation of geometrical figures, and shew the relation which one line bears to another, as well as the effect produced by the intersection or combination of lines in the figure itself.

A box of geometrical solids may now be presented to the children, and the nature of each figure fully explained; and, by questions, lead them to discover the difference between superficial and solid geometry, as well as the method of measuring plane and solid figures.

§ 4. OF GEOGRAPHY.

WHEN children enter on the science of geography, the *natural* divisions of the earth only should be attended to.

If an elevated situation should be near the scene of instruction, the children may be taken to the summit of the hill or mountain, and from thence view the surrounding country.

In the first instance, it will be essential to give them an idea of *north, east, south,* and *west;* and, for this purpose, let them face the north; then inform them that the east is on their right, the west on their left, and the south immediately behind them; and assist them in taking an attentive survey of the surrounding country, progressively pointing out the elevation of hills or mountains, and by questions lead them to declare whether they are conical, spherical, or pyramidical; whether adjacent or at a distance from each other; whether the base be of great extent, and the sides gradually or abruptly inclined; and whether the pinnacles or summits of the mountains resemble towers, spiral points, round points, &c.

Then the form of the plains should be described, whether they are perfectly even, or in waves, and if the waves are parallel or oblique. Also the appropriate terms of the valleys and defiles, both as to their form and relative situation to the hills and mountains, by which they are formed. Then all the water which can be seen from the selected spot should be taken notice of, agreeable to its extent, &c.

While the relative situation of all the visible objects are under consideration, it will be essential to point out and illustrate the geographical definitions or denominations of LAND; as, *continents, islands, peninsulas, isthmuses, capes, promontories, shores, coasts,* &c.: also of WATER; as, *oceans, seas, straits, gulfs, bays, harbours, creeks, lakes, rivers, streams, springs,* &c.

They should next be taught to form a notion of distance, by measuring, in the field, feet, yards, fathoms, miles, and leagues; so as to extend their ideas to the relative proportion of these denominations: square and solid measure should be considered in a similar manner, and made perfectly familiar to their comprehension. Then direct them to consider the objects previously noticed from their chosen station, in association with these measurements.

From the above observations, the pupils may easily be led to perceive that all the elevations are so trifling, compared to the extent, that a plain surface may be used as a representation of the country with sufficient accuracy, and more convenience, than by delineating hills or mountains in the map.

The children should now be required to name the bearings of such particular objects as have been pointed out to them, whether north, east, south, or west; and how they are situated with regard to water, &c.

If no elevated spot be near, a map and a globe must be used; and then question them in the following manner:

Can you inform me whether the earth is round or square?

Did you ever hear that it was round, similar to that globe?

Have you ever seen an eclipse of the moon?

Do you know what it is that darkens the light of the moon?

Is the moon round?

Is the sun round?

Will a square produce a round shadow?

Does an eclipse of the moon present to your view a round or a strait shadow?

If an object presents a circular shadow, what shape will that object be?

Tell me then what is the form of the earth?

Did you ever see the sun rise?

Where does it rise?

And where does it set?

What is the middle point between its rising and setting, or between the east and the west?

Do you know when the sun is at the highest point?

At what hour of the day is your shadow the shortest?

Can you tell by the sun when it is twelve o'clock? At what hour then is the sun highest?

What point is the sun in when at the highest?

How often in the day is the sun at the highest, or
n the south?

Can you inform me whether the sun moves round
the earth, or the earth round the sun?

Which do you conceive to be the largest, the
sun or the earth?

It may be necessary to inform you that the diameter of the sun is about 1,000 times larger than
that of the earth. Now draw a horizontal line on
your slate as long as it will admit of; divide that
line by nine points into ten equal parts; take the
first tenth of that line, and divide it by nine points
into ten equal parts; now take one tenth of that
division, and divide it by nine points into ten equal
parts, and one of these tenths will bear the same
proportion to the whole line, as the diameter of the
earth bears to the diameter of the sun. Tell me
which you suppose most rational, that the greater
body should move round the less, or the less round
the greater?

Did you ever see a top spinning?

While it moves in circles upon the floor, has it any
other motion?

Drive a brass nail into the outer edge of a top,
spin it, and see whether the nail looks like a circle
while the top is in motion, and tell me why it is so?

You are right; because it spins round on its own
centre, while revolving in circles upon the floor.
This is the case with the earth, while moving round
the sun it moves also round its own axis.

Now suppose the earth to move round the sun
once in 365 days, and that a given place (name the
spot where you reside) has had the sun 365 times
in the south of it during that period, how many
times will the earth have turned upon its axis in
that time?

How long then does the earth take to turn once
round upon its axis?

Do you know the exact time the earth takes to revolve once round its axis?

It is generally called 24 hours, but the true time is 23 hours, 56 minutes, 3 seconds, and 23 thirds.

What proof have you that the earth has turned once round in every day?

As the earth turns completely round once every day, can you inform me whether it moves from east to west, or from west to east?

Why from west to east?

You are right, because we see the sun rise in the east every morning, and set in the west every evening; therefore the motion of the earth must be from west to east, and this occasions an apparent motion of the sun and heavenly bodies from east to west.

If a place on the earth's surface, suppose London, has passed the sun, and gone round till it comes to the sun again, will it not have described a circle similar with the nail in the edge of the top?

Suppose this circle to be divided into 360 equal parts or degrees, which is the common division of every circle, and that number to be divided by 24, the number of hours in one day, the quotient will give you the number of degrees that a place moves from the sun in one hour, namely, 15.

If a place has its shadow at the shortest, and the sun in its south two hours after it has been to the south of us, how many degrees will that place be distant from us?

Where did you say the sun sets?

Will the place that has the sun two hours after us be east or west from us?

How much to the west will that place be which has the sun nine hours after us?

Now suppose the circumference of the earth to be 25,000 miles; divide that number by 360, and the quotient will give you 69$\frac{4}{9}$, which, for the sake of whole numbers, call 69, or the number of miles contained in one degree; that quotient multiplied by 15, the number of degrees the sun travels in one hour, will give you the number of miles, namely, 1,035, which a place that has the sun one hour later or earlier than we have, would be from us in an easterly or westerly direction. If the distance of all the lines upon the earth's surface were equal, this measurement would be correct with regard to places situated east and west, and is called LONGITUDE.

In a map of the world, as well as on the globe, the upper point is called the north, or north pole; and the lower the south, or south pole; the east is on the right, and the west on the left; the line that is supposed to pass through the centre of the earth, and the globe, from north to south, is called the axis.

If I draw a line in the centre from east to west, how much of a circle will be intercepted between the north and south points each way?

Can you inform me what that circle is called which, passing from east to west, divides the earth into two equal parts, and is itself equally distant from each pole?

True, it is called the EQUATOR.

How many degrees will each pole be from this circle?

Right, ninety degrees or one fourth of a circle. Places therefore, north or south of the equator, are said to be so many degrees north or south of the equator; this measurement is called LATITUDE.

Here it will be essential to explain the circles that are drawn on the globes and maps of the world, beginning with the

TROPIC OF CANCER and the TROPIC OF CAPRICORN; each of which are twenty-three degrees and a half from the equator; the former is also called the SUMMER and the latter the WINTER

SOLSTICE, because when the sun approaches to one of these boundaries, it is supposed to stand still for a few days, and then gradually recedes.

The ARCTIC CIRCLE on the north, and the ANTARCTIC CIRCLE on the south, the former twenty-three degrees and a half from the north pole, and the latter twenty-three degrees and a half from the south pole.

The ECLIPTIC shews the earth's apparent annual path in the heavens, and is drawn from tropic to tropic. They should then be shewn how this line is divided into twelve parts called SIGNS, each containing thirty degrees, which are explained by Dr. Watts, in the following lines:

" The *Ram*, the *Bull*, the heavenly *Twins*,
And next the *Crab*, the *Lion* shines,
  The *Virgin* and the *Scales;*
The *Scorpion*, *Archer*, and *Sea Goat*,
The man that holds the *Watering-pot*,
  The *Fish* with glittering tails."

Next inform them that the broad space between the two tropics is called the TORRID or BURNING ZONE, because the sun being always over some part of it, makes it exceedingly hot and scorching. That the space between the arctic circle and the tropic of Cancer is called the NORTH TEMPERATE ZONE, and the space on the south, between the tropic of Capricorn and the antarctic circle, is called the SOUTH TEMPERATE ZONE; they are thus named because the sun never comes directly over the heads of the inhabitants, which renders the heat temperate.

The circular spaces bounded by the two polar circles are the two FRIGID or FROZEN ZONES, so called on account of the extreme cold and ice always found there.

Dryden has given us a translation from Ovid, explaining the zones, in the following lines:

" And as five zones the etherial region bind,
 Five correspondent are to the earth assigned :
 The sun with rays *directly* darting down,
 Fires all beneath, and fries the middle zone ;
 The two beneath the *distant* poles complain
 Of endless winters and perpetual rain ;
 Betwixt the *extreme* two happier climates hold
 The *temper* that partakes of hot and cold."

Now place a map of England, on a large scale, before the children, and desire them to name the principal river that runs near the place where they reside. If in London, or its vicinity, the THAMES will naturally be named.

Then trace that river on the map, beginning at the spring or head, which, according to Dr. Campbell, takes its source from four rivulets, rising in the Cotswold hills in Gloucestershire, and, connecting together, form one stream, near Lechlade. About a mile below the source of the river, is the first corn mill, which is called Kemble mill. Here the river may properly be said to form a constant current, from Somerford the stream winds to Cricklade, where it unites with many other rivulets. Approaching Kemsford, it again enters its native county, dividing it from Berkshire at Inglesham. It widens considerably in its way to Lechlade; and being there joined by the Lech and Coln, at the distance of 138 miles from London, it becomes navigable for vessels of 90 tons. At Ensham, in its course N. E. to Oxford, is the first bridge of stone, having three arches. Passing near the ruins of Godstow nunnery, the river reaches Oxford, in whose academic groves its poetical name of *Isis* has been repeatedly invoked. Being there joined by the Cherwell, it proceeds S. E. to Abingdon, where it receives the Ork, and thence to Dorchester, where it is joined by the Tame. Continuing its course S. E. by Wallingford to Reading, and forming a boundary to the counties of Berks, Bucks, Surrey, Middlesex, Essex, and Kent, it waters the towns of Henley, Marlow, Maidenhead, Windsor, Eton, Egham, Staines, Laleham, Chertsey, Weybridge, Shepperton, Walton, Sunbury, East and West Moulsey, Hampton, Thames-Ditton, Kingston, Teddington, Twickenham, Richmond, Isleworth, Brentford, Kew, Mortlake, Barnes, Chiswick, Hammersmith, Putney, Fulham, Wandsworth, Battersea, Chelsea, and Lambeth. Then, on the north bank of the river, are Westminster and London; and on the opposite side, Southwark; forming together one continued city, extending to Limehouse and Deptford; and hence the river proceeds to Greenwich, Erith, Greenhithe, Gray's-Thurrock, Gravesend, and Leigh, into the ocean. It receives, in its course from Dorchester, the rivers Kennet, Loddon, Coln, Wey, Mole, Wandle, Lea, Roding, Darent, Medway, &c. &c. &c.

The children must now return to the spring or head of the river, and prepare to represent the course of that river on their slates, which should be carefully ruled, so as to include a sufficient number of degrees, both of longitude and latitude; and shew the various streams that flow into the Thames, as it passes on from county to county, until it flows into the sea; as well as the several towns and villages that stand on or near the banks of it. Straight lines will answer this purpose, such as they have been accustomed to use in drawing exercises, so as to shew the course of the river and its principal branches, and to ascertain the longitude and latitude of each point where two of these lines meet.

A short description of every city, town, and village, with such anecdotes or remarkable events as have occurred in either, should be communicated

to the pupils; and when they have completed their
plan of the river, and entered the longitude and
latitude of each place in the columns prepared for
that purpose, they should be shewn how to apply
the principal bends belonging to each straight line,
so as to give the river its real character.

Lastly, let them trace all the brooks that run into
the Thames, by straight lines, shewing the longitude
and latitude where two lines meet, and then add
the curvature belonging to each line. Hills, towns,
and villages, within a few miles of the Thames, may
be inserted, agreeably to their longitude and latitude, or by measured distances, taking six miles in
the map in direct course for seven miles on the
road, allowing one mile for the curvature of the
road; until the surrounding country, belonging to
the river, is filled up in a general map.

Thus every principal river should be traced, with
such streams as run into them, until a general
knowledge of the British Empire is acquired.

Arrowsmith's large map of the world may now
be presented to the children, and a conspicuous
river on the continent named for them, suppose the
RHINE; beginning at the spring or head of that
river in the Grison Alps, where the three streams
that form it unite in one; shew them where its
principal branch descends from the mountain of
St. Gothard, and passes through the lakes of Con-
stance and Zell. After it has crossed part of
Germany and the Netherlands, watering Basil,
Huninguen, Strasburg, Worms, Mentz, Coblentz,
Bonne, Cologne, Dusseldorf, Rees, Emmerick, &c.,
it separates into two branches, one of which preserves the name of the Rhine, and loses itself in the
sands west of Leyden, the supposed *Lugdunum
Batavorum* of Ptolemy; the other takes the name
of the Lech or Leck, and falls into the Merwe, five
miles N. W. of Dordrecht

Here they should be directed to shew the course of the river, as before directed, in straight lines; and fill it up in every respect as described when speaking of the Thames. And upon coming to such parts of other rivers whose territories are adjacent to that of the Rhine, they should not be too minute in their detail; but make such remarks only as may be necessary for the purpose of extending their observation with respect to the extent of the continent.

It may now be essential to take a globe in your hand, let the north or south pole be placed immediately opposite the children, and by questions lead them to discover that the meridians have the appearance of straight lines, and the parallels that of circles described round the globe. This view will give them a comprehensive idea of the polar projection; and they should then be required to trace every line in that projection which they have laid down on the globular or Mercator's projection.

The attention of the children should also be led to observe the general outline or boundary of the earth; and to select such points as will enable them to lay down the whole of Europe, Asia, Africa, and America, in straight lines, extending each of them as long as possible, without omitting any prominent feature in the form of the country. The points where the lines meet should be capes, harbours, or places of consequence; and an index of the longitude and latitude entered on their slates.

When the boundary of the continent of a country or an island has been delineated by the children in straight lines, and every degree of information given them relative to places of consequence, they should be directed to notice the situation of the mountains, and to trace them on their maps by straight lines, noting the longitude and latitude similar with those of the rivers.

They should then classify the rivers whose waters fall into the sea; as, for example, those which fall into the Mediterranean, the Baltic, the Black Sea, &c.

In the same manner let them lay down the mountains or banks which separate the rivers into their respective territories, and lay them down in straight lines as before.

These lines, when the curvatures or bends belonging to each are added to the map, will complete the simple outline of all the natural features of the earth.

It will be essential to exercise the attention of the children on a large globular as well as a polar projection, at least sixty inches diameter, on a board or canvass, painted black with white meridians and parallels; and from recollection direct them to draw with chalk certain countries, islands or continents, in straight lines, with the rivers and mountains expressed in the same way; then to introduce the curvatures or bends belonging to each line, and name every object as they delineate them on the map, relating such circumstances or particular anecdotes concerning each place as may be worthy of observation.

In this manner lead them on by degrees, enlarging the sphere of observation. And as the details of large skeleton maps are thus day by day filled up, they should be exercised upon it each day, recapitulating the preceding day's work, by naming the particulars of such places as the parent or teacher may direct them to explain; by which means in a short time they will receive a perfect knowledge of every place and object worthy of note on the surface of the globe.

In teaching the principles of UNIVERSAL HISTORY, maps corresponding with those they have already delineated, shewing the face of the habitable world should be drawn, describing the political divisions of the several kingdoms and states in Europe, Asia, Africa, and America, in which the pupils should write the names of all the emperors, kings, princes, or rulers, with the leading events of their respective reigns.*

§ 5. OF NUMBERS.

PESTALOZZI's method of teaching " THE RELATIONS OF NUMBERS," by TABLES, conveys to the comprehension of children the most clear and convincing proofs of the nature and use of every species of calculation, from the most simple to the most complex combination of numbers.

A series of units are presented to the eye of the pupil, on the FIRST TABLE, arranged in compartments corresponding in the aggregate with those on the multiplication table. In each compartment of the upper horizontal row, there is " *one unit;*" in the second, " *two;*" in the third, " *three;*" increasing progressively to " *twelve units*" in each compartment.

On the SECOND TABLE squares representing whole numbers, are presented to the eye, and these are divided into " *simple fractions;*" namely, *halves, thirds, fourths, fifths, &c.* to *twelfths.*

On the THIRD TABLE these squares are subdivided into compound fractions, or " *fractions of a fraction,*" such as *halves* into *fourths, thirds* into *sixths, fourths* into *eighths, &c.*

On each table there are various exercises, each

* A series of geographical and historical exercises on Pestalozzi's plan, with sections of maps for this instructive study, is nearly ready for the press, and will shortly be published, price 12s. quarto.

of which is calculated to awaken the understanding and cultivate the reasoning faculties of children, proceeding INTUITIVELY from units and simple quantities to the most complicated relations of abstruse or mixed numbers.

As soon as children are capable of observation, they may begin with the table of units, assisted in the first instance by " VISIBLE OBJECTS," such as pebbles, beans, &c.; and for this purpose, twelve rods, or pieces of wood, each about an inch and half broad, three quarters thick, and eighteen inches long, must be prepared. In the upper part of each rod, make twelve oval or circular compartments to hold the pebbles, and place them in such a manner that they may severally correspond with the lines of units on the table.

By these simple, yet demonstrative means, children may be taught to count any number, from the least to the greatest, as well as to *add*, *subtract*, *multiply*, and *divide* numbers, preparatory to their commencing with the tables.

They should be accustomed to count forwards to 10, 20, 30, &c., and then to read them backward with perfect ease; and let them be frequently questioned respecting the situation of numbers, as, what is the next number less than 18? the next greatest number above 27, &c. Desire them to repeat all the odd numbers in 30, beginning with 1, 3, 5, &c.; then all the even numbers, forward and backward, until they do it with precision.

In counting on the table, they must be exercised on the third line with the odd and even numbers, beginning with 3, 9, 15, &c., and then with 6, 12, 18, &c., until they are acquainted with all the three-fold numbers; and the same with the other numbers contained in each horizontal line on the table.

In commencing with ADDITION, they should add

1 to 1, 1 to 2, 1 to 3, &c.; then 2 to 1, 2 to 2, 2 to 3, &c., and thereby lead them to discover every possible way of forming a number.

You may then take any number of rods, suppose five, and put beans or pebbles in one compartment of each; as, 3, 5, 2, 7, 4; and desire them to inform you how many there are in all by adding them together; then shew them how these visible objects are represented on the table by units, and prove one operation by the other; let them vary the mode of adding by placing the rods in different positions, until they can add with precision, and demonstrate the truth of the operation on the table, as well as with the visible objects.

It will be proper to inform the children, that to assist us in making calculations we use certain characters called figures, namely, 1, 2, 3, 4, 5, 6, 7, 8, 9, 0; and prove to them why these characters are used as the signs of a given number of visible objects; inform them of their simple value when they stand alone; and that when two or more figures are taken collectively they increase in a ten-fold proportion; for this purpose direct them to write certain figures one under the other in columns, between upright lines, on the slate, as for example,

I.		1		II.		3	
		2				7	
		3				5	
		4				2	
		6				9	
1	6			2	6		

then take the rods, and place the same number of visible objects in compartments immediately following each other, as are represented by the signs or figures on the slates, as in the annexed columns; and let these be added together, and declare the amount of the first, namely, sixteen, and inform them that in the number sixteen, there is one ten and six units, and therefore one on the left of the six represents ten; that in all calculations the first figure on the right represents so many units, the second figure on the left so many tens, the third so many hundreds, the fourth so many thousands, &c.

In the addition of the second example, they have two tens and six units, or twenty-six.

Then let them have five columns, and place such figures in them as the teacher may be pleased to direct, and have a corresponding number of pebbles placed on the rods; as for example,

		1	4	1
	3	2	1	5
5	7	3	7	2
		5	6	3
1	4	7	3	4
7	6	0	2	5

First direct the children to read downwards all the figures that stand in the unit column, namely, 1, 5, 2, 3, 4; then read them upwards, 4, 3, 2, 5, 1; proceed in a similar manner with the column of tens, of hundreds, of thousands, and of tens of thousands. Then direct them to add the figures in the unit column together, and declare the amount, namely, 1 ten and 5 units; direct them to put the 5 under the units, and add the ten to the column of tens, which, when added, amounts to 2 hundreds and 2 tens; place the tens under the column of tens, and add the 2 hundreds to the column of hundreds; add up that column, and the amount is 20, that is 2 thousands and no hundreds; put a cipher in the column of hundreds, and add 2 to the column of thousands, and that amount is 16, namely, 6 thousands and 1 tens of thousands; put down the 6 in the column of thousands and add 1 to the next column containing tens of thousands, and the sum is 7 tens of thousands, that is seventy thousands; set down the 7, and read the figures from right to left, namely, 5 units, 2 tens, no hundreds, 6 thousands, and 7 tens of thousands; then read them from left to right, namely, 76 thousands, and 25.

In this manner lead them on by increasing the number of columns, until they are acquainted with and perfectly comprehend the real value of all the figures used in calculations of every kind.

In SUBTRACTION we must begin like addition, merely reversing the operations by *decomposing* the numbers that were first *composed* in addition, and be extremely careful not to do it mechanically; prove to them that if you take 1 from 1, there will be no remainder, 1 from 2 and 1 remains, 1 from 3 and 2 remains, and so on through every variety of number, both with visible objects and on the table. Then, to exercise the thinking faculties, the questions may be varied, and direct them to subtract the third odd from the fifth even number, and inform you what remains. The third odd number is 5, the fifth even number is 10, then take 5 from 10 and 5 remains. Next direct them to add 5 to 7, and subtract the amount from 15. Also subtract the fifth even number from the eighth odd number, and add the third odd number to the remainder; in every example they must prove the truth of the operation by visible objects, by the table, and by figures on their slates, until they are perfectly acquainted with the nature and use of the characters by which we represent any number of real objects.

In MULTIPLICATION, which is a short method of performing several additions, they must be satisfactorily informed, and have it clearly proved to them by visible objects, and by the table, that 1 and 1, or twice 1, make 2; that 1 and 1 and 1, or 3 times 1, make 3, &c.; then that 2 and 2, or twice 2, make 4; also that 2 and 2 and 2, or 3 times 2, make 6, &c. Proceed thus with every line on the table, assisted by visible objects on the rods, until they are truly convinced that 12 times 12 are 144 times 1.

In this exercise, questions should be proposed on every line of the table: thus, in 4 times 2 how many times 1? answer, 8; why? because once 2 is twice 1, twice 2 is 4 times 1, 3 times 2 is 6 times 1, and 4 times 2 is 8 times 1; therefore 4 times 2 are 8 times 1. This must be proved by visible objects on the rods, as well as by the table.

They may be exercised next in multiplying even numbers by even numbers; odd numbers by odd numbers; then even by odd, and odd by even numbers. Also shew them the nature of square numbers, and prove to them how square numbers are formed, namely, by being composed of two even or two odd numbers; as for example, 4 is produced by twice 2; 9 by 3 times 3; 16 by 4 times 4; 25 by 5 times 5; 36 by 6 times 6, &c.

In DIVISION it may be proper to inform them that this rule is a short method of performing many subtractions. Here they may be desired to divide 12 by 4, and give them twelve visible objects for that purpose; then take three rods, and direct the children to inform you how many fours there are in 12, by putting four pebbles into one compartment of each rod, and they will discover by this means that four is contained in twelve three times; then explain to them how multiplication is proved by division, and division by multiplication; and this must be satisfactorily demonstrated on the table of units, as well as by visible objects.

Question them here in the same manner as in multiplication, and never permit them to answer any question without fully demonstrating the truth of the answer.

The tables may now be entered upon to shew them the relation and combination of numbers; most of the exercises on the table may be divided into three lessons; *first,* the introductory or preparatory lesson, which is designed to give the children a clear idea of what they are going to do. The *second,* or principal lesson, will afford them the power of advancing step by step through the exercise; and the *third* gives them facility and promptitude in answering questions applicable to the whole.

In the first step, the children are taught how to read the table; to shew how many units are contained in any whole or mixed number; and then to consider the units in composing a number as so many fractional parts of a whole.

The subsequent exercises consist in *composition, decomposition,* and *transformation* of numbers, in every possible variety, until they are perfectly acquainted with the several relations and proportions of numbers, and parts of a number with itself, as well as with other numbers; thereby enabling them mentally to answer questions with accuracy and precision, and to demonstrate the truth of it in less time than may be required to state or arrange the question by the *rules* given in our general systems of arithmetic.

The following questions will, it is presumed, fully prove the truth of the preceding remarks.

I. THE RULE OF PROPORTION. " *If six men weave 34 yards of cloth in 10 hours, how many yards may be wove by 20 men in 15 hours? Answer,* 170 *yards.*

Why? Because if 6 men will do it in 10 hours, 1 man will do it in 6 times 10, or 60 hours; and what 20 men can do in 15 hours, 1 man can do in 20 times 15, or 300 hours. Therefore, as often as 60 is contained in 300, namely, 5 times, so often must the number of yards be increased; and 5 times 34 are equal to 170 yards, the answer.

Or proportionally, 6 bears the same proportion to 34 that 20 bears to $113\frac{1}{3}$. And 10 bears the same proportion to $113\frac{1}{3}$ as 15 bears to 170.

" *If* 10 *men working* 4 *hours a-day, do a piece of work in* 3 *days, how long would* 6 *men be required to do it working* 5 *hours each day?*

SOLUTION. 1 man would do it in $10 \times 3 \times 4 = 120$ hours; 6 men multiplied by 5 hours are equal to 30 hours each day. Therefore 120 divided by 30 is equal to 4 days, the answer.

" *If* $\frac{3}{4}$ *of* $2\frac{1}{5}$ *of a Flemish ell cost* $1\frac{3}{11}l.$, *what will* $114\frac{3}{5}$ *English ells cost?*"

First, $\frac{3}{4}$ of $2\frac{1}{5} = \frac{33}{20}$ and $\frac{33}{20} \times \frac{3}{5} = \frac{99}{100}$.

And $114\frac{3}{5} = 5\frac{73}{5}$ and $5\frac{73}{5} \times 20 = \frac{11460}{100}$.

Then $\frac{99}{100} = 33$ times $\frac{3}{100}$
$\frac{11460}{100} = 3820$ times $\frac{3}{100}$

therefore 33 times $\frac{3}{100}$ $= 33$ times $\frac{1}{3820}$ of 3820 times $\frac{3}{100}$ and 3820 times $\frac{3}{100} = \frac{11460}{100} = 114\frac{3}{4}$.

Again, $1\frac{3}{11} = \frac{14}{11}$ and $\frac{14}{11} \times 33 = \frac{462}{363} = 33$ times $\frac{14}{363} = \frac{1}{3820}$ of 3820 times $\frac{14}{363} = \frac{53480}{363} = 147l.$ 6s. $6\frac{1}{4}d.$ $\frac{86}{121}$.

Therefore $\frac{3}{4}$ of $2\frac{1}{5}$ Flem. ell : $1\frac{3}{11}l.$: : $114\frac{3}{5}$ Eng. ell : $147l.$ 6s. $6\frac{1}{4}d.$ $\frac{86}{121}$.

II. INTEREST. " *What must the capital be that gains* 10s. *interest in* 1 *week at* $4\frac{1}{2}$ *per cent?*"

SOLUTION. 10s. in 1 week is equal to 20s. in 2 weeks, the half of 52 weeks is 26 weeks. Therefore as often as $4\frac{1}{2}$ is contained in 26, so often must the capital or 100l. be multiplied. $26 = \frac{52}{2}$ and $4\frac{1}{2} = \frac{9}{2}$. Now $\frac{52}{9} = 5\frac{7}{9}$ and $5\frac{7}{9}$ multiplied by 100l. $= 577l.$ 15s. $6\frac{1}{2}d.$ $\frac{6}{9}$.

III. PARTNERSHIP. " *Two persons enter into trade, one puts in* 400l., *the other* 900l., *they gained* 500l., *how much of the profits belong to each?*"

SOLUTION. 1 put in 4, the other $9 = 13$ parts, and the profits 500 divided by 13 is equal to $38\frac{6}{13}$.

Therefore 38 $\frac{6}{13}$ mul. by 4=153$\frac{11}{13}$=153*l.* 16*s.* 11*d.* $\frac{1}{13}$.
And   38$\frac{6}{13}$ mul. by 9=346$\frac{2}{13}$=346   3   0 $\frac{12}{13}$.

$$\overline{\qquad\qquad\qquad\qquad\qquad}$$

500*l.*   0   0

IV. SQUARE ROOT. " *Suppose a gentleman gave a class of boys 7s. 6¼d. to be divided equally between them, how many boys were there in the class, and how much did each receive?*"

SOLUTION.   7*s.* 6¼*d.* is equal to 361 farthings, and 19 times 19 are 361. Therefore there were 19 boys in the class, and each boy received 4¾*d.*

V. CUBE ROOT. *Charles borrowed of Henry a hay-rick that measured 6 yards every way, and returned him 2 cubical pieces, each of the sides of which measured 3 yards; did Charles pay Henry as much as he borrowed?*"

SOLUTION. $6 \times 6 \times 6 = 216$ yards borrowed.
$3 \times 3 \times 3 \times 2 = 54$ yards paid.

$$\overline{\qquad\qquad}$$

Consequently 162 yards, or ¾ of the quantity borrowed, hath not been returned.

Thus children who have been taught " *the relations of numbers*" according to PESTALOZZI's plan, will answer the most difficult questions where fractional parts of high denominations, and various coins, weights, and measures, are concerned, with accuracy and precision.

PART II.

ELUCIDATING THE SEVERAL PARTS OF SPEECH USED IN THE ENGLISH LANGUAGE.

§ 1.

GRAMMAR may be defined the art of communicating our ideas by certain sounds to the ear, or signs to the eye; its design is to teach us to speak and write agreeably to the most approved laws of language.

Men could not enjoy the advantages of their civil association if they had not easy means of fixing, by precise signs, their social relations, and of communicating their thoughts.

Language offers them these signs and means of communication; and it merits our attention principally on account of the important part it performs in the operations of the mind; it is the instrument of thought; and on its perfection depends also that of our intellectual faculties.

Persons unacquainted with the rules of grammar must always feel their inferiority in company and correspondence, and ever speak and write in fear; whereas those who are familiar with them are unawed and confident in address.

It is in language that a child begins to think, that his reason developes itself, and that he acquires ideas of information.

Hence the necessity of acquiring a correct know-

---

* From the Greek word *Gramma*, a letter, picture, or painting.

ledge of the English language is obvious, it being universally admitted to be the gate of science, and the indispensable guide and ornament of literature.

The common division, or arrangement of all the words of our language, generally called PARTS OF SPEECH, are as follows :—

1. The *Noun.*
2. The *Article.*
3. The *Adjective.*
4. The *Pronoun.*
5. The *Verb.*
6. The *Participle.*
7. The *Adverb.*
8. The *Preposition.*
9. The *Conjunction.*
10. The *Interjection.*

§ 2. OF THE NOUN AND SUBSTANTIVE.

The NOUN* or NAME conveys to the mind an idea of whatever may be conceived to exist in the universe; and being the first object of conception, it is entitled to the first place in grammar, and especially as it is " *the* ROOT *of all words, and the* REGISTER *of all ideas.*"

A SUBSTANTIVE represents a SUBSTANCE, something that really exists, and not a quality.

The first process in the communication of knowledge was to contrive NAMES for all the SUBSTANCES.

The ANIMAL substances received their names from **ADAM.**

Under the comprehensive term ANIMAL we arrange all *living creatures;* those in a live state we call NATURAL SUBSTANCES; and the parts of animals in a dead state used by various mechanics, such as *bones, hair, horns, leather,* &c., also retain the name of ANIMAL SUBSTANCES, but in an ARTIFICIAL STATE.

---

* From the Latin word *Nomen,* a name.

D

Animal substances are divided into classes; as *man*, *beast* or *cattle*, *birds*, *insects* or *reptiles*, *fishes*, and *amphibious animals* ; each class is subdivided into various species.

Every substance which springs from a root, and bears branches, leaves, &c., from a blade of grass to the lofty cedar, is called a VEGETABLE SUBSTANCE.

Vegetable substances are divided into classes, such as *trees*, *shrubs*, *flowers*, *garden vegetables*, *grasses*, *grains*, *moss*, and *funguses* ; each class is subdivided into different species.

The next class of SUBSTANCES are MINERALS or FOSSILS; under this general head are included *earth*, *stones*, *sand*, *salts*, *metals*, *crystals*, and *petrifactions*.

The fourth and last classification is that of FLUID SUBSTANCES; under this head are included *water*, *wine*, *oil*, *blood*, *quicksilver*, &c.

Every SUBSTANCE or SUBSTANTIVE must be either a NATURAL or an ARTIFICIAL PRODUCT; thus a QUILL is a natural product, but a PEN is an artificial product.

Of the division of Nouns.

Nouns are divided into four classes, *proper*, *particular*, *common*, and *abstract*.

PROPER NAMES are appropriate to individuals; as, John, James, Philip.

PARTICULAR NAMES to places and things; as, London, Dublin, Edinburgh; the *Thames*, a river; the *Royal George*, a stage coach; the *Globe*, a daily paper.

COMMON NOUNS belong to the whole class which they express; as, *man*, *house*, *garden*, *chair*; for the name of *man* belongs to every *man* ; *house* to every *house* ; *garden*, to every *garden* ; and *chair*, to every *chair*.

ABSTRACT NAMES contemplate qualities as detached beings, having laws and regulations within themselves; such as faith, hope, charity, virtue, honour, mercy, height, depth, &c. Hence we say, " the rules of decency," " the laws of propriety," with the same confidence as we say " the laws of England."

The just shade of distinction between common and abstract nouns will appear by considering that an *animal* may be compared with an *animal*, and a *tree* with a *tree*; but *virtue* cannot so properly be compared with *vice*. The relation of abstract nouns to the adjectives from which they are formed; as, *goodness* from *good*, is obvious from the consideration that the adjective *good* denotes a quality inherent in the noun substantive to which it is applied; as, a *good* man, a *good* book, &c.; and the abstract noun *goodness* expresses a quality common to all the noun substantives to which it is competent to apply the adjective.

Almost every adjective in the English language will form an abstract noun; as,

Adjective.	Abstract Noun.	Adjective.	Abstract Noun.
Cheerful,	cheerfulness;	virtuous,	virtue ;
bright,	brightness ;	proud,	pride ;
smooth,	smoothness ;	healthy,	health ;
high,	height ;	slothful,	sloth ;
wise,	wisdom ;	grateful,	gratitude.

Some nouns are called *verbal nouns;* as, *observation, observance*, &c. When *to observe* signifies " to remark," the verbal noun is *observation;* when it signifies " to obey," or " to keep," the verbal is *observance*. To this class may be added *participial nouns;* as, *hearing, reading, writing, beginning*, &c. This class of nouns, however, are bettet distinguished as abstract nouns.

Nouns have three properties, *number, case,* and *gender.*

Of Number.

NUMBER distinguishes objects singly or collectively. When it represents a single idea, as one pen, one book, one slate, it is of the SINGULAR NUMBER: but when two or more persons or things are represented, as boys, books, pens, slates, it is of the PLURAL NUMBER.

The most common way of forming the *plural* is by some change in the terminations of the nouns.

When the singular ends in *ss* or *s, x, ch* soft, or *sh,* the plural is formed by adding the syllable *es;* as miss, miss*es*; tax, tax*es*; peach, peach*es*; fish, fish*es*: also nouns ending in *o,* preceded by a consonant, require *es*; as, hero, hero*es*; but when preceded by a vowel the *s* only is added; as, folio, folio*s.*

When the singular ends in *f* or *fe,* the plural is formed by changing *f* or *fe* into *ves*; as, half, hal*ves*; life, li*ves*; except dwarf, grief, hoof, &c., which, with *ch* hard, and *ff,* require the *s* only; as, dwarf, dwarf*s*; monarch, monarch*s*; muff, muff*s*; except staff, which makes sta*ves.*

When the singular ends in *y,* preceded by a consonant, the plural is formed by changing the *y* into *ies*; as, lady, lad*ies*; fly, fl*ies*; but the *y* is not changed when there is another vowel in the syllable; as, key, key*s*; attorney, attorney*s.*

The plural of many other English nouns is formed by changing the vowels; as, man, men; tooth, teeth; goose, geese; foot, feet: sometimes by adding the syllable en, as ox, oxen: sometimes by changing the vowels and consonants; as, mouse, mice; penny, pence.

Many of our nouns, from the nature of the things

which they express, are used only in the singular form; as, gold, pitch, pride, sloth, wheat, &c.: others only in the plural form; as, alms, ashes, bellows, ethics, matins, news, scissors, &c.

Some nouns are the same in both numbers; as, deer, sheep, swine.

The distinction between the singular and the plural number in the following foreign words, used chiefly in books of science, requires to be studied with attention.

Singular.	Plural.	Singular.	Plural.
Animalcu-lum,	Animalcula;	Erratum,	Errata,
		Focus,	Foci;
Antithesis,	Antitheses;	Genius,	Genii*;
Appendix,	Appendices;	Genius,	Geniuses;
Apex,	Apices;	Genus,	Genera;
Arcanum,	Arcana;	Hypothesis,	Hypotheses
Automaton,	Automata;	Index,	Indices†;
Axis,	Axes;	Lamina,	Laminæ;
Basis,	Bases;	Magus,	Magi;
Beau,	Beaux;	Medium,	Media;
Calx,	Calces;	Memoran-dum,	Memoranda;
Cherub,	Cherubim;		
Crisis,	Crises;	Metamor-phosis,	Metamor-phoses;
Criterion,	Criteria;		
Datum,	Data;	Phenome-non,	Phenomena
Desidera-tum,	Desiderata;		
		Radius,	Radii;
Diæresis,	Diæreses;	Seraph,	Seraphim;
Effluvium,	Effluvia;	Stamen,	Stamina;
Ellipsis,	Ellipses;	Stratum,	Strata;
Emphasis,	Emphases;	Vortex,	Vortices.
Encomium,	Encomia;	Virtuoso,	Virtuosi.

* *Genii*, when denoting aërial spirits; *Geniuses*, when signi-fying persons of genius.

† *Indices*, when referring to algebraic quantities; *Indexes*, when it signifies pointers, or tables of contents.

Of Case.

Nouns admit of three cases, the *nominative*, the *possessive*, and the *objective*.

The NOMINATIVE CASE* simply names the person or thing whose action, passion, or existence, is pointed out by the verb; as, *I* write; *Ann* sings; *James* plays.

The POSSESSIVE or GENITIVE CASE† expresses the relation of property, possession, or descent, and has an apostrophe with the letter *s* after it; as, *Philip's* horse; *Murray's* grammar; *Mary's* harp.

The OBJECTIVE or ACCUSATIVE CASE is the same in form as the nominative, but points out the object of the action, and consequently follows the verb; it is very frequently preceded by a preposition; as, Ann is gone to *Paris;* George wrote a letter to his *father;* Charles gave his whip to *Henry.*

Nouns are declined in the following manner :—

Singular.	Plural.
Nom. A mother.	*Nom.* Mothers.
Poss. A mother's of a mother.	*Poss.* Mothers' of mothers.
Obj. A mother.	*Obj.* Mothers.

Of Genders.

Nouns admit of three varieties with regard to gender‡; namely, the *masculine*, the *feminine*, and the *neuter*.

The MASCULINE§ speaks of the male kind; as, man, lion, horse.

The FEMININE‖ speaks of females; as, woman, lioness, mare.

All other nouns belong to the NEUTER GENDER,

---

* From *nominativus,* (*a nomino*) naming.
† From *genitivus,* (*à gigno,*) natural, or belonging to.
‡ From *genus,* a sex or kind.
§ From *mas,* the male-kind.
‖ From *femina,* a woman.

which is a negation of the other two; as, slate, form, desk.

The MASCULINE GENDER is given to some NEUTER nouns when used figuratively, which are conspicuous for the attributes of imparting or communicating; and are by nature strong and efficacious, either of good or evil, or which have a claim to some eminence, whether laudable or otherwise. Those again we make FEMININE which are conspicuous for the attributes of containing and of bringing forth, having more of the passive in their nature than of the active—which are peculiarly beautiful or amiable—or which have respect to such excesses as are rather feminine than masculine. Upon these principles, the *sun* is said to be masculine; and the *moon*, being the receptacle of the sun's light, to be feminine. The *earth* is generally feminine. A *ship*, a *country*, a *city*, &c., are likewise made feminine, being receivers or containers. *Time* is always masculine, on account of its mighty efficacy. *Virtue* is feminine from its beauty, and its being the object of love. *Fortune* and the *church* are generally put in the feminine gender.

The gender of English nouns are classed in Kirkman's grammar, under different heads, from which the following are selected.

1st. By appropriate names; as,

Masculine.	Feminine.	Masculine.	Feminine.
Batchelor,	Maid;	Husband,	Wife;
Boy,	Girl;	King,	Queen;
Brother,	Sister;	Lad,	Lass;
Buck,	Doe;	Lord,	Lady;
Dog,	Bitch;	Man,	Woman;
Drake,	Duck;	Master,	Mistress;
Earl,	Countess;	Nephew,	Niece;
Father,	Mother;	Ram,	Ewe;
Friar,	Nun;	Son,	Daughter;
Gander,	Goose;	Uncle,	Aunt.
Horse,	Mare;		

D 4

2d. Genders are distinguished by different terminations; as,

Masculine.	Feminine.	Masculine.	Feminine.
Abbot,	Abbess;	Hero,	Heroine;
Actor,	Actress;	Host,	Hostess;
Administra-tor,	Administra-trix;	Jew,	Jewess;
Adulterer,	Adulteress;	Lion,	Lioness;
Ambassa-dor,	Ambassa-dress;	Marquis,	Marchio-ness;
Baron,	Baroness;	Mayor,	Mayoress;
Bridegroom,	Bride;	Patron,	Patroness;
Benefactor,	Benefac-tress;	Peer,	Peeress;
Caterer,	Cateress;	Priest,	Priestess;
Count,	Countess;	Prince,	Princess;
Deacon,	Deaconess;	Prophet,	Prophetess;
Duke,	Duchess;	Shepherd,	Shepherd-ess;
Emperor,	Empress;	Songster,	Songstress;
Executor,	Executrix;	Tiger,	Tigress;
Governor,	Governess;	Viscount,	Viscountess;
Heir,	Heiress;	Widower,	Widow.

Many names of this class have *no feminine*; as, arbitrator, guide, guardian, &c.; and some have *no masculine*; as, laundress, sempstress, &c.

3d. The gender is distinguished by prefixing nouns, pronouns, &c., employed as adjectives; as,

A turkey-cock,	A turkey-hen;
A dog-fox,	A bitch-fox;
A he-wolf,	A she-wolf;
A man-servant,	A maid-servant;
A male-child,	A female-child;
Male-descendants,	Female-descendants.

4th. When the gender is not distinguished by an appropriate name, we do it by adding the proper or the common name; as,

Maternal grandfather,	Maternal grandmother;
Cousin John,	Cousin Mary;
Uncle Thomas,	Aunt Sarah;
Neighbour James,	Neighbour Ann.

It sometimes happens that the same noun is either masculine or feminine; as, parent, child, cousin, friend, neighbour, servant, and several others, are indiscriminately used for either.

Questions.

1. What is grammar?
2. Repeat the parts of speech.
3. What is a noun?
4. What is a substantive?
5. What are animal substances?
6. What is a natural substance?
7. What is an artificial substance?
8. How are animal substances divided?
9. What is a vegetable substance?
10. How are vegetable substances divided?
11. What are fossil substances?
12. How are fossil substances divided?
13. What are fluid substances?
14. How are fluid substances divided?
15. What is a natural product?
16. Write ten examples.
17. What is an artificial product?
18. Write ten examples.
19. How are nouns divided?
20. What are proper nouns?
21. Give me ten examples.
22. What are particular nouns?
23. Write ten examples.
24. What are common nouns?
25. Write ten examples.
26. What are abstract nouns?
27. How are abstract nouns distinguished?

28. Can adjectives be converted into abstract nouns?

29. Write ten examples.

30. Write ten abstract nouns.

31. What must we consider in nouns?

32. What is number?

33. How many numbers are there?

34. Give me ten examples in the singular, and ten in the plural number.

35. What is the most common way of forming the plural number?

36. How are plurals formed when the singular end in ss, x, ch soft, and sh, and o?

37. Write eight examples.

38. How are plurals formed when the singular ends in f, or fe?

39. Write six examples.

40. How in ch hard, and ff?

41. Write four examples in each.

42. When the singular ends in y, how is the plural formed?

43. Write ten examples.

44. How are plurals formed by changing the vowel or vowels?

45. Give me examples in each.

46. Write all the nouns you are acquainted with that have no plural.

47. Write all the nouns you can recollect that have no singular.

48. Write all the nouns that are the same in both numbers.

49. How are the plurals formed in foreign words?

50. Give all the examples you are acquainted with.

51. How many cases are there?

52. What is the nominative case?

53. Write ten examples.

54. What is the possessive case?
55. Write ten examples.
56. What is the objective case?
57. Write ten examples.
58. Decline the nouns you have written.
59. How many genders have English nouns?
60. How many modes of distinguishing gender are there?
61. What is the first mode?
62. Give me ten examples.
63. What is the second mode?
64. Give me ten examples.
65. What is the third mode?
66. Give me ten examples.
67. What is the fourth mode?
68. Write two examples.
69. What nouns are the same in both genders?
70. Write an example.
71. What nouns have no masculine?

§3. OF THE ARTICLE.

ARTICLES* are little words prefixed to nouns, to enlarge or circumscribe their meaning; they are *a* or *an*, and *the*.

The article *a* or *an* is called the *general* or *definite article*, because it refers the object to its species only, and denotes our conceptions of it no further than the common qualities of the species extends; as, *a* hat, *a* book, *a* glove.

The article *the* is called the *particular* or *definit article*, because it discriminates the object to which it is prefixed from all others of the same species and denotes our previous acquaintance with it, or its own particular characteristics; as, *the* hat which

---

* From *articulus*, a joint, or small part.

my father wore yesterday; *the* book in which Jane is reading; *the* glove which I left on the sofa.

Nouns require no article when they stand alone; as, Milton, Knox, Blair; temperance, fortitude, prudence, justice.

The article *the* sometimes precedes the adjective and the adverb; as, *the* good man is applauded; *the* more I study *the* more I improve.

Questions.

1. How many articles are there?
2. Repeat them.
3. Write proper articles before ten nouns of each class, singular and plural.
4. How is the general article used?
5. Give five examples.
6. How is the particular article used?
7. Give five examples.

§ 4.   OF ADJECTIVES.

An ADJECTIVE* is a term of quality generally put before nouns, and are by some called *adnouns*, because they serve to notify the qualities or attributes, and to define and illustrate the meaning of the noun; as, a *fragrant* flower; a *plentiful* harvest; a *serene* sky.

All adjectives which denote qualities susceptible of augmentation or diminution admit of degrees of comparison, called the comparative and superlative.

An adjective in its SIMPLE or POSITIVE STATE expresses the quality without any increase or diminution; as, dear, happy, sweet.

The COMPARATIVE increases or lessens the po-

---

* From *ad*, to, and *jacio*, to put.

sitive; as, dearer, or less dear; happier, or less happy; sweeter, or less sweet.

The SUPERLATIVE increases or lessens the positive to the highest or lowest degree; as, dearest, or least dear; happiest, or least happy; sweetest, or least sweet.

The adverbs *more, most, less* and *least, very, infinitely*, &c., are frequently used in comparing adjectives.

The *fourth* or *absolute* degree of comparison is when we say, *Holy, Holy, Holy;* which is the same as when we say *the Most Holy;*—most wise, most gracious, and most mighty, are of the absolute degree.

The philosophy of language does not allow us to compare the superlative degree; yet that expression in the Psalms, "THE MOST HIGHEST," has been much admired. St. Paul also takes the same liberty: " Unto me, who am *less than the least* of all saints, is this grace given."

You may easily know an adjective by joining it with an article to the name of any person or thing; thus, a *pretty* girl; a *lovely* woman; a *beautiful* picture.

Adjectives are compared in the following manner:

Positive.	Comparative.	Superlative:
High,	Higher,	Highest.
Fine,	Finer,	Finest.
Good,	Better,	Best.
Amiable,	More amiable,	Most amiable.
Bad,	Worse,	Worst.

Questions.

1. What is an adjective?
2. Name the degrees of comparison.
3. Write ten adjectives in the positive state.
4. ——————————— the comparative state.
5. ——————————— the superlative state.

6. What is the fourth or absolute case?
7. Give me an example.
8. How are adjectives known?

§ 5.   OF PRONOUNS.

Pronouns* have no other use in language but to represent nouns; and of course they are commonly called to occupy the stations of the nouns they represent.   They should therefore be marshalled agreeably to the stations in which their principals would appear.

There are three kinds of pronouns, namely, the personal, the relative, and the adjective.

Personal Pronouns.

The principal PERSONAL PRONOUNS are four, *I,* *thou* or *you, he, she.*   To these *it* is added when we do not know the gender.   Their plurals are, *we, ye* or *you, they.*

Personal pronouns are subject to the same modifications as nouns, with regard to *number, case,* and *gender.*

I is the sign of the first person, and the speaker.

Thou or *you* is the sign of the second person, and the person spoken to.

He, she, or *it,* is the sign of the third person, or thing spoken of, and is the subject of the discourse; as, *I* have read your book, and feel pleasure in informing *you* that *it* met my approbation.

As the pronouns of the first and second person refer to persons who are present to each other when they speak, their sex must appear, and therefore needs not to be marked by a *masculine* or *feminine*

* From *pro,* for, and *nomen,* a name.

pronoun. But as the third person may be absent or unknown, the distinction of gender then becomes necessary, and accordingly in English the third person hath all the genders belonging to it; namely, *he, she, it.*

The personal pronouns are declined as follows :—

First Person.

	Singular.	Plural.
Nom.	I,	We.
Poss.	Mine,	Ours.
Obj.	Me,	Us.

Second Person.

	Singular.	Plural.
Nom.	Thou *or* you,	Ye *or* you.
Poss.	Thine,	Yours.
Obj.	Thee,	You.

Third Person.

	Singular.	Plural.
Nom.	He, she, it,	They.
Poss.	His, hers, its,	Theirs.
Obj.	Him, her, it,	Them.

The personal pronouns illustrated.

SING. *I* learn; *thou* teachest, or, in polite language, *you* teach; *he* ciphers; *she* sings; *it* stands.

PLUR. *We* dance; *ye* or *you* read; *they* improve.

SING. *My* knife; *thy* hat, or *thine* house; *his* whip; *her* fan.

PLUR. *Our* coach; *your* farm; *their* boat.

SING. He instructs *me*; he directs *thee*; she loves *him*; he teaches *her.*

PLUR. They impeach *us*; they scourge *them*; they forgive *you.*

A TABLE OF PRONOUNS.

		PERSONAL.		POSSESSIVE.	
		Nominat. Case.	Object. Case.	With a Noun.	Without a Noun.
First person {	Sing.	I	Me	My	Mine
	Plur.	We	Us	Our	Ours
Second person {	Sing.	Thou	Thee	Thy	Thine
	Plur.	Ye *or* you	You	Your	Yours
Third person { Sing. {		He	Him	His	His
		She	Her	Her	Hers
		It	It	Its	Its
	Plur.	They	Them	Their	Theirs
Interrog. of persons.		Who	Whom	Whom	Whose
Interrog. of things.		What	What	Whereof.	

Relative Pronouns.

The RELATIVE PRONOUNS are so called because they relate to some preceding word or phrase, which is the antecedent to the pronoun. They are, *who, which, that,* and *what.*

Who, which, and *what,* when used in asking questions, are called *interrogatives.*

Who is thus declined; *Nom.* who; *Poss.* whose; *Obj.* whom.

Which relates to things, and *who* to persons; as, *which* book do you prefer? *who* read last?

In asking questions, *which* is distinguished from *what,* by its always following a noun expressed or understood; as, where is the book *which* I gave you?

Whose refers to property; as, *whose* coach is that? *whose* horse do you ride?

Whom refers to the object of discourse, and is

used in the following manner; those *whom* I have greatly served have proved ungrateful.

That is frequently used to prevent the repetition of *who* and *which*, and is applied both to persons and things; as, the book *that* he read last is very instructive; those *that* love virtue are esteemed.

That, without exception, is used after an adjective of the superlative degree; as, Milton was the most sublime poet *that* ever wrote in the English language.

Whether was formerly used as an interrogative; as, *whether* of these shall I choose? but *which* is now generally substituted for it.

Pronominal Adjectives.

The PRONOMINAL ADJECTIVES are of a mixed nature, participating the properties both of pronouns and adjectives; they are divided into four sorts, namely, the *possessive*, the *distributive*, the *demonstrative*, and the *indefinite*.

The POSSESSIVE relate to possession or property; as, *my, thy, his, her, its, our, your, their*; and are used in the following manner; *my* hat is new; *thy* shoes are worn out; he attends to *his* learning; she minds *her* work; that book is not in *its* place; we have lost *our* kite; *your* map is well finished; I admire *their* parsing.

Own and *self* are used in conjunction with pronouns. *Own* is added to POSSESSIVES singular and plural; as, my *own* book; our *own* house.

Compound pronouns confer emphasis on the noun, and the pronoun; as, God *himself* is my judge; I did this *myself*.

The following examples shew the manner in which they are used in our language.

SING. *I myself* witnessed the deed.

PLUR. *We ourselves* were present at the election.

SING. *Thou thyself*, or *you yourself*, or *he himself*, saw the ship launched.

PLUR. *Ye* or *you yourselves* have been appointed arbitrators to settle this dispute.

The DISTRIBUTIVE specify the persons or things that make up a number; they are, *each, every, either.*

Each generally relates to two persons or two things taken separately: as, *each* of his farms is well stocked; *each* of her brothers is very humane.

Every alludes to several persons or things taken separately; and he gave to *every* man a penny; *every* boy in the class was attentive to the lecture.

Either signifies one of two persons or things; as, " *either* you or I must be mistaken;" " no man can serve two masters, for *either* he will hate the one and love the other, or else he will hold to the one and despise the other."

Neither signifies not either, that is, not one or the other; as, *neither* you nor I attended the meeting.

The DEMONSTRATIVE point out the subject to which they refer; *this* and *that*; *these* and *those* are of this class.

This refers to the nearest person or thing, *that* to the most distant; as, *this* gem has a brighter lustre than *that*. For the sake of distinction, *that* is used in reference to the former, and *this* to the latter; as,

> Self-love, the spring of motion, acts the soul;
> Reason's comparing balance rules the whole.
> Man but for *that* no action could attend,
> And but for *this* were active to no end.
>
> Some place the bliss in action, some in ease;
> *Those* call it pleasure, and contentment *these*.

The INDEFINITE express their subjects in a general manner; they are, *some, other, any, one, all, such*, &c.

The following examples will elucidate the indefinite pronouns; as, *some* are attentive; *others* are inattentive; I will not knowingly offend *any* man;

we are commanded to love *one* another; *all* the earth should worship Thee the Father everlasting; *such* as are obedient will be rewarded.

Questions.

1. What are pronouns?
2. How many kinds of pronouns are there
3. Repeat the personal pronouns.
4. How many persons are there?
5. Give me an example.
6. Do pronouns admit of number, case, and gender?
7. What pronouns admit of gender?
8. Decline the pronouns.
9. Give me an example of their use in composing sentences.
10. What are relative pronouns?
11. Name the interrogative pronouns.
12. Decline *who.*
13. Give me an example how the pronouns *who, which, that* and *what,* are used.
14. What are pronominal adjectives?
15. How many sorts are there?
16. Repeat them.
17. What are the possessive?
18. How are they used?
19. What are the distributive?
20. How are they used?
21. What are the demonstrative?
22. How are they used?
23. What are the indefinite?
24. How are they used?

§ 6. OF THE VERB.

The verb* is a word which denotes action or

---

* From *verbum,* a word; a verb being the principal word in a sentence.

energy; consequently every thing we do is a verb; as, "I *read;*" "you *write;*" "he *ciphers;*" "we *talk;*" "ye *laugh;*" "they *play.*"

Verbs are either *active, passive,* or *neuter.* They are also divided into *regular, irregular,* and *defective.*

ACTIVE VERBS denote the action or condition begun, and necessarily implies an *agent,* and an *object* acted upon; as, "George *cleans* the slate."

In this example it is evident that the action performed by the agent *George,* passes to the *slate,* which is the object acted upon; and as *cleans* is the word that shews the action, it must be an active verb.

An active verb is said to be *transitive,* when the action passes from the subject to the object; as, "I worship God;" "I esteem virtue."

PASSIVE VERBS shew the action has been completed, and necessarily implies an object acted upon; as, "the slate was *cleaned* by George."

When an action is expressed by a passive verb, the agent, or doer of the action, is pointed out by a preposition, which governs the agent by whom the action was performed, as in the above example.

NEUTER VERBS express neither action nor passion, but being, or a state of being, and may properly be called *intransitive,* because the effect is confined within the subject, and does not pass to any object; as, "I *grow;*" "you *stand;*" "they *run.*"

Neuter verbs sometimes indicate an action more plainly than active verbs; as, "that boy *swims* swiftly, and he will undoubtedly *reach* the shore."

In this example, swims is a verb neuter, because the action expressed by it remains with the person who performs it; *will reach* is a verb active, because the circumstance declared by it passes from the agent to the object, namely, the shore.

In the grammatical order of words, it is required that the agent, or nominative, shall first make its appearance; the agent is followed by the action of the verb, and the verb is succeeded by the subject, or objective case, on which the action is exerted. In this logical order, an English writer, paying a compliment to Pestalozzi, might say, " It is impossible for me to pass over in silence so remarkable a system of education; such a singular and un-heard-of mode of cultivating the understanding, and awakening the attention of youth, and such unusual moderation in the exercise of instruction." Here we have, in the first instance, presented to us the person who speaks: " It is impossible for *me*," next, what that person has to do, "*impossible for him to pass over in silence;*" and lastly, the object which moves him to do so, " *the system, the mode of cultivating the understanding, and moderation of Pestalozzi in the exercise of instruction.*"

In the verb are to be considered, *number, person, mood*, and *tense*; the two latter require particular attention.

Verbs have two numbers, the *singular* and the *plural*; and in each number there are three persons; as,

	Sing.	Plur.
First Person,	I praise,	We praise.
Second Person,	Thou praisest,	Ye or you praise.
Third Person,	He praises,	They praise.

The MOOD* signifies the MODE, or manner, in which the action, passion, or suffering, is expressed by the verb.

There are five moods; namely, the *indicative,* the *imperative*, the *potential,* the *subjunctive,* and the *infinitive.*

The INDICATIVE MOOD† simply expresses an

---

* From *modus,* a manner.
† From *indico,* to shew.

action or passion, as present, past, or future; as, " I praise;" " I did praise;" " I shall praise." Or it asks a question; as, "do I praise?" " did I praise?" " shall I praise?"

The IMPERATIVE MOOD* employs the language of authority and command. It entreats, exhorts, and permits; as, "let not mercy and truth forsake thee;" "fear the Lord, and depart from evil;" " go, humble thyself before the Lord;" rise, take up thy bed and walk."

The POTENTIAL MOOD† implies power, ability, will, or obligation; as, "it may be a fine day to-morrow;" " I can read;" " we should obey our teachers."

The SUBJUNCTIVE MOOD‡ is so called because it depends on some other verb which is subjoined in the beginning, or at the end, to a conjunction, to make the sense complete; as, " though I bestow all my goods to feed the poor, and though I give my body to be burned, and have not charity, it profiteth me nothing;" " unless he repent, he will not be forgiven."

The INFINITIVE MOOD§ requires no agent to be prefixed or understood in the form of a nominative. It expresses all action or passion without limitation or restraint. In computing the time of the infinitive, we employ the present, the past, and the future, according as the action which it denotes happens to be of the same, of prior, or of posterior time, to that of the antecedent verb; as, " I am happy to see him;" " I am happy to have seen him;" " I am happy to be about to see him."

In relating an action, it is requisite to notify

---

* From *impero*, to command.
† From *poten alis (à possum)*, to be able.
‡ From *sub*, under, and *jungo*, to join.
§ From *infinitivus*, without bounds.

whether it is finished, is finishing, or will be finished. Hence arose the necessity that the verb, along with the signification of action, should likewise express *time* or *tense*.

The three grand divisions of TIME are the *present*, the *past*, and the *future*. These are all employed to express the Divine existence; as, " the Lord which is,—and which was,—and which is to come."

The PRESENT TENSE confines the agency of the verb to the minutest instant; as, " I praise;" " you pray;" " they kneel."

The IMPERFECT TENSE denotes the time past, and represents the action or event, either finished, or as remaining unfinished, at a certain time past; as, " I loved her for her modesty and virtue; " I dined after you arrived."

The PERFECT TENSE not only refers to what is completely past, but also conveys an allusion to the present time; as, " I have taken my walk;" " you have learned your lesson;" " she has finished her sampler."

The PLUPERFECT TENSE is so called because it expresses an action as past, prior to another action with which the time is compared; as, " I had taken my tea before you came."

The FIRST FUTURE TENSE represents the action as yet to come, either with or without respect to the precise time, and is expressed by the auxiliaries *shall* and *will*; as, " I *will* examine the book, and you *shall* have my opinion."

The SECOND FUTURE TENSE has relation to the time of another future action, with which it is compared; as, " then cometh the end, when he shall have delivered up the kingdom to God."

The CONJUGATION of a verb is the regular combination and arrangement of it with regard to mood, tense, number, and person.

Before we enter on the conjugation, it is proper

first to explain the force and power of the auxiliary verbs.

The AUXILIARY VERBS* are, *do, have, shall, will; may, can, let,* and *must,* all of which have INFLECTIONS† or variations, except *must;* as, *do, did, didst, doing, done.*

The peculiar force of the several auxiliaries will appear from the following account of them.

Those of the INDICATIVE MOOD are *do, did; have, had; shall, will.*

Do and *did* mark the action itself, or the time of it, with greater energy and positiveness; as, "I *do* speak truth;" I *did* respect him;" " here am I, for thou *didst* call me."

Have and *had* mark time; the former denoting that the action is finished just now, the latter that some interval has elapsed since it was completed; as, "I *have* read the book;" "I *had* completed the exercise before the master came."

Shall and *will* express futurity, but with some affection or disposition of the agent. Thus, in the first person, *shall* barely foretells or predicts performances; as, "I *shall* walk;"—hereafter I am to perform the action of walking." Will implies promise or engagement; as, "I *will* walk;"—"I am determined hereafter to walk." In the second and third persons, these auxiliaries exchange their additional significations; and *shall* denotes promise or engagement; as, "thou *shalt* walk;"—*will* expresses futurity; as, "he *will* read;—that is to say, according to promise or engagement, "thou *shalt* walk;" and " he *will* hereafter read."

The auxiliaries of the POTENTIAL are *may* and *can; might, could, would, should.*

May and *can* denote capacity or ability; as, " I

---

* From *auxilior,* to help.
† From *inflecto,* to change the ending.

may write;" " I *can* read."   *Might* and *could* express the perfect time of *may* and *can*; and like them, are significant of ability or capacity; but the execution depends on circumstances which have not yet come into existence; as, " I *might* see him," " I *could* tell him," expresses that my capacity *to see* and *tell* him is complete, and I only wait for an opportunity to put it in action.

Would denotes inclination, *should* obligation, but the performance hangs upon some incident, or power, not under the control of the agent; as, " I *would* read, if I had a book;" " I *should* walk, if I had leave."

Ought is used in the following example in preference to *should*, because it is the stronger to express obligation and duty, and obviates a recurrence of the same word. " We *ought* to forget injuries, lest the remembrance of them *should* excite revenge."

Should is often followed by *would*; as, " if you *should* take the town to-day, the castle *would* be yours to-morrow."

They are sometimes used promiscuously, as, " it *should* seem;" " it *would* seem."   Both these forms express a shade of belief and confidence.

Should refers to duty and propriety, and *would* to choice, a delicacy of distinction is required. Hence *would* is not improperly used in the following example out of *Camoens:*

" Vain world ! did we but rightly feel,
  What ills thy treach'rous charms conceal,
How would we long from thee to steal,
  To death and sweet repose !"

Would is sometimes suppressed by making *were* the leading verb; as, " it *were* well if this could be ascribed to the overflowings of a rich imagination ;"

E

" it *were* no virtue to bear calamities, if we did not feel them;" that is, "*it would be.*"

The auxiliary TO BE, usually called a *substantive verb*, because it is confined to the signification of existence only, is generally and naturally an auxiliary of the passive form of the verb. In this case it is always attended with the perfect participle of the same form; as, " I *am* contented;" " I have *been* contented;" " I shall *be* contented."   But, added to the present participle of the active form, and supported by the other auxiliaries, there is not a mood or tense of the active form of the verb, which *to be* may not denote; as, " I am praising;" " I may be praising;" " be thou praising;" " to be praising;" are expressions equivalent to, I praise; I may praise; praise thou: to praise.

The CONJUGATION of the auxiliary and ACTIVE VERB

TO HAVE.

INDICATIVE MOOD.

Present Tense.

Singular.	Plural.
1 *Person,* I have.	1 We have.
2 *Person,* Thou hast*.	2 Ye, *or* you have.
3 *Person,* He, she, *or* it hath†, *or* has.	3 They have.

---

* In polite language, for the second person singular we now say " *you* have; *you* had; *you* will, or shall have." But the people called quakers retain *thou* in addressing individuals of all ranks.

† *Hath* reads remarkably well in the solemn style; as, " he *hath* shewed strength with his arm; he *hath* scattered the proud in the imagination of their hearts." It reads better than *has* after the conjunction *as;* " as hath been already observed." But we mostly prefer the ellipsis, and say, " as already observed."

Imperfect Tense.

Singular.	Plural.
1 I had.	1 We had.
2 Thou hadst.	2 Ye, *or* you had.
3 He had.	3 They had.

Perfect Tense.

1 I have had.	1 We have had.
2 Thou hast had.	2 Ye, *or* you have had.
3 He has had.	3 They have had.

Pluperfect Tense.

1 I had had.	1 We had had.
2 Thou hadst had.	2 Ye, *or* you had had.
3 He had had.	3 They had had.

First Future Tense.

1 I shall, *or* will have.	1 We shall, *or* will have.
2 Thou shalt, *or* wilt have.	2 Ye, *or* you shall, *or* will have.
3 He shall, *or* will have.	3 They shall, *or* will have.

Second Future Tense.

1 I shall have had.	1 We shall have had.
2 Thou wilt have had.	2 Ye, *or* you will have had.
3 He will have had.	3 They will have had.

IMPERATIVE MOOD.

1 Let me have.	1 Let us have.
2 Have, *or* have thou, *or* do thou have.	2 Have, *or* have ye, *or* do ye, *or* you have
3 Let him have.	3 Let them have.

E 2

POTENTIAL MOOD.

Present Tense.

Singular.	Plural.
1 I may, *or* can have.	1 We may, *or* can have.
2 Thou mayst, *or* canst have.	2 Ye, *or* you may, *or* can have.
3 He may, *or* can have.	3 They may, *or* can have.

Imperfect Tense.

1 I might, could, would, *or* should have.	1 We might, could, would, *or* should have.
2 Thou mightst, couldst, wouldst, *or* shouldst have.	2 Ye, *or* you might, could, would, *or* should have.
3 He might, could, would, *or* should have.	3 They might, could, would, *or* should have.

Perfect Tense.

1 I may, *or* can have had.	1 We may, *or* can have had.
2 Thou mayst, *or* canst have had.	2 Ye, *or* you may, *or* can have had.
3 He may, *or* can have had.	3 They may, *or* can have had.

Pluperfect Tense.

1 I might, could, would, *or* should have had.	1 We might, could, would, *or* should have had.
2 Thou mightst, couldst, wouldst, *or* shouldst have had.	2 Ye, *or* you might, could, would, *or* should have had.
3 He might, could, would, *or* should have had.	3 They might, could, would, *or* should have had.

SUBJUNCTIVE MOOD.

Present Tense.

Singular.	Plural.
1 If I have.	1 If we have.
2 If thou have.	2 If ye, *or* you have.
3 If he have.	3 If they have.

The remaining tenses of this mood are, in every respect, similar to the correspondent tenses of the indicative mood, except the second person singular of the first future, which is *shall or will* in the subjunctive, and "*shalt* or *wilt*" in the indicative. See subjunctive mood, conjugated page 83.

INFINITIVE MOOD.

Present Tense. To have.   *Perfect Tense.* To have had.

PARTICIPLES.

Present, Active, Having.   *Perfect,* Had.
Compound Perfect, Having had.

The conjugation of the auxiliary and NEUTER VERB

TO BE.

INDICATIVE MOOD.

Present Tense.

Singular.	Plural.
1 I am.	1 We are.
2 Thou art.	2 Ye, *or* you are.
3 He, she, *or* it is.	3 They are.

Imperfect Tense.

1 I was.	1 We were.
2 Thou wast.	2 Ye, *or* you were.
3 He was.	3 They were.

E 3

Perfect Tense.

Singular.	Plural.
1 I have been.	1 We have been.
2 Thou hast been.	2 Ye, *or* you have been.
3 He hath, *or* has been.	3 They have been.

Pluperfect Tense.

1 I had been.	1 We had been.
2 Thou hadst been.	2 Ye, *or* you had been.
3 He had been.	3 They had been.

First Future Tense.

1 I shall, *or* will be.	1 We shall, *or* will be.
2 Thou shalt, *or* wilt be.	2 Ye, *or* you shall, *or* will be.
3 He shall, *or* will be.	3 They shall, *or* will be.

Second Future Tense.

1 I shall have been.	1 We shall have been.
2 Thou wilt have been.	2 Ye, *or* you will have been.
3 He will have been.	3 They will have been.

IMPERATIVE MOOD.

1 Let me be.	1 Let us be.
2 Be thou, *or* do thou be.	2 Be ye, *or* you, *or* do ye be.
3 Let him be.	3 Let them be.

POTENTIAL MOOD.

Present Tense.

1 I may, *or* can be.	1 We may, *or* can be.
2 Thou mayst, *or* canst be.	2 Ye, *or* you may, *or* can be.
3 He may, *or* can be.	3 They may, *or* can be.

Imperfect Tense.

Singular.	Plural.
1 I might, could, would, *or* should be.	1 We might, could, would, *or* should be.
2 Thou mightst, couldst, wouldst, *or* shouldst be.	2 Ye, *or* you might, could, would, *or* should be.
3 He might, could, would, *or* should be.	3 They might, could, would, *or* should be.

Perfect Tense.

1 I may, *or* can have been.	1 We may, *or* can have been.
2 Thou mayst, *or* canst have been.	2 Ye, *or* you may, *or* can have been.
3 He may, *or* can have been.	3 They may, *or* can have been.

Pluperfect Tense.

1 I might, could, would, *or* should have been.	1 We might, could, would, *or* should have been.
2 Thou mightst, couldst, wouldst, *or* shouldst have been.	2 Ye, *or* you might, could, would, *or* should have been.
3 He might, could, would, *or* should have been.	3 They might, could, would, *or* should have been.

SUBJUNCTIVE MOOD.

Present Tense.

1 If I be.	1 If we be.
2 If thou be.	2 If ye, *or* you be.
3 If he be.	3 If they be.

E 4

Imperfect Tense.

Singular.	Plural.
1 If I were.	1 If we were.
2 If thou wert.	2 If ye, *or* you were.
3 If he were.	3 If they were.

Perfect Tense.

1 If I have been.	1 If we have been.
2 If thou have been.	2 If ye, *or* you have been.
3 If he have been.	3 If they have been.

Pluperfect Tense.

1 If I had been.	1 If we had been.
2 If thou had been.	2 If ye, *or* you had been.
3 If he had been.	3 If they had been.

INFINITIVE MOOD.

Present Tense, To be.   *Perfect Tense,* To have been.

PARTICIPLES.

Present, Being.   *Perfect,* Been.
Compound Perfect, Having been.

Conjugation of regular Verbs.

Verbs active are called regular when they form their imperfect tense of the indicative mood, and their perfect participles by adding to the verb *ed,* or *d* only when the verb ends in *e;* as,

Present.	Imperfect.	Perf. Participles.
I consider.	I considered.	Considered.
I praise.	I praised.	Praised.

A REGULAR ACTIVE VERB is conjugated in the following manner:

TO PRAISE.

INDICATIVE MOOD.

Present Tense.

Singular.	Plural.
1 I praise.	1 We praise.
2 Thou praisest, *or* you praise.	2 Ye, *or* you praise.
3 He praises.	3 They praise.

Imperfect Tense.

1 I praised.	1 We praised.
2 Thou praisedst.	2 Ye, *or* you praised.
3 He praised.	3 They praised.

In conjugating both the above tenses, we often use the auxiliary do, when we have occasion to confer superior emphasis; as, " I *do* praise; thou *dost* praise; he *doth* or *does* praise;" and, " I *did* praise; thou *didst* praise; he *did* praise." Also in questions; as, "*do* I praise? *dost* thou praise? *did* I praise? *didst* thou praise?" &c.

Perfect Tense.

1 I have praised.	1 We have praised.
2 Thou hast praised.	2 Ye, *or* you have praised
3 He hath, *or* has praised.	3 They have praised.

Pluperfect Tense.

1 I had praised.	1 We had praised.
2 Thou hadst praised.	2 Ye, *or* you had praised.
3 He had praised.	3 They had praised.

First Future Tense.

Singular.	Plural.
1 I shall, *or* will praise.	1 We shall, *or* will praise.
2 Thou shalt, *or* wilt praise.	2 Ye, *or* you shall, *or* will praise.
3 He shall, *or* will praise.	3 They shall, *or* will praise.

Second Future Tense.

1 I shall have praised.	1 We shall have praised.
2 Thou wilt have praised.	2 Ye, *or* you will have praised.
3 He will have praised.	3 They will have praised.

These tenses are called simple tenses, which are formed of the principal verb, without an auxiliary: as, "I praise; I praised." The compound tenses are such as cannot be formed without an auxiliary verb; as, "I *have* praised; I *had* praised; I *shall* or *will* praise; I *may* praise; I *may be* praised; I *may have been* praised;" &c. These compounds are, however, to be considered as only different forms of the same verb.

IMPERATIVE MOOD.

1 Let me praise.	1 Let us praise.
2 Praise, *or* praise thou, *or* do thou praise.	2 Praise, *or* praise ye, *or* you, *or* do ye praise.
3 Let him praise.	3 Let them praise.

POTENTIAL MOOD.

Present Tense.

1 I may, *or* can praise.	1 We may, *or* can praise.
2 Thou mayst, *or* canst praise.	2 Ye, *or* you may, *or* can praise.
3 He may, *or* can praise.	3 They may, *or* can praise.

Imperfect Tense.

Singular.
1 I might, could, would, *or* should praise.

2 Thou mightst, couldst, wouldst, *or* shouldst praise.

3 He might, could, would, *or* should praise.

Plural.
1 We might, could, would, *or* should praise.

2 Ye, *or* you might, could, would, *or* should praise.

3 They might, could, would, *or* should praise.

Perfect Tense.

1 I may, *or* can have praised.

2 Thou mayst, *or* canst have praised.

3 He may, *or* can have praised.

1 We may, *or* can have praised.

2 Ye, *or* you may, *or* can have praised.

3 They may, *or* can have praised.

Pluperfect Tense.

1 I might, could, would, *or* should have praised.

2 Thou mightst, couldst, wouldst, *or* shouldst have praised.

3 He might, could, would, *or* should have praised.

1 We might, could, would, *or* should have praised.

2 Ye, *or* you might, could, would, *or* should have praised.

3 They might, could, would, *or* should have praised.

SUBJUNCTIVE MOOD.

Present Tense.

1 If I praise.
2 If thou praise.
3 If he praise.

1 If we praise.
2 If ye, *or* you praise.
3 If they praise.

Imperfect Tense.

Singular.	Plural.
1 If I praised.	1 If we praised.
2 If thou praised.	2 If ye, *or* you praised.
3 If he praised.	3 If they praised.

Perfect Tense.

1 If I have praised.	1 If we have praised.
2 If thou have praised.	2 If ye, *or* you have praised.
3 If he have praised.	3 If they have praised.

Pluperfect Tense.

1 If I had praised.	1 If we had praised.
2 If thou had praised.	2 If ye, *or* you had praised.
3 If he had praised.	3 If they had praised.

First Future Tense.

1 If I shall, *or* will praise.	1 If we shall, *or* will praise.
2 If thou shall, *or* will praise.	2 If ye, *or* you shall, *or* will praise.
3 If he shall, *or* will praise.	3 If they shall, *or* will praise.

Second Future Tense.

1 If I shall have praised.	1 If we shall have praised.
2 If thou shall have praised.	2 If ye, *or* you shall have praised.
3 If he shall have praised.	3 If they shall have praised.

Notwithstanding the conjunction *if* only has been used in the above conjugation, it may be necessary to remark, that any other conjunction proper for the subjunctive mood may, with equal propriety, be occasionally used.

INFINITIVE MOOD.

Present Tense, To praise.   *Perfect Tense,* To have praised.

PARTICIPLES.

Present, Praising.   *Perfect,* Praised.
Compound Perfect, Having praised.

A PASSIVE VERB is conjugated by adding the perfect participle to the auxiliary verb TO BE, through all its changes of number, person, mood, and tense, in the following manner:

TO BE CONTENTED.

INDICATIVE MOOD.

Present Tense.

Singular.	Plural.
1 I am contented.	1 We are contented.
2 Thou art contented.	2 Ye, *or* you are contented.
3 He is contented.	3 They are contented.

Imperfect Tense.

1 I was contented.	1 We were contented.
2 Thou wast contented.	2 Ye, *or* you were contented.
3 He was contented.	3 They were contented.

Perfect Tense.

1 I have been contented.	1 We have been contented.
2 Thou hast been contented.	2 Ye, *or* you have been contented.
3 He hath, *or* has been contented.	3 They have been contented.

Pluperfect Tense.

Singular.	Plural.
1 I had been contented.	1 We had been contented.
2 Thou hadst been contented.	2 Ye, *or* you had been contented.
3 He had been contented.	3 They had been contented.

First Future Tense.

1 I shall, *or* will be contented.	1 We shall, *or* will be contented.
2 Thou shalt, *or* wilt be contented.	2 Ye, *or* you shall, *or* will be contented.
3 He shall, *or* will be contented.	3 They shall, *or* will be contented.

Second Future Tense.

1 I shall have been contented.	1 We shall have been contented.
2 Thou wilt have been contented.	2 Ye, *or* you will have been contented.
3 He will have been contented.	3 They will have been contented.

IMPERATIVE MOOD.

1 Let me be contented.	1 Let us be contented.
2 Be thou contented, *or* do thou be contented.	2 Be ye, *or* you contented, *or* do ye be contented.
3 Let him be contented.	3 Let them be contented.

POTENTIAL MOOD.

Present Tense.

Singular.

1 I may, *or* can be contented.
2 Thou mayst, *or* canst be contented.
3 He may, *or* can be contented.

Plural.

1 We may, *or* can be contented.
2 Ye, *or* you may, *or* can be contented.
3 They may, *or* can be contented.

Imperfect Tense.

1 I might, could, would, *or* should be contented.
2 Thou mightst, couldst, wouldst, *or* shouldst be contented.
3 He might, could, would, *or* should be contented.

1 We might, could, would, *or* should be contented.
2 Ye, *or* you might, could, would, *or* should be contented.
3 They might, could, would, *or* should be contented.

Perfect Tense.

1 I may, *or* can have been contented.
2 Thou mayst, *or* canst have been contented.
3 He may, *or* can have been contented.

1 We may, *or* can have been contented.
2 Ye, *or* you may, *or* can have been contented.
3 They may, *or* can have been contented.

Pluperfect Tense.

1 I might, could, would, *or* should have been contented.
2 Thou mightst, couldst, wouldst, *or* shouldst have been contented.
3 He might, could, would, *or* should have been contented.

1 We might, could, would, *or* should have been contented.
2 Ye, *or* you might, could, would, *or* should have been contented.
3 They might, could, would, *or* should have been contented.

SUBJUNCTIVE MOOD.

Present Tense.

Singular.	Plural.
1 If I be contented.	1 If we be contented.
2 If thou be contented.	2 If ye, *or* you be contented.
3 If he be contented.	3 If they be contented.

INFINITIVE MOOD.

Present Tense, To be contented.
Perfect Tense, To have been contented.

PARTICIPLES.

Present, Being contented. *Perfect,* Contented.
Compound Perfect, Having been contented.

Conjugation of the irregular verb,

TO WRITE.

INDICATIVE MOOD.

Present Tense.

1 I write.	1 We write.
2 Thou writest.	2 Ye, *or* you write.
3 He writeth, *or* writes.	3 They write.

Imperfect Tense.

1 I wrote.	1 We wrote.
2 Thou wrotest.	2 Ye, *or* you wrote.
3 He wrote.	3 They wrote.

Perfect Tense.

1 I have written.	1 We have written.
2 Thou hast written.	2 Ye, *or* you have written
3 He hath, *or* has written.	3. They have written.

Pluperfect Tense.

Singular.	Plural.
1 I had written.	1 We had written.
2 Thou hadst written.	2 Ye, *or* you had written.
3 He had written.	3 They had written.

First Future Tense.

1 I shall, *or* will write.	1 We shall, *or* will write.
2 Thou shalt, *or* wilt write.	2 Ye, *or* you shall, *or* will write.
3 He shall, *or* will write.	3 They shall, *or* will write.

Second Future Tense.

1 I shall have written.	1 We shall have written.
2 Thou shalt have written.	2 Ye *or,* you shall have written.
3 He shall have written.	3 They shall have written.

IMPERATIVE MOOD.

1 Let me write.	1 Let us write.
2 Write thou, *or* do thou write.	2 Write ye, *or* you, *or* do ye write.
3 Let him write.	3 Let them write.

POTENTIAL MOOD.

Present Tense.

1 I may, *or* can write.	1 We may, *or* can write.
2 Thou mayst, *or* canst write.	2 Ye, *or* you may *or* can write.
3 He may, *or* can write.	3 They may, *or* can write.

Imperfect Tense.

1 I might, could, would, *or* should write.	1 We might, could, would, *or* should write.
2 Thou mightst, couldst, wouldst, *or* shouldst write.	2 Ye, *or* you might, could, would, *or* should write.

Singular.

3 He might, could, would, *or* should, write.

Plural.

3 They might, could, would, *or* should write.

Perfect Tense.

1 I may, *or* can have written.

2 Thou mayst, *or* canst have written.

3 He may, *or* can have written.

1 We may, *or* can have written.

2 Ye, *or* you may, *or* can have written.

3 They may, *or* can have written.

Pluperfect Tense.

1 I might, could, would, *or* should have written.

2 Thou mightst, couldst, wouldst, *or* shouldst have written.

3 He might, could, would, *or* should have written.

1 We might, could, would, *or* should have written.

2 Ye, *or* you might, could, would, *or* should have written.

3. They might, could, would, *or* should have written.

SUBJUNCTIVE MOOD.
Present Tense.

1 If I write.
2 If thou write.
3 If he write.

1 If we write.
2 If ye *or* you write.
3 If they write.

Infinitive Mood.

Present tense, To write. *Perfect tense*, To have written.

Participles.

Present, Writing. *Perfect*, Written.
Compound perfect, Having written.

Of Irregular Verbs.

IRREGULAR VERBS are those which do not form their *imperfect tense*, or their *perfect participle*, by the addition of *d* or *ed* to the verb ; as,

Present.	Imperfect.	Perfect Participle.
I begin,	I began,	Begun.
I know,	I knew,	Known.
I drive,	I drove,	Driven.

Of Participles.

The *participle** is a certain form of the verb, and derives its name from its participating, not only of the properties of a verb, but also those of an adjective.

When participles describe the action of an agent, they are called ACTIVE ; as, *writing, reading, ciphering ;* the active participle always ends in " *ing*." But when they describe the reception of an agency, they are called PASSIVE ; as, *praised, adored, beloved.*

Irregular verbs are of various sorts; the first class have the present, the imperfect, and perfect tenses active, like the passive participle.

Present Tense.	Imperfect.	Perf. and Pass. Part.
I burst,	I burst,	I have burst.
cast,	cast,	cast.
cost,	cost,	cost.
cut,	cut,	cut.
hit,	hit,	hit.
hurt,	hurt,	hurt.
knit,	knit,	knit.
let,	let,	let.
put,	put,	put.
read,	read,	read.
rent,	rent,	rent.
rid,	rid,	rid.

* From *participo,* to partake.

Present Tense.	Imperfect.	Perf. and Pass. Part.
I set,	I set,	I have set.
shed,	shed,	shed.
shred,	shred,	shred.
shut,	shut,	shut.
slit,	slit,	slit or slat.
split,	split,	split.
spread,	spread,	spread.
thrust,	thrust,	thrust.

The second class of irregular verbs have the imperfect, the perfect active tenses, and the passive participles alike.

Present Tense	Imperfect.	Perf. and Pass. Part.
I abide,	I abode,	I have abode.
awake,	awoke,	awoke, having a-woke.
befall,	befell,	befell.
behold,	beheld,	beheld.
bend,	bent,	bent.
bereave,	bereft,	bereft.
beseech,	besought,	besought.
bide,	bode,	bode.
bind,	bound,	bound.
bleed,	bled,	bled.
bless,	blessed, blest,	blessed, blest.
breed,	bred,	bred.
bring,	brought,	brought.
build,	built,	built.
burn,	burnt,	burnt.
buy,	bought,	bought.
catch,	catched caught,	catched, caught.
clothe,	clad, clothed,	clad, clothed,
cling,	clung,	clung.

Present Tense.	Imperfect.	Perf. and Pass. Part.
I creep,	I crept,	I have crept.
curse,	curst,	curst.
dare,	dared, durst,	dared.
deal,	dealt,	dealt.
dig,	dug,	dug.
dip,	dipt,	dipt.
dream,	dreamt,	dreamed, dreamt.
drop,	dropped, dropt,	dropped, dropt.
dwell,	dwelt,	dwelt.
feed,	fed,	fed.
feel,	felt,	felt.
fight,	fought,	fought.
find,	found,	found.
flee,	fled,	fled.
fling,	flung,	flung.
fright,	frighted, fraught,	frighted, fraught,
gild,	gilt,	gilt.
gird,	girt, girded,	girt, girded.
grind,	ground,	ground.
hang,	hung,	hung, hanged
have,	had,	had.
hear,	heard,	heard.
keep,	kept,	kept.
kneel,	knelt,	knelt.
lay,	laid,	laid, lain.
lead,	led,	led.
leap,	leapt,	leapt.
leave,	left,	left.
lend,	lent,	lent.
lop,	lopt,	lopt.
lose,	lost,	lost.
make,	made,	made.

Present Tense.	Imperfect.	Perf. and Pass. Part.
I mean,	I meant,	I have meant.
meet,	met,	met.
pay,	paid,	paid.
quit,	quitted, quit,	quitted, quit.
rend,	rent,	rent.
say,	said,	said.
seek,	sought,	sought.
sell,	sold,	sold.
send,	sent,	sent.
shine,	shone,	shone.
shoe,	shod,	shod.
shoot,	shot,	shot.
sit,	sat,	sat.
sleep,	slept,	slept.
sling,	slung,	slung.
slink,	slunk,	slunk.
slip,	slipt,	slipt.
smell,	smelled, smelt,	smelled. smelt.
speed,	sped,	sped.
spell,	spelt,	spelt.
spend,	spent,	spent.
spill,	spilt,	spilt.
spin,	spun,	spun.
stamp,	stampt,	stampt.
stand,	stood,	stood.
stick,	stuck,	stuck.
sting,	stung,	stung.
stink,	stunk,	stunk.
string,	strung,	strung.
strip,	stript,	stript.
sweat,	swet,	swet.
sweep,	swept,	swept.
swing,	swung,	swung.
teach,	taught,	taught.
tell,	told,	told.

Present Tense.	Imperfect.	Perf. and Pass. Part.
I think,	I thought,	I have thought.
understand,	understood,	under-stood.
weep,	wept,	wept.
whip,	whipt,	whipt.
win,	won,	won.
wind,	wound,	wound.
work,	wrought,	wrought.
wring,	wrung,	wrung

The third class vary the present, the imperfect, and the perfect tense, and the passive participle.

Present Tense.	Imperfect.	Perf. and Pass. Part.
I am,	I was,	I have been.
arise,	arose,	arisen.
bake,	baked,	baken. baked.
bear*,	bare,	borne.
bear†,	bore, bare,	borne.
bear‡,	bore,	borne.
beat,	beat,	beaten, beat.
become,	became,	become.
begin,	began,	begun.
bid,	bade,	bidden, bid.
bite,	bit,	bitten, bit.
blow,	blew,	blown.
break,	broke,	broken.
chide,	chid,	chidden, chid.
choose,	chose,	chosen.
cleave,	clove, clave,	cloven, cleft.
cling,	clang,	clung.

---

* An infant.　　† Witness.　　‡ A burden.

Present Tense.	Imperfect.	Perf. and Pass. Part.
I come,	I came,	I have come, came.
crow,	crew,	crowed.
dare,	dared, durst,	dared.
die,	(he) died,	(he is) dead.
do,	did,	done.
draw,	drew,	drawn.
drive,	drove,	driven.
drink,	drank,	drunk.
eat,	eat, *or* ate,	eaten.
fall,	fell,	fallen.
fly,	flew,	flown.
fold,	folded,	folded, folden.
forbear,	forbore,	forborn.
forget,	forgot,	forgotten, forgot.
forgive,	forgave,	forgiven.
forsake,	forsook,	forsaken.
freeze,	froze.	frozen.
get,	got,	gotten.
give,	gave,	given.
go,	went,	gone.
grave,	graved,	graven.
grow,	grew,	grown.
heave,	hove,	hoven, hove.
help,	helped,	helped, holpen.
hew,	hewed,	hewn.
hide,	hid,	hidden, hid.
hold,	held,	holden.
know,	knew,	known.
lade,	loaded,	laden.
lie, (down,)	lay,	lain.
load	loaded,	laden.

Present Tense.	Imperfect.	Perf. and Pass. Part.
I melt,	I melted,	I have molten.
mix,	mixed,	mixt.
mow,	mowed,	mown.
overcome,	overcame,	over- come.
owe,	owed,	owed, owen.
pass,	passed,	past.
ride,	rode,	ridden, rode.
ring,	rang,	rung.
rise,	rose,	risen.
rive,	rived,	riven.
run,	ran,	run.
saw,	sawed,	sawn.
see,	saw,	seen.
seethe,	seethed,	sodden.
shake,	shook,	shaken.
shape,	shaped,	shaped. shapen.
shaved,	shaved,	shaved. shaven.
shear,	sheared, shore,	shorn.
show,	showed,	shown.
shrink,	shrank, shrunk,	shrunk.
shrive,	shrove,	shriven.
sing,	sang,	sung.
sink,	sank, sunk,	sunk.
slay,	slew,	slain.
slide,	slid,	slidden.
smite,	smote,	smitten.
snow,	snowed,	snown.
sow,	sowed,	sown.
speak,	spoke, spake,	spoken.
spit,	spit, spat,	spitten, spit.
spring,	sprang,	sprung.

Present Tense.	Imperfect.	Perf. and Pass. Part.
I steal,	I stole,	I have stolen.
stink,	stank,	stunk.
strew,	strewed,	strewn.
stride,	strode,	stridden.
strike,	struck,	stricken.
strive,	strove,	striven.
strow, or strew,	strowed, or strewed,	strown, strowed. strewed.
swear,	swore,	sworn.
swell,	swelled,	swollen.
swim,	swam,	swum.
take,	took,	taken.
tear,	tore,	torn.
thrive,	throve,	thriven.
throw,	threw,	thrown.
tread,	trod,	trodden.
wax,	waxed,	waxen.
wear,	wore,	worn.
weave,	wove,	woven.
write,	wrote,	written,
writhe,	writhed,	writhen.

The DEFECTIVE VERBS are those which are used only in some of the moods and tenses.

Present Tense.	Imperfect.	Perf. and Pass. Part.
Can,	could.	
May,	might.	
Must,	must.	
Ought,	ought.	
Quoth,	quoth.	
Shall,	should.	
Will,	would.	
Wis,	wist.	
Wit, wot,	wot.	

Many of our regular verbs double the final con

sonant in the present participle, and in the past tense. Of this class we give the following selection :

Present Tense.	Past Tense, and Pass. Part.	Present Tense.	Past Tense and Pass. Part.
Abet,	abetted*.	Confer,	conferred.
Abhor,	abhorred.	Control,	controlled.
Acquit,	acquitted.	Counsel,	counselled.
Admit,	admitted.	Crop,	cropped.
Allot,	allotted.	Crum,	crummed.
Annul,	annulled.	Cup,	cupped.
Appal,	appalled.	Debar,	debarred.
Bar,	barred.	Defer,	deferred.
Barrel,	barrelled.	Disinter,	disinterred.
Beg,	begged.	Drop,	dropped.
Bet,	betted.	Drum,	drummed.
Bias,	biassed.	Dun,	dunned.
Blot,	blotted.	Enamel,	enamelled.
Bowel,	bowelled.	Enrol,	enrolled.
Brag,	bragged.	Equal,	equalled.
Bud,	budded.	Equip,	equipped.
Cabal,	caballed.	Fag,	fagged.
Cancel,	cancelled.	Fan,	fanned.
Cap,	capped.	Flit,	flitted.
Cavil,	cavilled.	Fulfil,	fulfilled.
Char,	charred.	Fur,	furred.
Chat,	chatted.	Gravel,	gravelled.
Chip,	chipped.	Gum,	gummed.
Clip,	clipped.	Handsel,	handselled.
Clot,	clotted.	Hem,	hemmed.
Commit,	committed.	Hip,	hipped.
Compel,	compelled.	Hovel,	hovelled.
Con,	conned.	Jam,	jammed.
Concur,	concurred.	Japan,	japanned.

* The active participle also doubles the final consonant; as, abetting, &c.

Present Tense.	Past Tense, and Pass. Part.	Present Tense.	Past Tense and Pass. Part.
Jar,	jarred.	Revel,	revelled.
Incur,	incurred.	Rebel,	rebelled.
Instil,	instilled.	Recur,	recurred.
Inter,	interred.	Refit,	refitted.
Knit,	knitted.	Regret,	regretted.
Libel,	libelled.	Ship,	shipped.
Map,	mapped.	Sin,	sinned.
Marvel,	marvelled.	Skip,	skipped.
Net,	netted.	Spot,	spotted.
Nib,	nibbed.	Sprig,	sprigged.
Nip,	nipped.	Star,	starred.
Occur,	occurred.	Stop,	stopped.
Omit,	omitted.	Submit,	submitted.
Parcel,	parcelled.	Sup,	supped.
Patrol,	patrolled.	Throb,	throbbed.
Permit,	permitted.	Tin,	tinned.
Plan,	planned.	Tinsel,	tinselled.
Plat,	platted.	Transfer,	transferred.
Prefer,	preferred.	Victual,	victualled.
Quit,	quitted.	Wed.	wedded.

Some verbs double the final consonant in the active participle, although irregular in the past tense and passive participle; as,

Present Tense.	Active Participle.	Past Tense.	Pass. Part.
Begin,	beginning,	began,	begun.
Bid,	bidding,	bade,	bidden.

Questions.

1. What is a verb?
2. How many sorts of verbs are there?
3. What is an active verb?
4. Give me an example.

5. Prove the verb to be active.
6. What is a passive verb?
7. Give me an example.
8. Prove it to be passive.
9. What are neuter verbs?
10. Why are they called intransitive?
11. Can neuter verbs indicate action?
12. Give me an example.
13. Have verbs any number?
14. Have these numbers any person?
15. Give me an example.
16. How many modes have verbs?
17. What does the indicative do?
18. Give me an example.
19. What does the imperative do?
20. Give me an example.
21. What does the potential do?
22. Give me an example.
23. What does the subjunctive do?
24. Give me an example.
25. What does the infinitive do?
26. Give me an example.
27. How are verbs divided with regard to time or tense?
28. How many variations of time or tense are there?
29. For what purpose do we use the present tense?
30. ———————————— imperfect tense?
31. ———————————— perfect tense?
32. ———————————— pluperfect tense?
33. ———————————— first future tense?
34. ———————————— second future tense?
35. What do you mean by the conjugation of a verb?
36. What are auxiliary verbs?
37. Repeat them.

F 3

38. What auxiliaries are used in the indicative mood?

39. Explain *do* and *did*.

40. Explain *have* and *had*.

41. Explain *shall* and *will*.

42. What auxiliaries are used in the potential mood?

43. Explain *may* and *can*.

44. Explain *would* and *should*.

45. What is the auxiliary verb " *to be*" called?

46. Give me an example.

47. What voice do you call the conjugation of an active verb?

48. Conjugate the *active verb* TO HAVE, indicative mood, present tense.

49. Repeat the imperfect tense.

50. Repeat the perfect tense.

51. Repeat the pluperfect tense.

52. The first future tense.

53. The second future tense.

54. Repeat the imperative mood.

55. Conjugate the potential mood.

56. Conjugate the subjunctive mood.

57. Conjugate the infinitive mood.

58. Repeat the participles.

59. Conjugate the neuter verb TO BE through all the moods and tenses.

60. What are regular verbs?

61. How are regular verbs known?

62. Conjugate the regular active verb TO PRAISE through all the moods and tenses.

63. What voice do you call the conjugation of passive verbs?

64. Conjugate the passive verb to BE CONTENTED, through all the moods and tenses.

65. Conjugate the irregular verb TO WRITE, through all the moods and tenses.

66. What are irregular verbs?
67. Give me some example in the first class.
68. What are the second class of irregular verbs?
69. Give me some examples.
70. How are the third class of irregular verbs distinguished?
71. Give me some examples.
72. What are defective verbs?
73. Give me some examples.
74. Do any of the regular verbs double the final consonant?
75. Give me some examples.

§ 7. OF THE ADVERB.

The chief use of the ADVERB*, as its name imports, is to modify the verb, just as the adjective qualifies the noun. The circumstances of the action expressed by tenses and moods are all of a nature too general to be sufficient for the purposes of communication. It is often necessary to be much more particular in ascertaining both the time and the manner, but particularly the place of the action. The important office of the adverb is to accomplish these ends.

Adverbs admit of degrees of comparison similar with adjectives; as,

Soon,	sooner,	soonest.
Often,	oftener,	oftenest.

Those ending in *ly* are commonly compared by *more* and *most*; as,

Carefully,	*more* carefully,	*most* carefully.

Adverbs, though very numerous, may be reduced to certain classes; as, *Affirmation, comparison, con-*

---

* From *ad*, to, and *verbum*, a verb.

tingency, *doubt, inference, interrogation, negation, number, order, place, preference, quality* and *manner, quantity, time*, &c.

I. *Affirmation,* assuredly, certainly, doubtless, indeed, really, surely, truly, undoubtedly, verily, yea, yes, &c.

II. *Comparison.* Alike, almost, best, better, equally, least, less, little, more, most, so, thus, very, worse, worst, &c.

III. *Contingency.* Perhaps, possibly, probably, &c.

IV. *Doubt.* Peradventure, perchance, &c.

V. *Inference.* Consequently, hence, therefore, &c.

VI. *Interrogation.* How, wherefore, whether, why, &c.

VII. *Negation.* By no means, in no wise, nay, no, not, not at all, &c.

VIII. *Number.* Frequently, often, once, rarely, thrice, twice, &c.

IX. *Order.* First, finally, fourthly, lastly, secondly, thirdly, &c.

X. *Place.* Above, anywhere, backward, below, downward, elsewhere, forward, hence, here, herein, hither, nowhere, somewhere, thence, there, thither, upward, whence, where, whither, whithersoever, within, without, &c.

XI. *Preference.* Chiefly, especially, principally, rather, &c.

XII. *Quality* and *Manner.* Foolishly, genteelly, gracefully, handsomely, highly, ill, justly, lordly, proudly, quickly, slowly, well, wisely, &c.

NOTE.—Adverbs of quality are of the most numerous kind, and they are generally formed by adding the termination *ly* to an adjective or participle, or changing *le* into *ly*; as, bad, badly; cheerful, cheerfully; true, truly,

XIII. *Quantity.* Abundantly, copiously, enough, how great, how much, less, little, more, much, plentifully, something, somewhat, sufficiently, &c.

XIV. *Time.* PRESENT. Now to-day, &c.

PAST. Already, before, heretofore, hitherto, lately, long ago, long since, yesterday, &c.

FUTURE. By-and-by, henceforth, henceforward, hereafter, immediately, instantly, not yet, presently, straightway, to-morrow, &c.

INDEFINITE. Again, always, daily, ever, hourly, monthly, never, oft, often, oftentimes, ofttimes, seldom, sometimes, soon, then, weekly, when, yearly, &c.

Adverbs may be divided into as many other classes as there are circumstances in an action, or bearings in argument; but a refined division would perplex the learner without any apparent advantage.

Many of our adverbs are formed by a combination of prepositions with adverbs of place, *here, there,* and *where;* as, *hereof, thereof, whereof, &c.*

There are also some adverbs compounded of nouns and the letter *a,* used instead of the preposition, *at, on,* &c.; as *abed, abroad, afloat, aground, aside, ashore,* &c.; meaning, **on** shore, *on one side,* &c.

One adverb is frequently employed to qualify another; as, *too confidently, very seldom;* and they are sometimes applied to circumscribe adjectives; as, *unmercifully severe, highly criminal, superlatively excellent.*

Questions.

1. For what purpose are adverbs used?
2. Can adverbs be compared like adjectives?
3. Give me an example of the modes of comparison.
4. Are adverbs divided into classes?
5. Repeat all the adverbs of number that you are acquainted with.
6. Repeat the adverbs of order.

7. Repeat the adverbs of place.
8. How are adverbs of time divided?
9. Repeat those of present time.
10. Repeat the adverbs of past time.
11. Repeat the adverbs of future time.
12. Repeat the indefinite adverbs.
13. Name the adverbs of quantity.
14. Repeat the adverbs of quality.
15. How are adverbs of quality generally formed?
16. Repeat the adverbs of doubt.
17. Name the adverbs of affirmation.
18. Repeat the adverbs of negation.
19. Repeat the adverbs denoting the passions.
20. Repeat the adverbs of interrogation.
21. Repeat the adverbs of comparison.
22. Repeat the adverbs of inference.
23. Repeat the adverbs of contingency.
24. Repeat the adverbs of preference.
25. What adverbs are formed by the aid of prepositions?
26. Give me an example of all you are acquainted with.
27. Repeat the adverbs that are compounded of nouns and prepositions.

§ 8. OF PREPOSITIONS

The chief office of PREPOSITIONS* is to denote the relations of substantives to one another; they are therefore placed generally between the related objects, immediately before the one that bears the relation, and as near as possible to the other to which the relation is borne. " A man *of* honour." " Success *to* industry." " Genius *with* judgment."

Prepositions may be divided into two classes.

---

* From *præ*, before, and *pono*, to place.

The first expresses the connexion of things, and will bear a comparison with the adjective; as, " monarchs are *above* the law, but criminals are *under* its sentence."

The second class express the connexion of actions, and has some affinity to the verb; " as, I study language *according to* the principles of the best grammarians, and *consonant to* their examples."

When the prepositions *out, near, far, even,* &c. precede another preposition, they become adjectives; as, *out of* sight; *near to* London; *far from* home; *even till* midnight.

The principal prepositions are contained in the following list:—

Above,	before,	down,	over,
About,	behind,	except,	through,
According	below,	excepting,	till,
to,	beneath,	for,	to,
After,	beside,	from,	toward, to-
Against,	besides,	in, into,	wards,
Amid,	between,	near,	up, upon,
amidst,	betwixt,	of and off,	under, un-
Among,	beyond,	on,	derneath,
Amongst,	by,	out of,	with, within,
Around,	concerning,	outside,	without.
At,			

The necessity and use of prepositions will appear from the following examples; as, " he writes a pen ;" " they run the river ;" " the monument fell the men ;" " the man is the house." In each of these expressions there is observable either a total want of connexion, or such a connexion as produces nonsense or falsehood; and it is evident that before they can be turned into sense, the vacancy must be filled up by some connecting word; as thus, " he writes *with* a pen ;" " they run *towards* the river ;" " the monument fell *upon* the men ;" " the man is *within* the house:" hence we see prepositions are necessary to connect words which in their signification are not naturally connected.

The importance of prepositions will be further perceived by the explanation of a few of them.

Against, opposed, hostile, contrary; as, " to swim *against* the stream."

By implies agent, instrument; as, " goods are sold *by* weight and measure."

For is used in various forms; as, " bitter *for* sweet."

In relates to time, place, the state or manner of being or acting; as, " he resides *in* the city."

Into is used after verbs that imply motion of any kind; as, " the horse went *into* the stable."

Of denotes possession; " as, " the house *of* my friend."

To or *unto* is opposed to from; as, " he rode *from* Tunbridge-wells *to* London."

Through implies to pass; " as he went to Kensington *through* the Park."

With signifies association; as, " Ann walked *with* Sarah."

Compound prepositions are exemplified in the following manner.

A is often improperly used for *on* or *of*; as, " set *a* going;" John *a* Gaunt."

Be is used in besprinkle, betoken, &c.

For in forbid, forlorn, forsake, &c.

Fore in forebode, forefather, forewarn, &c.

Mis in misdemeanor, mishap, mistake, &c.

Over, in overcome, overreach, overtake, &c.

Out, in outdo, outstrip, outwit, &c.

Un, in undo, unheard, unlike, unmanly, &c.

Up, in uphold, upland, upward, &c.

With, in withdraw, withhold, withstand, &c.

Questions.

1 What is a preposition?

2. What are prepositions used for?

3. Give me an example.

4. How are the first class of prepositions used?

5. Give an example.

6. What is the second class used for?

7. Give an example.

8. Repeat the simple prepositions.

9. What preposition is used to denote opposition?

10. Give an example.

11. What preposition is used to denote the agent or instrument?

12. Give an example.

13. What preposition is used to mark the cause or motion of an action?

14. Give an example.

15. What preposition is used to express the manner of being or acting?

16. Give an example.

17. What preposition is used to imply motion?

18. Give an example.

19. What preposition is used to denote possession?

20. Give an example.

21. How are prepositions used to denote opposition?

22. Give an example.

23. What preposition is used to imply passing?

24. Give an example.

25. What preposition is used to denote association?

26. Give an example.

27. What preposition is used to mark separation?

28. Give an example.

29. Is *a* ever used for a preposition?

30. Give an example.
31. Repeat the compound prepositions.

§ 9. OF CONJUNCTIONS.

Conjunctions* are used to connect nouns, clauses of sentences, or members of periods; and to give notice of the succession of those members in a distinct and expressive manner; as, " house *and* garden!" " never depart from the truth, *nor* associate with naughty children;" " you cannot learn *unless* you pay attention.

In the first of these examples the conjunction *and* is copulative, and joins house and garden; in the second, *nor* is disjunctive, being designed to separate good from bad children; and the third, *unless*, is conditional.

Conjunctions as well as adverbs are divided into various classes, but the division should not be extended too far; the following list contains the principal conjunctions :—

I. COPULATIVE. *Also, and, because, both, for, if, since, that, then, therefore, wherefore.*

II. DISJUNCTIVE. *As, but, either, lest, neither, nor, notwithstanding, or, that, though, unless, yet.*

The *conditional* class of conjunctions comprises the following words; except, if, though, unless, whether.

Conjunctions are also subdivided in the following manner to denote
Addition. Besides, besides that.
Comparison. Neither, nor, than.

---

* From *con*, with, and *jungo*, to join.

Conclusion. Now, so that, therefore, thus.

Connexion. Also, and.

Division. Either.

Doubt. If, in case that, provided, suppose that.

Exception. Although, except, save.

Mind or *intention.* For fear that, to the end that.

Necessity or *motive.* Because, for, seeing that, since.

Opposition. In the meanwhile, nevertheless, yet.

Time. Again, since that, when, while.

The copulative class of conjunctions serve to connect or to continue a sentence by expressing an addition, a supposition, or cause; as, " Mary *and* Charles are very attentive;" " we will go if you will accompany us."

The disjunctive class are used not only to connect and continue the sentence, but also to express opposition of meaning in different degrees; as, " *though* he was frequently admonished *yet* he did not reform." This class runs mostly in pairs; as, " give me *neither* poverty *nor* riches."

Some conjunctions have corresponding conjunctions belonging to them either expressed or understood.

As is often followed by *so*, expressing comparison; " *as* the stars *so* shall thy seed be."

As is sometimes followed by *that*; " *as* soon as you have read my apology, you will be convinced *that* I have not neglected your commission."

As is sometimes followed by *as*, expressing comparison of equality; " she is *as* amiable *as* her sister, and *as* much respected."

Either is sometimes followed by *or*; " I will *either* send the book *or* bring it myself;" " *either* the one *or* the other must be to blame."

Neither is followed by *nor*: " *neither* he *nor* I am able to answer the question."

No is often followed by *nor*; " *no* man can preserve his reputation, *nor* protect his character from censure, unless he faithfully discharges his duty to GOD and man."

So is followed by *that*, expressing a consequence; " the truth of HIS doctrine was *so* persuasive, *that* it engrossed the attention of every hearer."

Though is mostly followed by *yet*; " *though* HE was rich, *yet* for our sakes HE became poor."

Whether is followed by *or*; " I have not heard *whether* your sister returns to-day *or* to-morrow."

Questions.

1. What are conjunctions used for ?
2. Give me an example.
3. Are conjunctions divided into classes ?
4. Repeat the copulative conjunctions.
5. Repeat the disjunctive conjunctions.
6. Repeat the conditional conjunctions.
7. What conjunctions denote connexion ?
8. ———————————————— opposition ?
9. ———————————————— division ?
10. ———————————————— exception ?
11. ———————————————— comparison ?
12. ———————————————— addition ?
13. ———————————————— mind or intention ?
14. ———————————————— time ?
15. What conjunctions shew necessity or motive ?
16. ———————————— doubt ?
17. What conjunctions are used to conclude ?
18. What are the copulative conjunctions used for ?
19. Give an example.
20. What are the disjunctive conjunctions used for ?
21. Give an example.

22. Explain the corresponding conjunction— though.
23. ——————————————— whither,
24. ——————————————— either.
25. ——————————————— neither.
26. ——————————————— no.
27. ——————————————— so.
28. ——————————————— as.

§ 10. OF INTERJECTIONS.

Interjections* indicate those impressions which so suddenly and violently affect the mind of the speaker or writer as to burst asunder the regular train of his thoughts and expressions, and thence demand immediate utterance.

Interjections vary according to the feelings they excite.

Those which intimate *earnestness* or *grief* are, O! oh! ah! alas! well-a-day! lack-a-day! alas, alas!

Such as are expressive of *aversion, disgust,* or *contempt,* are, pish! tush! pshaw! foh! fie! away!

Of *wonder* or *surprise;* aye! heigh! really! strange! indeed! do you say so! what!

Of *calling;* hem! ho! soho! halloo!

Of *laughter;* ha, ha, ha!

Of a call of the *attention;* lo! behold! hark!

Of requesting *silence;* hush! hist!

Of *salutation* or *greeting;* welcome! hail! all hail!

Of *mirth* and *applause;* hey! bravo! well done! huzza!

Of *veneration;* O!

Of *parting;* farewell! adieu!

---

* From *inter,* between, and *jacio,* to throw.

Questions.

1. What are interjections?
2. What interjections are used to express earnestness, grief, &c.?
3. ———————————— aversion, contempt, &c.?
4. ———————————— wonder or surprise?
5. ———————————— calling?
6. ———————————— laughter?
7. ———————————— attention?
8. ———————————— silence?
9. ———————————— salutation?
10. ———————————— mirth and applause?
11. ———————————— veneration?
12. ———————————— parting?

§ 11. GRAMMATICAL EXERCISES.

Nouns, Adjectives, Verbs, and Adverbs.

Write a number of abstract nouns, the adjectives from whence they are derived, the corresponding adverb, and verb, in the following order:

Ab. Nouns	Adjectives.	Verbs.	Adverbs.
Attention	attentive	they are attentive	attentively
Breadth	broad	it is broad	broadly
Care	careful	I am careful	carefully
Cheerfulness	cheerful	he is cheerful	cheerfully
Decency	decent	it is decent	decently
Diligence	diligent	she is diligent	diligently
Gratitude	grateful	ye are grateful	gratefully
Heat	hot	it is hot	hotly
Height	high	they are high	highly
Humility	humble	ye are humble	humbly
Joy	joyful	we are joyful	joyfully
Luxuriance	luxurious	it is luxurious	luxuriously
Modesty	modest	she is modest	modestly

Ab. Nouns.	Adjectives.	Verbs.	Adverbs.
Noise	noisy	they are noisy	noisily
Pride	proud	he is proud	proudly
Simplicity	simple	ye are simple	simply
Strictness	strict	you are strict	strictly
Truth	true	it is true	truly
Virtue	virtuous	she is virtuous	virtuously
Wisdom	wise	he is wise	wisely

These exercises should be continued until the children have written several lessons including ten or twelve of each class of words in a lesson, taking them alphabetically.

From this exercise, lead them to compose simple sentences, taking the first line in the preceding list of words, in the following manner:

Ab. Noun.   A good child studies with *attention.*

Adj.   A good child studies in an *attentive* manner.

Verb.   A good child *is attentive* to his studies.

Adv.   A good child studies *attentively.*

This will be found an amusing and truly useful exercise, giving the pupils a taste for composition, as well as transposition.

Exercises of the above kind should be given to the pupils, until they compose simple sentences with facility.

Of Prepositions.

Direct the children to name all the persons or things they can associate with other persons and things, by placing the prepositions *above, about, according to, adown, afore, after, against, aloft, amid, amidst, among, amongst, around, at, athwart, atween, atwixt, bating, before, behind, below, beneath, beside, besides, between, betwixt, beyond, by, concerning, cross, down, except, excepting, for, from, 'gainst, in, into, near, nigh, of, off, on, over, out of, past, round, since, thorough, through, throughout, till, to, touching, toward, towards, traverse, under, underneath, unto, up, upon, with, within, without,* &c., between them; as for example,

" In building a wall one stone is placed *above* another."

" The children walk *about* the garden."

" She studies *according to* rule," &c.

Of Conjunctions.

When the pupils have completed the exercise on prepositions, they should be directed how to apply conjunctions. And here they should be informed that certain persons may perform more actions than one; and that more persons than one may perform the same action.

Then direct them to connect a number of actions with persons performing them, and the circumstances under which they are performed, to other actions, persons, and circumstances, by using the copulative conjunctions, *and, because, both, for, if, since, that, then, therefore, wherefore,* &c.; as for example,

" Ladies walk in the park, *and* their footmen follow them."

" Men love darkness rather than light, *because* their deeds are evil."

Both the horse and rider were exhausted.

As soon as they have given examples applying all the copulative conjunctions, exercise them in a similar manner by using the disjunctive conjunctions; and direct them to separate or divide a number of actions, together with the persons performing them, by the use of the words, *as, but, either, lest, neither, nor, notwithstanding, or, than, though, unless, yet,* &c.; as for example,

" In singing *as* well *as* playing you excel."

" John is as intelligent as James, *but* not so communicative."

" Your sister is more attentive to her studies *than* your brother."

When the pupils are well versed in the change of words, and their association with one another, they may be required to compose sentences by adding certain parts of speech to a given noun, at the discretion of the parent or teacher; as for example, let us suppose we were walking near the sea, and saw a ship in full sail, destined for the East Indies, and from thence to return to England. Write on your slates two adjectives qualifying the noun substantive ship, preceded by an article, " *a beautiful majestic ship*"—now add a preposition, two adjectives, a noun, and verb, descriptive of some action performed by the ship, qualified by an adverb, " *with wide spreading canvass sails swiftly*"— describe the place where she sails by a preposition, article, adjective, and noun, " *across the great deep*" —explain the object of the voyage by an active participle, article, noun, preposition, and noun, " *conveying the produce of England*"—enlarge this description by a copulative conjunction, active participle, article, noun, preposition, possessive pronoun, adjective, and noun, " *and extending the commerce of our native land*" — conclude this member of the sentence by a preposition, article, adjective, noun, preposition, article, and noun, "*to the eastern extremity of the world :*"—To complete this sentence we must take a view of the pleasure that Albion's sons will receive on the arrival of a vessel from England, with intelligence from their families and friends, and then shew the grand design of the merchants in such an undertaking, by adding an

active participle, noun, preposition, possessive pronoun, noun, active participle, preposition, pronominal adjective of the demonstrative kind, and a
noun, "*administering comfort to our countrymen
residing in those parts*"—then take a copulative
conjunction, preposition, adverb, noun, preposition,
article, noun, preposition, noun, verb, article, noun,
copulative conjunction, noun, article, noun, preposition, article, and noun, "*and from thence return
with the treasures of Asia, to enrich the owners and
increase the wealth of the empire.*"

Now let me hear what you have written,

"*A beautiful majestic ship, with wide spreading
canvass, sails swiftly across the great deep, conveying
the produce of England, and extending the commerce
of our native land to the eastern extremity of the
world, administering comforts to our countrymen
residing in those parts, and from thence return with
the treasures of Asia, to enrich the owners and increase the wealth of the empire.*"

In this manner they should be instructed in the
composition of sentences, more or less complex at
the discretion of the parent or teacher.

When reading, they should be frequently called
upon to point out the principal features of a sentence, and by interrogation lead them on to shew
what degree of importance the subordinate members associated with it are to the matter intended
to be conveyed.

They should also be required to change the most
important verbs into different numbers, persons,
tenses, &c. And then explain what changes that
will necessarily make in the other parts of the sentence. This will enable them to discover the several rules which are used to shew the government
and agreement of words with each other, commonly
called SYNTAX," the nature of which will be fully
explained in the following pages.

PART III.

§ 1. OF SYNTAX, THE CONSTRUCTION OF SENTENCES, and PUNCTUATION.

The word SYNTAX * imports the reciprocal arrangement of words in a SENTENCE, which in all cases should be agreeable to the order of nature, and the present forms of speech.

The rules of syntax may be comprised under two heads; the *first* respects the concord or agreement of words, the *second* the government or dependance of words.

CONCORD consists in the agreement of words with one another, in *person*, *number*, *gender*, and *case*.

GOVERNMENT consists in the influence which one word has over another, by causing it to be in some particular *case*, *number*, *mood*, or *tense*.

The terms *sentence* and *period* are nearly synonymous, both denoting the quantity of words or members comprehended between two full points, in writing or printing; and convey a complete sense of themselves, independent of the words that either precede or follow them.

Both the sentence and the period may consist of sub-divisions, clauses, or members, which are commonly separated from one another; these more closely connected, by commas, those more slightly, by semicolons.

In every sentence or period there must be an AGENT, an *action*, and an OBJECT or SUBJECT on which the agent operates; that is, there must be a

---

* From *syntaxis*, a joining.

nominative case, a verb, and an objective case; as, " Wellington conquered Buonaparte."

Here *Wellington* is the agent,—*conquered* is the action,—and *Buonaparte* the object towards whom the action was directed.

If there are *two classes* of agents, actions, and subjects, in the sentence, one class depending on the other, the sentence will consist of *two members*, which are separated from one another by a comma; as, " If Julius Cæsar had employed as much policy and cruelty as Augustus, he might have prevented the conspiracy formed against his life."

If there are *three classes* of agents, actions, and subjects, the sentence will consist of *three members*, separated by semicolons; as, " If Julius Cæsar had employed as much policy and cruelty as Augustus; if he had proscribed every suspicious person under his government; he might have prevented the conspiracy formed against his life."

If there are *four classes* of agents, actions, and subjects, the sentence will consist of *four members* separated by semicolons; as, " If Julius Cæsar had employed as much cruelty and policy as Augustus; if he had proscribed every suspicious person under his government; he might have prevented the conspiracy formed against his life; and he might have lived, like that emperor, to old age, flattered, obeyed, and adored by the Roman people."

In the above example it is obvious, that though the pressure of an agent, an action, and a subject, be requisite to constitute a member, yet they do not prohibit the attendance of explanatory words, particularly of adjectives or participles, which denote some quality or property of an agent or the subject. Accordingly, in the last member, " he might have lived, like that emperor, to old age, flattered, obeyed, and adored by the Roman people;" the participles *flattered, obeyed, adored*, encroach not on the unity of the member, but tend merely to modify or illustrate its principal parts.

When a sentence contains one member only, it is called SIMPLE; when it contains more members than one, it is called COMPLEX; when it contains three, four, or more members, it generally takes the name of PERIOD.

SIMPLE SENTENCES are best adapted to express the controversial and reprehensive parts of an oration. The period is adapted to the more splendid and pathetic parts, particularly the introduction and the conclusion.

A *sentence* or *phrase* is the smallest quantity of words which can express one entire proposition; that is, which can exhibit an agent as performing some action, or which can convey the affirmation of some truth.

If, for example, the verb be *intransitive*, and preceded by its nominative, a proposition will be expressed, and a sentence will be formed; because an agent will be represented as performing an action, and a complete meaning will be communicated; as, " the sun rises;" " the morning lowers;" " I eat, drink, walk," &c.

But if the verb be *transitive*, the nominative and the verb will not form a sentence, a proposition, or complete sense; because a subject will be wanting on which the action must be exerted.

Thus the words, " Cato killed," " Cicero banished," exhibit inefficient actions, and incomplete sentences. They leave the mind totally in suspense, till the subjects are subjoined on which the actions " killed" and " banished" are given.

But if we say " Cato killed himself," " Cicero banished Catiline," we present complete sentences, and communicate knowledge and information.

Again, if I assert, " I am going to," I exhibit

an incomplete sentence, or an imperfect affirmation, till I add the words " do it, buy it, fetch it," &c.; which furnish an entire affirmation, and a perfect sentence.

Hence it appears that the object of a sentence is to convey one proposition, and one only; that it generally contains an agent, an action, and a subject; and *must* contain an *agent* and an *action*. This constitutes what is called the unity of a sentence.

In constructing COMPLEX SENTENCES, which consist of different classes of agents, actions, and subjects, the unity will be preserved, and only one proposition, with all its circumstances, will be expressed, if such sentences, however complex, be properly composed.

To accomplish this end, the different members of a simple sentence, or the different classes of agents, actions, and subjects, so depend on one another, that the sense is not fully communicated, till they are all perfectly arranged and conjoined.

The following member of a sentence, " *if religion constitutes the supreme good,*" conveys no complete sense, and the hearer continues in suspense, till it is added, " *all wise men will prefer it to every other acquisition;*" the sentence, thus completed, exhibits two classes of agents, actions, and subjects, but contains only one full meaning, or one proposition.

Again, " *if religion constitute the supreme good; if it can communicate the most substantial comfort and support;*" still these two members leave the sense imperfect, and the mind hesitates, till it is added, " *all wise men will prefer it to every other acquisition;*" this completes both the proposition and the meaning.

The inconclusive members may be farther augmented; " *if religion constitute the supreme good; if it can communicate the most substantial comfort and support; if it can procure the approbation of all good men in this world and the favour of heaven hereafter;"* still the sense is incomplete, till the efficient member is subjoined, *" all wise men will prefer it to every other acquisition;"* which produces an entire proposition, fully satisfies the mind, and preserves the unity of the period.

From these observations it is evident, that the unity of a sentence is not impaired by its length, and that it will naturally be longer or shorter as the leading agent or member is attended with more or less dependent or explanatory agents, or members. No more members must ever be accumulated than are consistent with unity and perspicuity; neither should the meaning nor the cadence be intercepted by a frequent recurrence of abrupt sentences of one or two members. The sense is the main regulating principle of the length, the sound is only a secondary consideration; if, however, the former be preserved, the latter may be consulted, by a variety of modulation, as great as possible.

SHORT SENTENCES impart animation and energy to style. They are contrasts to periods, simple and perspicuous, and the ideas which they convey are usually lively, forcible, or dignified. They are also employed chiefly to deliver maxims of wisdom and sublime sentiments, which, supported by their natural importance and elevation, spurn the pomp and ornament of language.

THE FULL PERIOD of several members possesses most dignity and modulation, and conveys also the greatest degree of force, by admitting the closest compression of thought. The members are generally conditional, and denote supposition and contrast.

By *supposition* is understood, that the preceding members furnish a foundation on which the conclusion is built; or that they operate as a climax, by which it is raised to the highest elevation.

By *contrast* is understood, that the preceding members are opposed to the concluding member, which, notwithstanding, possesses such energy, that the contrast takes place with irresistible effect.

If, besides, such periods are properly constructed; if the members are so formed as to swell one above another in sound, as well as in sentiment; the impression will become exceedingly powerful, and cannot escape the most inattentive observer.

In the following example, the members increase both in extent and cadence; the rising series of contrasts convey much dignity and energy to the conclusion. "*Though the people should riot, and produce insurrection; though the tyrant should rage, and threaten destruction; though the hurricane should lay open the bed of the sea, and the earthquake tear the globe in pieces; though the stars should fall from their spheres, and the frame of nature be dissolved; yet* RELIGION *will protect her votaries, and those who faithfully trust in the* ROCK OF AGES, *the* SAVIOUR *and* REDEEMER *of man, will remain tranquil amid the ruins of the world.*"

All the parts of a sentence should correspond to each other; a regular and dependent construction throughout should be carefully pursued. The most important words in all members, sentences, and periods, are almost invariable. The AGENT *appears first, the* ACTION *succeeds, and the* SUBJECT, *if there be one, takes its station* last.

If the agent or subject be modified or illustrated by adjectives, or the action be extended or restricted by adverbs, the dependent words assume their stations as closely connected to their principals as possible; the adjectives to their nouns, and the adverbs to their verbs.

The ADJECTIVE is placed *before* its correspondent noun, when no circumstance depends on it; but is situated *after* the noun, when it is followed by some modification; as, " a *wise* man;" " a *good* book;" " a *spacious* apartment;" that is, " a man *wise* for himself;" " a book *good* for instruction;" " an apartment *convenient* for company."

ADVERBS generally *follow* neuter, but *precede* active verbs; as, " Wellington fought *bravely*;" " Buonaparte *rashly* engaged him at Waterloo." English adjectives have no inflections, and therefore they must be placed close to their nouns.

Though in every member of a sentence there must be an *agent*, an *action*, and a *subject*, unless the action be intransitive, there are to be found in many members *two*, in some *three* classes of *agents*, *actions*, and *subjects*, that explain, restrict, or otherwise depend on the primary class, by which the member is discriminated.

Ex. " It is usual," says Addison, Spectator, No. 131, " for a man who loves country sports, to preserve the game on his own grounds, and divert himself on the grounds of his neighbours. My friend, Sir Roger, generally goes two or three miles from his own house, and gets into the frontiers of his estate, before he beats about for a hare or a partridge, on purpose to spare his own fields, where he is always sure of finding diversion when the worst comes to the worst."

In the former of these sentences, there is one class only of agents, actions, and subjects; " a man who loves country sports;" but there are not less than three such classes in the first clause of the latter sentence; " Sir Roger generally goes two or three miles; he gets into the frontiers of his estate, before he beats about for a hare or a partridge." These dependent classes, like dependent words, adjectives, and adverbs, are placed as near to the primary class as is consistent with the intimacy of their relation.

Of the arrangement of the *pronouns, participles, prepositions* and *conjunctions,* no directions can be given that will not be liable to many exceptions. The following principles seem to include every thing which can, with any confidence, be advanced on the subject.

The chief use of PREPOSITIONS is to denote the relations of nouns to one another; they are, therefore, placed generally between the related objects, immediately before the one that bears the relation, and as near as possible to the other, to which the relation is borne; as, " the house *of* industry;" " destruction *to* vice;" " govern *with* discretion."

PARTICIPLES in general assume the situations of adjectives, of the nature of which they very much partake; but they are also employed to introduce clauses dependent on preceding verbs; as, " a *loving* father," " a *learned* man;" " he *passed* through life, *adored* by his friends, and *respected* by all good men."

CONJUNCTIONS are often introduced to connect single nouns, but more commonly to connect clauses of sentences. From their nature, they require a situation between the things of which they form an union.

The INTERJECTION, in a grammatical sense, is totally unconnected with every other word in a sentence. Its arrangement, of course, is altogether arbitrary, and cannot admit of any theory.

If two adverbs attend upon a single verb, one significant of place or time, the other of some modification of the verb, the former is mostly situated *before* the verb, the latter, more intimately connected with the verb, is placed immediately *after* it, to the exclusion even of the subject, when some circumstance depends upon the subject; as, "Cæsar *often* reprehended *severely* the ingratitude of his enemies;" "he every where declared *publicly* his inclination to preserve the constitution of his country."

If one auxiliary attend a verb, along with one adverb, the adverb is generally placed between the auxiliary and the verb; as, "folly has *always* exposed her author;" "wealth may *often* make friends, but can *never* produce true peace of mind."

If there be two auxiliaries, the adverb is commonly situated between them; as, "he should *certainly* have come;" "he might *easily* have known." In passive sentences, however, the adverb is placed after both the auxiliaries; as, "he will be *uncommonly* delighted;" "I shall be *completely* ruined."

If there be three auxiliaries, when the sentence must again be passive, the adverb is placed after them all; as, "I might have been *correctly* informed;" he might have been *completely* educated in that branch of science;" "it should have been *well* authenticated."

If two adverbs, with two auxiliaries, attend upon the same verb, the adverbs will be intermixed with the auxiliaries; as, "I have *always* been *much* embarrassed by these inconveniences;" "he can *never* be *sincerely* disposed to promote peace;" "he might at *least* have *plainly* told him."

In the arrangement of two or more prepositions, the relation of concomitance seems to be the most intimate, and therefore takes the precedency of all others; as, "he went *with* him *to* France; he came *with* him *from* Rome; he lived *with* him *at* Naples, and fought *with* him *in* Flanders; he contended *with* him *for* fame, but fought *with* him *against* his enemies." The relation denoted by *from*, precedes that signified by *to*. "He came *from* Rome *to* Paris, and *from* Paris *to* London;" "*from* a beginning very unpromising, he rose *to* great influence and wealth;" "society proceeds *from* barbarity *to* refinement, *from* ignorance *to* knowledge, *from* wealth *to* corruption, and *from* corruption *to* ruin."

OF PUNCTUATION.

Punctuation is the art of marking in writing the the several pauses, or rests, between sentences and the parts of sentences, according to their proper quantity or proportion, as they are expressed in a just and accurate pronunciation.

The several degrees of connexion between sentences, and between their principal constructive parts, are

the Period,		.
the Colon,	marked thus,	:
the Semicolon,		;
the Comma,		,

The *Period* is the whole sentence, complete in itself, wanting nothing to make a full and perfect sense, and not connected in construction with a subsequent sentence.

The *Colon*, or member, is a chief constructive part, or greater division, of a sentence.

The *Semicolon*, or half-member, is a less constructive part, or sub-division, of a sentence or member.

A sentence, or member, is again sub-divided into *Commas*, or segments; which are the least constructive parts of a sentence, or member, in this way of considering it; for the next subdivision would be the resolution of it into phrases and words.

The proportional quantity, or time, of the points,

with respect to one another, is determined by the following general rule :—The period is a pause, in quantity or duration, double the colon; the colon is double the semicolon; and the semicolon is double the comma.

In order to understand the meaning of the points, and to know how to apply them properly, we must consider the nature of a sentence as divided into its principal constructive parts, and the degrees of connexion between those parts upon which such division of it depends.

To begin with the least of these principal constructive parts, the *Comma*. In order the more clearly to determine the proper application of the point which marks it, we must distinguish between an imperfect phrase, a simple sentence, and a compound sentence.

An imperfect phrase contains no assertion, or does not amount to a proposition or sentence.

A simple sentence has but one subject, and one finite verb.

A compounded sentence has more than one subject, or one finite verb, either expressed or understood; or it consists of two or more simple sentences connected together.

In a sentence, the subject and the verb may be each of them accompanied with several adjuncts; as the object, the end, the circumstances of time, place, manner, and the like; and the subject or verb may be either immediately connected with them, or mediately; that is, by being connected with some thing which is connected with some other; and so on.

If the several adjuncts affect the subject or the verb in a different manner, they are only so many imperfect phrases; and the sentence is simple

A simple sentence admits of no point by which it may be divided or distinguished into parts.

If the several adjuncts affect the subject or the verb in the same manner, they may be resolved into so many simple sentences; the sentence then becomes compounded, and it must be divided into its parts by points.

For, if there are several subjects belonging in the same manner to one verb, or several verbs belonging in the same manner to one subject, the subjects and verbs are still to be accounted equal in number; for every verb must have its subject, and every subject its verb; and every one of the subjects, or verbs, should or may have its point or distinction.

Ex.—"The passion for praise produces excellent effects in women of sense." In this sentence *passion* is the SUBJECT, and *produces* the VERB; each of which is accompanied and connected with its adjuncts. The subject is not passion in general, but a particular passion determined by its adjunct of specification, as we may call it; the passion *for praise*. So likewise the verb is immediately connected with its object, *excellent effects*; and mediately, that is, by the intervention of the word *effects*, with *women*, the subject in which these effects are produced; which again is connected with its adjunct of specification; for it is not meant of women in general, but of women *of sense only*. Lastly, it is to be observed, that the verb is connected with each of these several adjuncts in a different manner; namely, with *effects*, as the object; with *women*, as the subject of them; with *sense*, as the quality or characteristic of those women. The adjuncts, therefore, are only so many imperfect phrases; the sentence is a simple sentence, and admits of no point, by which it may be distinguished into parts.

Ex.—" The passion for praise, which is so very vehement in the fair sex, produces excellent effects in women of sense." Here a new verb is introduced, accompanied with adjuncts of its own; and the subject is repeated by the relative pronoun *which.* It now becomes a compound sentence, made up of two simple sentences, one of which is inserted in the middle of the other; it must therefore be distinguished into its component parts by a point placed on each side of the additional sentence.

Ex. " How many instances have we (in the fair sex) of chastity, fidelity, devotion! How many ladies distinguish themselves by the education of their children, care of their families, and love of their husbands, which are the great qualities and achievements of womankind; as the making of war, the carrying on of traffic, the administration of justice, are those by which men grow famous, and get themselves a name* !"

In the first of these two sentences the adjuncts *chastity, fidelity, devotion,* are connected with the verb by the word *instances,* in the same manner, and in effect make so many distinct sentences ; " how many instances have we of chastity ! how many instances have we of fidelity ! how many instances have we of devotion !" They must therefore be separated from one another by a point. The same may be said of the adjuncts, " education of their children, &c." in the former part of the next sentence ; as likewise of the several subjects, " the making of war, &c.," in the latter part ; which have in effect each their verb ; for each of these " is an achievement by which men grow famous."

As sentences themselves are divided into simple and compounded, so the members of sentences may be divided likewise, into simple and compounded members; for whole sentences, whether simple or

---

* Addison, Spect. No. 73.

compounded, may become members of other sentences by means of some additional connexion.

Simple members of sentences closely connected together in one compounded member or sentence, are distinguished or separated by a *comma*; as in the foregoing examples.

So likewise the case absolute, nouns in opposition, when consisting of many terms, the participle with something depending on it, are to be distinguished by the *comma*, for they may be resolved into simple members.

When an address is made to a person, the noun, answering to the vocative case in Latin, is distinguished by a *comma*; as in the following example from Milton:

> Ex: " This said, He form'd thee, Adam; thee, O man,
>   Dust of the ground."
> " Now morn, her rosy steps in th' eastern clime
>   Advancing, saw'd the earth with orient pearl."

Two nouns, or two adjectives, connected by a single copulative or disjunctive, are not separated by a point; but when there are more than two, or where the conjunction is understood, they must be distinguished by a *comma*.

Simple members connected by relatives and comparatives, are for the most part distinguished by a *comma*; but when the members are short in comparative sentences, and when two members are closely connected by a relative restraining the general notion of the antecedent to a particular sense, the pause becomes almost insensible, and the *comma* is better omitted.

Ex. " Raptures, transports, and ecstasies, are the rewards which they confer: sighs and tears, prayers and broken hearts, are the offerings which are paid to them."

" What is sweeter than honey? and what is stronger than a lion?"

A circumstance of importance, though no more than an imperfect phrase, may be set off with a *comma* on each side, to give it greater force and distinction.

Ex. " The principle may be defective or faulty; but the consequences it produces are so good, that, for the benefit of mankind, it ought not to be extinguished."

A member of a sentence, whether simple or compounded, that requires a greater pause than a *comma*, yet does not of itself make a complete sentence, but is followed by something closely depending on it, may be distinguished by a *semicolon.*

Ex. " But as this passion for admiration, when it works according to reason, improves the beautiful part of our species in every thing that is laudable; so nothing is more destructive to them, when it is governed by vanity and folly."

Here the whole sentence is divided into two parts by the *semicolon*; each of which parts is a compounded member, divided into its simple members by the *comma.*

A member of a sentence, whether simple or compounded, which of itself would make a complete sentence, and so requires a greater pause than a *semicolon*, yet is followed by an additional part making a more full and perfect sense, may be distinguished by a *colon.*

Ex. " Were all books reduced to their quintessence, many a bulky author would make his appearance in a penny paper : there would be scarce any such thing in nature as a folio : the works of an age would be contained on a few shelves : not to mention millions of volumes that would be utterly annihilated."

Here the whole sentence is divided into four parts by *colons :* the first and last of which are compounded members, each divided by a *comma*; the second and third are simple members.

When a *semicolon* has preceded, and a greater pause is still necessary, a *colon* may be employed, though the sentence be incomplete.

The *colon* is also commonly used when an example, or a speech, is introduced.

When a sentence is so far perfectly finished as not to be connected in construction with the following sentence, it is marked with a *period*.

In all cases, the proportion of the several points in respect to one another is rather to be regarded, than their supposed precise quantity, or proper office, when taken separately.

Besides the points which mark the pauses in discourse, there are others which denote a different modulation of the voice in correspondence with the sense. These are

The interrogation point ⎫   ⎧ ?
The exclamation point   ⎬ thus marked ⎨ !
The parenthesis   ⎭   ⎩ ()

The *interrogation* and *exclamation* points are sufficiently explained by their names : they are indeterminate as to their quantity or time, and may be equivalent in that respect to a *semicolon*, a *colon*, or a *period*, as the sense requires. They mark an elevation of the voice.

The *parenthesis* encloses in the body of a sentence a member inserted into it which is neither necessary to the sense, nor at all affects the construction. It marks a moderate depression of the voice, with a pause greater than a *comma*.

§ 2.   RULES OF SYNTAX.

To produce the agreement and right disposition

of words in a sentence, the following rules must be strictly observed.

RULE I.

The first and most important rule of syntax is, that the NOMINATIVE CASE *must take the lead of the verb; and the* VERB *must agree with its nominative in number and person.*

Ex. Anne is industrious. Susan sings well. Alexander is a promising boy. The fields are green. The park is crowded.

In most sentences the NOMINATIVE is ascertained by asking the question, *who, which,* or *what;* as, " Who is industrious ?" " *Anne.*" " What are green ?" " The *fields,*" &c.

When the same verb applies to several nouns, they are all of the nominative case.

Ex. " I am the Lord THY GOD which brought thee out of the land of Egypt, out of the house of bondage." Here the pronoun I, and the nouns LORD and GOD, are in the nominative case to the verb *am.* Nouns thus circumstanced are said to be in APPOSITION, that is, they are put in the same case. See *Rule* xix.

RULE II.

The infinitive mood, or part of a sentence, is sometimes put as the nominative case to the verb.

Ex. 1. " To obey is better than sacrifice." 2. " To improve is commendable." 3. " To be temperate in eating and drinking, to use exercise in the open air, and to preserve the mind free from tumultuous emotions, *are* the best preservatives of health.

In the first example notwithstanding the infinitive mood is put in the nominative case to the verb *is,* yet the noun or pronoun is understood, namely, " For *me* or *thee* to obey, *&c.*"

In the last example the members of the sentence that precede the verb *are,* are put in the nominative case to that verb.

However ancient this mode of writing or speaking may be, it appears strange to apply the *infinitive mood* as the subject or nominative case to the verb! It would certainly be more correct to say, that " *the nominative is understood before the infinitive mood.*"

Rule III.

Every verb, except in the infinitive mood, or the participle, ought to have a nominative case expressed or understood.

Ex. 1. " Awake." 2. " Arise." 3. " Write." That is, " Awake, thou that sleepest." " Arise, and let us be doing." " Write your letter."

When the ellipsis is supplied, the nominative necessarily takes the lead.

If a nominative is used without a verb, it must be in allusion to some other member of the sentence which determines its meaning; it frequently occurs when persons are walking together, on seeing particular objects that an exclamation is made ; as, " The castle." " The sea." " The monument." That is, " Do you see the castle," &c.

In these examples the pronoun *you* is understood as the nominative to the implied verb. And whatever expressions we may find contrary to the first rule of grammar, it is either through an ellipsis, transposition, or parenthesis, which is not allowed to govern, but admitted simply to vary the forms of narrative and modes of interrogation, as in the following examples, where the nominative follows the verb.

I. In asking questions when the verb is the principal; as, "Say you so?" "Betrayest thou the Son of man with a kiss?" "Believest thou the prophets?" When a proper name is introduced, it does not supersede the pronoun as the nominative, because it names him as the third person, and addresses him as the second; as, "Jane, say you so?" "Judas, betrayest thou the Son of man with a kiss?" "King Agrippa, believest thou?"

Here is an exception to this rule when the nominative or subject of inquiry is preceded by a relative, or an auxiliary; as, "Who can find out the Almighty to perfection?" "Does virtue exalt a character?" "How delightful is the morning!" Here the nominative *virtue* follows the auxiliary *does*.

II. In many forms when both a transposition and an ellipsis occur together; as, "Were we not under the necessity?" that is, "If we were not under the necessity."

III. When adverbs of place precede the verb; as, "*Here* am I." "*There* is the man." "*Where* are the books?" "*Then* were the days of unleavened bread." The following sentence has a double transposition, "Let *there* be light, and *there* was light." Also when the idea is sudden and striking; as, "*There* happened a total eclipse of the sun during the battle."

IV. Many of the conjunctions precede the verb, as adverbs, and cause the nominative to follow the verb, chiefly by transposition; as, "*likewise* went they." "*As* was the master, *so* was the man.

V. Sometimes an adjective, or an adverb of number, occasions a transposition of the verb; as, "*Great* is the love." *At once* broke forth the light."

These examples are sufficient to prove, that it is *transposition* which occasions the *nominative* to follow the verb, and that nearly the whole of the examples may revert back to the regular form, by saying, "The light broke forth at once." "As the master was, so the man is," &c.

Were not the rules of grammar absolute, " *that the* NOMINATIVE *must take the lead, and* GOVERN *the* VERB," the powers of language would be destroyed.

RULE IV.

When the nominative case has no personal tense of a verb, but is put before a participle, independently on the rest of the sentence, it is called THE CASE ABSOLUTE.

Ex. " The system having been examined, *was* approved and adopted." " Shame being lost, all virtue is lost." " He being dead, yet speaketh." Supply the ellipsis, " Abel being dead, *or* though dead, speaks to posterity;" and the CASE ABSOLUTE is no case at all. It is merely the fragment of a phrase not reducible to law till the ellipsis is supplied; hence several learned writers on this subject do not mention *the case absolute.*

RULE V.

Two or more nouns or pronouns in the singular number, joined by copulative conjunctions, expressed or implied, must have verbs, nouns, and pronouns, agreeing with them in the plural number.

Ex. 1.—" Fire, air, water, earth, *are* the four elements."—2. " Wisdom, virtue, and happiness, *dwell* with the golden mediocrity."—3. " Religion and virtue, our best support and highest honour, *confer* on the mind principles of noble independence."—4. " Sand and salt, and a mass of iron, *are* easier to bear than a man without understanding."

Sometimes after an enumeration of particulars thus connected, the verb follows in the singular number; and is understood as applied to each of the preceding terms.

Ex.—" The glorious inhabitants of those sacred palaces, where nothing but light and blessed immortality, no shadow of matter for tears, discontentments, griefs, and uncomfortable passions to work upon; but all joy, tranquillity, and peace, even for ever and ever *doth dwell.*"

Rule VI.

When a noun or pronoun of the singular number is separated by a disjunctive conjunction, it requires a singular verb.

Ex. 1.—" Let it be remembered, that it is not the uttering, *or* the hearing of certain words, that *constitutes* the worship of the Almighty."— 2. " When sickness, infirmity, *or* reverse of fortune, *affects* us, the sincerity of friendship is proved."— 3.—" Want of judgment, *or* want of inquiry, *was* the occasion of his error."

Rule VII.

A noun of multitude may have a verb or pronoun agreeing with it either of the singular or plural number, unless it conveys the idea of plurality, in which case it must have a plural verb or pronoun.

Ex. 1.—" The British parliament *is* composed of King, Lords, and Commons."—2. " The flock and not the fleece, *is* or ought to be the object of the shepherd's care."—3. " The assembly *was* very numerous."

This rule indulges authors with liberty to use the

plural or the singular verb with a collective noun, as may be best adapted to the complication or the unity of the idea. It is, however, advisable for speakers to take the plural; because, when using a noun of multitude with a singular verb, they are in danger, while pursuing the idea in the warmth of eloquence, of committing themselves by using plural verbs or pronouns; as in the following sentence: "The world *considers* him as a man of application and talents; and being prepossessed in his favour, to which the lustre of title and the splendour of office contribute not a little, *they* cannot but *admire* the wisdom and propriety of his conduct." In this sentence Addison has used a singular and a plural verb.

In most cases where the word *whole* precedes a noun of multitude, the plural verb has the preference, because of the plural verbs, nouns, and pronouns, which generally follow; as, "The *whole* nation *were* thrown into confusion by the Cato-street conspirators; *all classes* of *men*, except the Radicals, *were* grateful for the interposition of Providence in revealing the diabolical plot, and *all were* ready to lend *their* aid in bringing the perpetrators of it to condign punishment."

Rule VIII.

Personal pronouns must occupy the position which their antecedents would fill, if repeated, agree with them in number, gender, and person, and with the pronouns, governed in the objective case.

Ex. 1.—" I am he."—2. " I waited on the ladies before they left town, and have since heard that they arrived safe."—3. " I that speak unto thee am he."

In the first example, *I* and *he* are both in the nominative case. *I* is sufficiently known as the speaker, but *he* requires the antecedent to be named, as in the answer of our Saviour to the woman of Samaria, " I that speak unto thee am H E."

In the second, *I* is likewise known; but it is omitted before *have*, as the mind can carry forward the idea.

The confusion which exists in this country between our written language and the oral phrases of the less-instructed, lies chiefly in the objective case, which is frequently used instead of the nominative; as, " no one was present but *him* and *me;*" instead of " no one was present but *him* and *I; that is, " *I* was present and *he* was present." To say *me* was present and *him* was present, would be highly improper. " Charles and *me* went together" —" He is happier than *me*"—" It is *me*." In each of these examples, instead of the objective *me*, the nominative *I* should be used.

A pronoun must not be used in the same phrase with a noun, unless it be to confer superior energy and emphasis on the subsequent noun; as, " the Lord, *he* is God."

RULE IX.

The relative pronoun, being of the same person with its antecedent, should immediately follow it, and the verb agree with it accordingly.

Ex. 1.—" Milton *who* wrote Paradise Lost."— 2. " The characters *which* he drew."—3. " The men and books *that* he studied."

Milton is the antecedent of *who*, in the first example. *Characters* of *which*, in the second. In the third, *men* require the relative *who*, and *books* the relative *which*, but as the pronoun *that* applies to either, it is allowed here, for the sake of brevity, to apply to both.

This rule *that the relative must follow its antece-dent,* does not exclude an additional member from falling between; as, " Arrowsmith, the geographer, *who* drew the maps."

Sometimes the antecedent is understood; as, " who conquers passion conquers all;" that is, " *he* or *she* who conquers passion conquers all."

When a proper name or surname occurs, not in immediate reference to the person, it should be followed by *which;* as, " he is considerably improved by reading Pestalozzi, *which* is the most persuasive and instructive system of education ever revealed to the public."

When a noun falls between the relative and its antecedent, it must not be of the same person and gender; as, " I recollect a parallel passage in Isaiah to the same effect with that of Malachi, *which* has given me great pleasure."

Rule X.

The relative is the nominative to the verb, when no nominative comes between it and the verb.

Ex. 1.—" They to *whom* much is given, will have much to answer for."—2. " The gentleman *who* purchased the house is gone to France."—3. " The servant *who* robbed his master, has been justly punished."—4. " The tidings of peace are welcome to those *who* have long groaned under the pressure of public calamity."

Rule XI.

When the nominative comes between the relative and the verb, the relative is governed by some word in its own member of the sentence.

Ex. 1.—" George the third, *who* did so long fill the British throne, *whose* power was paternal, and to *whom* all allegiance was due, has bequeathed to his people a high example of personal virtue and of family dignity."

In the first member of this sentence, the relative stands in its nominative form to represent the agent who filled the throne;—in the second, it stands in the possessive case to represent the possession of paternal power:—in the third, it stands in the objective form, to express the object of allegiance.

Ex. 2.—" The public often despise persons who appear to be avaricious and sordid characters."— 3. " Whom shall we appoint the teacher, and which class shall he take first?"

The relative *whom* is by some writers frequently used instead of *who*, when it follows a noun in the objective case; as, " he *whom* we have greatly served hath neglected us ;" " *who* shall we send?" In the first example, it should be *who*, and in the last, *whom*, the preposition *by* being understood, " by *whom* shall we send ?"

Rule XII.

When both the antecedent and relative become nominatives, each to different verbs, the relative is the nominative to the former, and the antecedent to the latter verb.

Ex. 1.—" True *Religion, which* is the ornament of our nature, *consists* more in the love of our duty and the practice of virtue, than in great talents and extensive knowledge."—2. " *They who have laboured* to make us wise and good, *are* the persons we ought to love and respect."—3. " *He who* faithfully *discharges* his duty *is* truly happy."

Rule XIII.

When the relative is preceded by two nominatives

of different persons, the relative and verb may agree in person with either according to the sense.

Ex. 1.—" I perceive thou art a pupil who possesses bright parts, but who *has* cultivated them but little."—2. " Thou art He, the Lord of Hosts, who *breathes* on the earth with the breath of spring, and who *covers* it with verdure and beauty."— 3. " I acknowledge that I am the person *who* approve and use Pestalozzi's system of intuitive and intellectual instruction."

Rule XIV.

When the relative is of the interrogative kind, the noun or pronoun containing the answer must be in the same case as that which contains the question.

Ex. 1. " *Whose* books are these? They are *Mary's.*" 2. " *Who* gave them to her? *We.*"

This rule will be easily comprehended by completing the answers; thus, " Whose books are these? They are *Mary's* books." " *Who* gave them to her? *We* gave them to her."

In all interrogatives, where the proper name is unknown, the relative takes the lead; as, " *who* is coming?" " *who* broke the slate?" " *which* of the boys threw the stone?"

Rule XV.

Every adjective, and every pronominal adjective, belongs to a noun expressed or understood; and must agree with it in number.

Ex. 1. " A *kind* parent." 2. " An *indulgent* master." 3. " A *beautiful* garden." 4. " *This* book, these books." 5. " *That* sort, those sorts." 6. " Another road, other roads."

Adjectives, as well as pronominal adjectives, mostly precede the noun, as in the above examples.

Many occasions, however, occur in which they are more emphatic when transposed; as, " *George* the *Fourth* ;" " a master *indulgent* to his pupils ;" " this list includes the *whole* of the conspirators."

There is in many phrases an ellipsis of the adjective, which prevents the student from determining the part of speech to which a word belongs; as, " such looks," " such behaviour," " such roads." In each of these examples a word is wanting to complete the sense; as, " such *haughty* looks," " such *rude* behaviour," " such *bad* roads."

Many polished writers obtrude adverbs into their composition, written as adjectives; but the latter may readily be distinguished from the former by putting an article before them, or by changing the word for another which is known to be an adjective or an adverb; as, " I scarce know ;" " I hardly, or barely, or only know." Here it should be " I scarcely know."

The following examples may assist the pupil in ascertaining an adverb from an adjective.

" He had the *previous* offer, because I had met him *previously*." " He is an *agreeable* man, because he conducts himself *agreeably*." " His feelings are *acute*, and he does *acutely* feel the slight." " His opinion is *right*, and he had *rightly* informed himself on the subject." " He is a *prudent* man, as is apparent from his conducting himself so *prudently* in the late delicate affair."

When the above method is found inadequate, the verb TO BE, in some one of its tenses, by becoming a substitute for the regular verb, will farther assist in determining the point; as, " The apricot tastes *delicious—is* delicious." " How *delightful* the clouds appear—the clouds *are* delightful." " How *terrible appeared* the breakers rolling over the latent rocks—how terrible *were* the breakers," &c.

H

Here we cannot say, " how *terribly* the breakers were," &c.; therefore *delicious, delightful, terrible,* and all words of a similar nature, ought to be written as adjectives.

Adjectives expressive of unity sometimes require singular, and sometimes plural nouns; as, " one calamity;" " other friends;" but adjectives expressive of number always require plural nouns; as, "*few* afflictions and *many* comforts."

Pronominal adjectives mostly precede the noun; as, "*my* book; *thy* house; *your* property; *their* country; *other* affairs." Many occasions, however, occur, in which they are more emphatic when transposed; as, "the task is *mine*;" " the mistake is *yours*."

The adjective *many* sometimes signifies the whole; as, "they are *many* in family;" "by one man's disobedience *many* were made sinners;" and sometimes it means a part; as, " some are gone, but *many* are left."

All implies the whole, or the whole in general; as, " *all* the harvest is saved," " *all* the fleet arrived safe;" " *all* men are satisfied of his innocence;" *all* men held John for a prophet; "he is addicted to *all* kinds of vice."

Any is always joined to the singular number, expressed or understood; as, " *any* pen;" " *any* number of pens." " *Any* accidents," meaning any number of accidents; as, "if these pages shall in *any* measure contribute to the satisfaction of *any* of the friends of truth and virtue," &c.

Both is confined to two objects; as, " *both* the sisters;" " *both* kinds;" " *both* ways."

Each is mostly restricted to two persons, or two things, taken separately; as, " *each* hat;" " *each* house."

Either signifies one of the two persons or

objects; as, " *either* Jane or Mary may go;" " you may go *either* to the play or to the concert."

Enough, whether used as a noun, an adjective, or an adverb, has the same import; as, " he walks enough;" " he is ready enough."

Enow, though seldom used, is the plural of enough; as, " he has friends *enow*."

Every signifies one **to each**; as, " to *every* house a lamb;" " *every* one shall have his share."

Rule XVI.

The distributive pronominal adjectives each, every, either, *agree with nouns, pronouns, and verbs, of the singular number only.*

Ex. 1. *Every* tree is known by its fruit."
2. " *Each* of the class receives instruction."
3. " *Either* of them is at your service."

Rule XVII.

When the adjective has a preposition before it, and the noun is understood, the adjective and preposition assume the nature of an adverb, and may be taken as such.

Ex. 1. " In general;" 2. " In particular;" 3. " In common;" that is, " generally, particularly, commonly."

Rule XVIII.

One noun governs another, signifying offspring, production, or property, in the possessive or genitive case.

Ex. 1. " Pestalozzi's tables." 2. " Murray's grammar;" " John's son." 3. " Henry's house."

Rule XIX.

When two nouns, signifying the same thing, come together, or are separated by a neuter verb, they are put in the same case by APPOSITION.

Ex. 1. " *Religion,* the *support* of adversity, adorns prosperity." 2. " *George* the IV. *King* of England, succeeded his father George the III. January 29th, 1820." 3. *Peace, joy,* and *content,* is the *offspring* of religion.

Rule XX.

Active verbs govern the objective case.
Ex. 1. " Religion elevates the soul." 2. " Virtue rewards her followers." 3. " Parents love their children."

Rule XXI.

Participles, like active verbs, govern the objective case.
Ex. 1. " Given to hospitality." 2. " Relieving the distressed." 3. " Esteeming themselves wise, they became foolish."

Participles are sometimes used as adjectives; as, " a *wounded* conscience;" "a *darling* child;" " a *pleasing* book."

Imperfect participles are sometimes used as abstract nouns; as, " plain *dealing;*" "a wise *saying.*"

By supplying the ellipsis in the last examples, the participles resume their regular places; as, " plain dealing with all men;" " a wise saying of Solomon's."

Rule XXII.

Prepositions govern the objective case.

Ex. 1. " Goliath was killed *by* David with a stone." 2. " I intend going *to* the Continent, and hope *to* reach Yverdun *by* Midsummer, and *to* return before Christmas." 3. " Charles went *to* Hendon *by* way *of* Hampstead, and returned *through* Kilburn."

RULE XXIII.

The governing prepositions to *and* for *are sometimes distinctly understood, especially after active verbs.*

Ex. 1. " Give them a holiday." 2. " Our Saviour fasted forty days." 3. " I have promised him my vote."

RULE XXIV.

The preposition is frequently separated by the relative which it governs.

Ex. 1. " He is an author *whom* I am much delighted *with*." 2. " The gentleman *whom* you were examined *by* is greatly esteemed." 3. " To have no one *whom* we heartily wish well *to,* and *whom* we are warmly concerned *for,* is a deplorable state."

RULE XXV.

Prepositions are sometimes allowed to conclude a sentence, because the relative who *or* which *is thereby often superceded.*

Ex. 1. " That is the person I gave it to." 2. " That is the book I spoke of." 3. " There are some material points in this system I have not spoken of."

Rule XXVI.

The primary verb TO BE *is always preceded and followed by a noun or pronoun in the same case.*

Ex. 1. "*I am* he."   2. "I thought it *was* him."
3. "Search the Scriptures; for in them ye think ye have eternal life; and they *are* they which testify of me."

In the first example, both the pronouns are in the nominative; and in the second, the two last are in the objective case.

Here it may also be essential to remark, that the pronouns *it* and *him* are in APPOSITION, because they refer to the same person, and are in the same case.

Rule XXVII.

One verb governs another that follows it, or depends upon it, in the infinitive mood.

Ex. 1. "We should be careful not to trifle with eternity."   2. "It is better to live on a little, than to outlive a great deal."   3. "We should be prepared to render an account of our actions."

Rule XXVIII.

Participles have the same government as the verbs from whence they are derived.

Ex. 1. " By *traducing* others we expose ourselves."   "Edward delights in *teaching* his sister."
2. "We should always feel pleasure in *relieving* the distress of others."   3. " *Esteeming* themselves wise, they became fools."

The verb or participle must agree with every other verb which it governs, in all the variations of mood and tense.

Ex. " I thought to buy the estate, but the buildings were too high." " Preferment will not be conferred on every candidate; but on those only who shall be qualified." " I purposed to ride." " I was desirous to give him a call."

The propriety of this rule will appear on comparing the tenses: " I thought *to have bought* the estate." When did I think to do it? Last week. But the phrase *to have bought* being in the past tense, expresses the action as already done, before I had even thought of the purchase. Hence, in relating our past actions, we should join the past tense with the infinitive mood; as, " I thought to buy the estate."

In the second example, it would not be correct to say, " those only who *are* qualified;" because in the interval between the claim and the grant of preferment, the candidate may make a rapid progress in the acquisition of qualifications; the construction requires " those only who *shall be* qualified."

Rule XXIX.

The auxiliary in the third person singular of the present and imperfect tense of the indicative mood, governs the principal verb by requiring it to be of the plural number.

Ex. 1. " Alexander *did* excel." 2. " Virtue *does* exalt a character." 3. " Religion *did* improve the man."

If the auxiliary were removed, the verb would be singular; as, " Alexander *excels*." " Virtue *exalts*." " Religion *improves*."

Auxiliary verbs are of a very limited nature, they are chiefly used to assist in the conjugation of principal verbs. The following conjugation of the auxiliary verbs will fully explain the foregoing rule.

TO BE.

Present Tense.

Sing. 1. I *am,*   2. Thou *art,*   3. He *is.*
Plur. 1. We *are,*   2. Ye *or* you *are,*   3. They *are.*

Imperfect Tense.

Sing. 1. I *was,*   2. Thou *wast,*   3. He *was.*
Plur. 1. We *were,*   2. Ye *or* you *were,*   3. They *were.*

Participles.

Present, *Being.*   Perfect, *Been.*

TO HAVE.

Present Tense.

Sing. 1. I *have,*   2. Thou *hast,*   3. He *hath* or *has*
Plur. 1. We *have,*   2. Ye *or* you *have,*   3. They *have.*

Imperfect Tense.

Sing. 1. I *had,*   2. Thou *hadst,*   3. He *had.*
Plur. 1. We *had,*   2. Ye *or* you *had,*   3. They *had.*

Participles.

Present, *Having.*   Perfect, *Had.*

SHALL.

Present Tense.

Sing. 1. I *shall**,   2. Thou *shalt,*   3. He *shall.*
Plur. 1. We *shall,*   2. Ye *or* you *shall,*   3. They *shall.*

Imperfect Tense.

Sing. 1. I *should,*   2. Thou *shouldst,*   3. He *should.*
Plur. 1. We *should,*   2. Ye *or* you *should,*   3. They *should.*

---

* *Shall* is here properly used in the present tense, having the same analogy to *should* that *can* has to *could, may* to *might,* and *will* to *would.*

WILL.

Present Tense.

Sing. 1. I *will,*   2. Thou *wilt,*   3. He *will.*
Plur. 1. We *will,*   2. Ye *or* you *will,*   3. They *will.*

Imperfect Tense.

Sing. 1. I *would,*   2. Thou *wouldst,*   3. He *would.*
Plur. 1. We *would,* 2. Ye *or* you *would,* 3. They *would.*

MAY.

Present Tense.

Sing. 1. I *may,*   2. Thou *mayst,*   3. He *may.*
Plur. 1. We *may,*   2. Ye *or* you *may,*   3. They *may.*

Imperfect Tense.

Sing. 1. I *might,*   2. Thou *mightst,*   3. He *might.*
Plur. 1. We *might,* 2. Ye *or* you *might,* 3. They *might.*

CAN.

Present Tense.

Sing. 1. I *can,*   2. Thou *canst,*   3. He *can.*
Plur. 1. We *can,*   2. Ye *or* you *can,*   3. They *can.*

Imperfect Tense.

Sing. 1. I *could,*   2. Thou *couldst,*   3. He *could.*
Plur. 1. We *could,* 2. Ye *or* you *could,* 3. They *could.*

TO DO.

Present Tense.

Sing. 1. I *do,*   2. Thou *dost,*   3. He *doth or does*
Plur. 1. We *do,*   2. Ye *or* you *do,*   3. They *do.*

Imperfect Tense.

Sing. 1. I *did,*   2. Thou *didst,*   3. He *did.*
Plur. 1. We *did,* 2. Ye *or* you *did.* 3. They *did.*

Rule XXX.

Conjunctions connect the same mood and tenses of verbs, and cases of nouns and pronouns.

Ex. 1. " Did he not tell me his fault, *and* entreat me to forgive him?" 2. " Your friend and I have called on the gentleman, *but* have not succeeded; *nor* have so much as obtained a promise, *or* you should have been informed of it immediately." 3. " Our season of improvement is short, *and,* whether used or not, it will soon pass away."

Rule XXXI.

Some conjunctions require the indicative, and some the subjunctive mood after them. It is a general rule that when the conjunction is of a doubtful nature, the verb must be put in the subjunctive mood; but when it is used to elucidate any member of the sentence, it will be in the indicative mood.

Ex. 1. " If this part of our trade were well conducted." 2. " If I were to write he would not regard it." 3. " He will not be pardoned unless he repent."

Rule XXXII.

The interjections O! oh! and alas! require the objective case of a pronoun in the first person after them; but the nominative in the second person.

Ex. 1. " Oh! me." 2. " What shall be done unto thee, O! thou lying spirit." 3. " Alas! unhappy *thou* who art deaf to the calls of duty and of honour.

Rule XXXIII.

Adverbs have no government. Their chief use is

to modify the verb.   *The circumstances of action ex-*
pressed by tenses and moods are all of a nature too
general to be sufficient for the purposes of communi-
cation.   It is often necessary to be much more parti-
cular in ascertaining both the time and the manner,
but particularly the place of the action.   The im-
portant office of the adverb is to accomplish this end.

In a sentence adverbs are placed before adjectives,
after verbs active or neuter, frequently between the
auxiliary and the verb, and sometimes after a pre-
position.

Ex. He made a *very* sensible discourse, he spoke
unaffectedly and *forcibly ;* and was *attentively* heard
by the whole assembly; the number of which
amounted to *near* a thousand.

Rule XXXIV.

The general article a *or* an, *must be joined to*
nouns of the singular number, or to nouns of multi-
tude which convey ideas of unity.

Ex. *A* soldier; *a* regiment; *an* army; *a* few;
a score ; *a* thousand.

The particular article the *may agree with nouns*
in the singular and plural number.

Ex. The sun, the moon, the stars.

The article is generally omitted before abstract
nouns; as, " virtue, honour, mercy."

When naming countries or cities, we say, England, France, Russia; London, Paris, Petersburgh :
speaking of rivers, we say, the Thames, the Rhine,
the Po : and of individuals, an Englishman, a
Frenchman, a Russian.

XXXV.

One of the double negatives used by our ancestors

H 6

is now generally superseded by the adjective any, *by* *the auxiliary* do, by *even*, or by *so much as*, &c.

Ex. I *never* gave him *no* cause of displeasure; that is, *any* cause of displeasure.

Lowth and *Murray* say that " *two negatives in English destroy one another, or are equivalent to an affirmative.*"

Ex. " I *cannot* by *no* means allow it." This does not fully prove the rule, but merely that *not* is superfluous, or that *any* should be substituted for *no.* " I have *not* found so great faith; *no not* in Israel." Here it is obvious that the first negative refers to the act of searching, and the second to the nation of Israel, and therefore no objection can be made to it.

RULE XXXVI.

In the use of words and phrases which, in point of time, relate to each other, a due regard to that relation should be observed.

The best rule that can be given for this purpose is the general one; " *to observe what the sense necessarily requires.*"

Ex. " I intended *to have written* last week." Though this is a common phrase it is not correct, the infinitive being in the past time, as well as the verb which it follows. It is immaterial as to the length of time since I thought of writing, " *to write*" was then present to me, and must still be considered as present when I bring back that time, and the thoughts of it. It ought therefore to be, " I intended *to write* last week."

To preserve consistency in the time of verbs, we must recollect that, in the subjunctive mood, the present and imperfect tenses often carry with them a future sense; and that the auxiliaries *should* and *would*, in the imperfect tenses, are to express the present and future as well as the past.

RULE XXXVII.

An ELLIPSIS, *as applied in grammar, is the omission of some words which must be supplied, either to complete the sense, or to make out the grammatical construction of the sentence.*

The principal design of the ellipsis is to avoid disagreeable repetitions, as well as to express our ideas in as few words, and in as pleasing a manner as possible.

In the application of this figure, great care should be taken to avoid ambiguity, for whenever it obscures the sense, it ought by no means to be admitted.

Almost all compound sentences are more or less elliptical.

THE ELLIPSIS OF THE NOUN.

" One thing perceived to be a cause, is connected with its several effects; some things are connected by contiguity of time, others by contiguity in space; some are connected by resemblance, some by contrast; some go before, some follow; not a single thing appears solitary and altogether devoid of connexion; the only difference is, that some are intimately connected, some more slightly, some near, some at a distance."

In the above example the noun *thing* is omitted in eight places.

The ellipsis of the *article* is thus used : " A man, woman and child;" that is, " *a* man, *a* woman, and *a* child." " The father and son." " The sun and moon." " The horse and gig."

In examples where the article has been once

omitted, the repetition of it would be unnecessary, unless some peculiar emphasis requires it.

" Not only the year, but *the* day and *the* hour." In this example the ellipsis of the last article would be improper. When a different form of the article is requisite, it should be repeated as, " *a* pear and *an* apricot," instead of " a pear and apricot."

The ellipsis of the *adjective* is used in the following manner : " A *delightful* orchard and garden ;" that is, " a delightful orchard and a delightful garden."

" A *little* man and woman." " *Great* wealth and power." In such elliptical expressions, the adjective ought to have exactly the same signification, and to be quite as proper, when joined to the latter as to the former nouns ; otherwise the ellipsis should not be admitted. Nor should we apply this ellipsis of the adjective to nouns of different members ; as, " A *magnificent* coach and horses." Here it would be better to say, " a *magnificent* coach and *fine* horses."

The following is the ellipsis of the *pronoun,* " *I* love and fear *him* ;" that is, " *I* love *him* and *I* fear *him.*"

" *My* house and lands." " *Thy* learning and wisdom." " *His* wife and daughter." " *Her* lord and master."

In all these instances the ellipsis may be introduced with propriety ; but if we would be emphatical, it must not be admitted ; as, " *My* sons and *my* daughters." " *His* friends and *his* foes."

In some of the common forms of speech the relative pronoun is usually omitted ; " as, " This is the man they hate ;" " these are the goods they bought ;" that is, " This is the man *whom* they hate ;" these are the goods *which* they bought."

The antecedent and the relative connect parts of a sentence together ; and should, to prevent confusion and obscurity, answer to each other with great exactness.

"We speak *that* we do know, and testify *that* we have seen." The ellipsis, in such instances, is manifestly improper; let it therefore be supplied, " we speak that *which* we do know, and testify that *which* we have seen."

The relative *what,* in the neuter gender, seems to include both the antecedent and the relative; as, " this is *what* you speak of ;" or, " the thing *which* you speak of."

The ellipsis of the *verb* is used in the following instances : " The man *was* old and crafty ;" that is, " the man *was* old, and the man *was* crafty." " She *is* young, and rich, and beautiful." " Thou *art* poor, and wretched, and miserable, and blind, and naked." When we are desirous to enumerate one property above the rest, that property should be put last, and the ellipsis supplied; as, " she *is* young and beautiful, and *she is* rich." If we would fill up the ellipsis in the last sentence, *thou art* ought to be repeated before each of the adjectives.

" I *recommend* the father and the son." " We *saw* the town and country." He *rewarded* the women and children." " You *ought* to love and serve him." " I *desire* to hear and learn."

" He *went* to see and hear ;" that is, " he *went* to see, and he *went* to hear." In this sentence there is not only an ellipsis of the governing verb *went,* but likewise of the sign of the infinitive mood, which is governed by it.

It may be proper to remark, that some verbs, through custom, seem to require the ellipsis of this sign.

" I *bid* you rise and go." " He *made* me go and do it." I *saw* her go that way." " You *need* not speak." In the preceding sentences the sign of the infinitive mood would be improper.

A singular verb in the first member of a sentence often leaves a plural verb to be understood in the second; as, " I *am* as thou *art,* and my people as thy people;" that is, " I am as thou art, and my people *are* as thy people."

The auxiliaries of the compound tenses are frequently used alone to spare the repetition of the verb; as, " she minds her work, but thou dost not;" that is, " dost not *mind it.*" " The first class was examined, but the others were not;" that is, " not *examined.*" " They must, and they shall be rewarded;" that is, " they must *be rewarded,* and they shall be rewarded."

The ellipsis of the *adverb* is shewn in the following examples: " He spake and acted *wisely;*" that is, " he spake *wisely,* and he acted *wisely.*" " They sing and play *most delightfully;*" that is, " they sing *most delightfully,* and they play *most delightfully.*" " *Thrice* I went and offered my service;" that is, " *thrice* I went, and *thrice* I offered my service." " He *soon* found and acknowledged his mistake;" that is, " he *soon* found, and he *soon* acknowledged his mistake."

The ellipsis of the *preposition* is thus used: " He went *into* the churches, halls, and public buildings;" that is, " he went *into* the churches, he went *into* the halls, and went *into* the public buildings. He also went *through* the streets and lanes of the city;" that is, " *through* the streets, and *through* the lanes of the city." " He spake *to* every gentleman and lady of the place;" that is, " he spake *to* every gentleman, and *to* every lady of the place."

" I did him a kindness;" that is, " I did *to* him a kindness." " He brought me the book;" that is, " he brought *to* me the book." " She gave him the cherries;" that is, " she gave *to* him the cherries."

The ellipsis of the *conjunction* is as follows,

" They confess the power, wisdom, goodness, and love of their Creator;" that is " they confess the power, *and* wisdom, *and* goodness, *and* love of their Creator." " May I speak of power, wisdom, goodness, truth?" The entire ellipsis of the conjunction, as in the last example, occurs but seldom.

" Though I love, I do not adore her;" that is, " though I love her, *yet* I do not adore her." " Though he went up, he could see nothing;" that is, "though he went up, *yet* he could see nothing."

The ellipsis of the *interjection* is not very common; we have however an example given by Milton; as, " O! pity and shame!" that is, " O pity! O shame!"

There is frequently an ellipsis of several words, or of a whole phrase.

" If good manners will not justify my long silence, policy, at least, will. And you must confess, there is some prudence in acknowledging a debt one is incapable of paying"—that is—" If good manners will not justify my long silence, policy, at least, will *justify it*. And you must confess, *that*, there is some prudence in acknowledging a debt, *which* one is incapable of paying."

" He will often argue, that if this part of our trade were well cultivated, we should gain from one nation; and if another, from another." That is—" He will often argue, that if this part of our trade were well cultivated, we should gain from one nation; and if another, *part of our trade were well cultivated, we should gain*, from another, *nation*."

" Could the painter have made a picture of me, capable of your conversation, I should have sat to him with more delight than ever I did to any thing in my life." That is—" Could the painter have made a picture of me, *which could have been*, capable of your conversation, I should have sat to him with more delight than ever I did, *sit*, to any thing in my life.".

As the ellipsis occurs in almost every sentence in the English language, the following examples will shew the application of all possible elliptical words.

" You must renounce the conversation of your friends, and every civil duty of life, to be concealed in gloomy and unprofitable solitude." That is— " You must renounce the conversation of your friends, and, *you must renounce*, every civil duty of life, to be concealed in gloomy *solitude*, and, *you must renounce the conversation of your friends, and you must renounce every civil duty of life, to be concealed in*, unprofitable solitude."

" When a man is thoroughly persuaded that he ought neither to admire, wish for, *or* pursue any thing but what is actually his duty; it is not in the power of seasons, persons, *or* accidents, to diminish his value." That is—" When a man is thoroughly persuaded that he ought neither to admire *any thing but what is actually his duty to admire, and when a man is thoroughly persuaded that he ought neither to* wish for *any thing but what is actually his duty to wish for*, or *when a man is thoroughly persuaded that he ought not to* pursue any thing but what is actually his duty, *to pursue;* it is not in the power of seasons *to diminish his value, and it is not in the power of* persons *to diminish his value*, or, *it is not in the power of* accidents to diminish his value.

The following examples are given to shew the impropriety of ellipsis in some particular cases.

" The learned gentleman, if he had read my essay quite through, would have found several of his objections might have been spared." It should have been " would have found, *that* several of his objections," &c.

" I scarce know any part of natural philosophy would yield more variety and use." " Any part of natural philosophy *which* would yield," &c.

" You and I cannot be of two opinions; nor, I think, any two men, used to think with freedom." " Nor, I think, any two men, *who are*, used to think," &c.

Some sentences, which seem to differ from the common forms of construction, are accounted for on the supposition of ellipsis.

" By preaching repentance."—" By *the* preaching *of* repentance." Both these are supposed to be proper and synonymous expressions, and I cannot but think the former is an ellipsis of the latter, in which the article and the preposition are both suppressed by custom.

By preaching of repentance, and by the preaching repentance, are both judged to be improper. These sentences are partly elliptical, and partly not so, and from hence the impropriety seems to arise. *Preaching*, in either form, is a noun distinguished by the sense, and a preposition prefixed to it; nor is the noun *repentance* governed by the supposed verbal force of the word *preaching*, but by the preposition expressed or understood.

" Well is him." " Woe is me." " Woe unto you." These sentences are all elliptical, and partly explain each other; as, " well is *it for* him;" " woe is *to* me;" " woe *is* unto you."

" My father is greater than I"—" greater than I am." " She loves him better than me"—" better than *she* loves me."

" To let blood." " To let down;" that is, " to let *out* blood ; or, to let blood *run out*." " To let *it fall* or *slide* down."

" To go a fishing;" that is, " to go a fishing *voyage*." " To go a hunting;" that is, " to go *on* a hunting *party*."

"To walk a mile."   "To sleep all night."
That is—"To walk *through the space of* a mile."
"To sleep *through* all *the* night."

"A hundred sheep."   "A thousand men."
That is—"A *flock of one* hundred sheep."   "A
company *of one* thousand men."

"That man has a hundred a year;" that is, "that
man has *an income of* a hundred *pounds in* a year."

"A few men."   "A great many men."   A *hundred,* a *thousand, few, many,* are to be considered
as collective nouns, and distinguished as such by
the singular article.

"A few men."   "A great many men."   That
is—"A *small number of* men."   "A *great number
of* men."

"He is the better for you."   "The deeper the
well, the clearer the water."   An article seems,
for the most part, to be the sign of a noun, either
expressed or understood; and the preceding sentences may be read thus: "He is the better *man*
for you."   "The deeper *well* the well *is,* the
clearer *water* the water *is.*"

"He descending, the doors being shut."   This
is commonly called the case or state absolute, and,
in English, the pronoun must be in the nominative.
The sentence seems to be elliptical, and the meaning is, "*While* he *was* descending, *while* the doors
were shut."

"He came into this world of ours."   "I am
justified in publishing any letters of Mr. Young's."
In the first of these examples, the possessive case
of the pronoun comes after the preposition, but
cannot be governed by it, for then it would be the
objective; it must therefore be governed by some
other word understood in the sentence: "He
came into this world of our *dwelling, habitation,*
&c.   And then omitting the noun, it will be,

this world of *ours,* by the common rules of construction.

The other sentence may be explained in the same manner. " I am justified in publishing any letters of Mr. Young's *writing, correspondence,* &c.; that is, of the writing or correspondence of Mr. Young.

The use of the possessive case, in such instances, seems to be a little uncouth. And though on some occasions, the possessive has its propriety and elegance, yet it should be used with caution, and much more sparingly than some authors have done.

---

§ 3. PARSING.

In all Parsing exercises, it is highly necessary to interrogate the pupils in the various parts of speech agreeably to the following plan.

1. *Nouns.*

Why a proper noun?   Why a particular noun?
Why a common noun?   What substance is it?
Why animal? Why vegetable? Why fossil?
Why fluid?
Why an abstract noun ? What is it derived from?
Is it an artificial or natural product? Why?
What person is it? What number? Why singular?
Why plural? What gender is it? Why masculine?
Why feminine ? Why neuter?
What case is it? Why nominative?
Why the genitive or possessive?
Why the accusative or objective?

Why is the apostrophic *s* omitted?
Why in apposition? Decline the noun.

2. *Articles.*

Why the definite or particular article?
Why the indefinite or general article?
Why is *n* added to the *a?* Why is the *n* omitted?
Why is the article omitted? Why repeated?
To what noun does it belong?

3. *Adjectives.*

Why an adjective? What noun does it qualify?
Why singular? Why plural?
Why omitted? Why repeated?
Why placed after the noun? What degree of comparison?
Why the comparative? Why the superlative?
Why in the positive state? Compare the adjective.

4. *Pronouns.*

Why a personal pronoun? Why a relative pronoun?
Why a pronominal adjective? Of what kind? Why?
What person? Why the first, second, or third person?
What case? Why the nominative? Why the possessive?
Why the objective?
What number? Why singular? Why plural?
What gender? Why masculine? Why feminine?
Why neuter? What is its antecedent? Why omitted?
Why repeated? Decline the pronoun.

5. *Verbs.*

Why is the verb regular? Why irregular?

Why active, neuter, or passive?

Why transitive or intransitive?

Why an imperfect verb?

Why a compound verb? What auxiliary is used with it?

Why is it in the indicative mood? Why imperative?

Why potential? Why subjunctive? Why infinitive?

What tense is it? Why the present? Why the imperfect? Why the perfect? Why the pluperfect? Why first future? Why the second future? Why first, second, or third person? Why singular? Why plural? Repeat the first person of the present tense, the imperfect tense, and the perfect and passive participle.

What is the nominative case to the verb?

What relation has it in point of time to another verb?

Conjugate the verb.

Why a participle?

From what verb is it derived?

Why active?

What action does it describe?

Why passive? What agency doth it refer to?

6. *Adverbs.*

Why an adverb? What verb does it qualify?

For what purpose is it used? What is its proper situation?

Why is the double negative used? Why rejected?

7. *Prepositions.*

What noun does it refer to?

What case does it govern? Why placed after the noun? Why omitted? Why repeated?

8. *Conjunctions.*

Why are conjunctions used? What do they connect?

What mood does it require? Why the subjunctive?

Why the indicative? Why omitted? Why repeated?

9. *Interjections.*

Why an interjection? What case follows it?

Why the nominative? Why the objective?

Why omitted? Why repeated?

PARSING EXERCISES.

RULE I.

The first and most important rule of syntax is, that the NOMINATIVE CASE *must take the lead of the verb; and the* VERB *must agree with its nominative in number and person.*

Ex. 1. *I learn.*

I is a personal pronoun, the sign of the first person singular, nominative case, to the verb "*learn.*" R. I. *Learn,* is a regular verb neuter, indicative mood, present tense, first person singular, and agrees with its nominative "*I.*" R. 1.

Ex. 2. TEMPERANCE *promotes health.*

Temperance is an abstract noun, third person singular, nominative case to the verb "*promotes.*" R. I. *Promotes,* is a regular verb active, indicative mood, present tense, third person singular, and agrees with its nominative "*temperance.*" R.I. *Health,* is an abstract noun, third person singular, objective case, governed by the verb "*promotes.*" R XX.

Ex. 3. JANE *behaved discreetly.*

Jane, is a proper noun substantive; the name is "*Jane,*" the substance "*animal,*" singular number, feminine gender, nominative case to the verb "*behaved,*" R. I. *Behaved,* is a regular verb neuter, indicative mood, imperfect tense, third person singular, and agrees with its nominative "*Jane,*" R. I. *Discreetly,* is an adverb of quality.

RULE II.

The infinitive mood, or part of a sentence, is sometimes put as the nominative case to the verb.

Ex. 4. To ERR *is human.*

To err, is the infinitive mood, and nominative case to the verb "*is,*" R. I. *Is,* is the neuter substantive verb*, indicative mood, present tense, third person singular, agreeing with its nominative "*to err,*" R. I. *Human,* is an adjective in the positive state, and belongs to the noun "nature" understood, R. XV.

---

* It is called the SUBSTANTIVE VERB, because of its peculiar power to denote being or existence; as, "*I am.*" "And the LORD said unto Moses, I AM that I AM. Thus shalt thou say unto the children of Israel, I AM hath sent me unto you."

I

Ex. 5. To walk in the park *is pleasant.*

To walk in the park, is part of a sentence put in the nominative case to the verb "*is,*" R. II. *Is,* is the neuter substantive verb, indicative mood, present tense, third person singular, and agrees with its nominative "*to walk in the park,*" R. I. *Pleasant,* is an adjective in the positive state, and belongs to its noun "*exercise,*" understood. R. XV.

Ex. 6. To countenance persons who are guilty of bad actions, *is scarcely one remove from actually committing them.*

To countenance persons who are guilty of bad actions, is part of a sentence, which is put in the nominative case to the verb "*is.*" R. II. *Is,* is the neuter substantive verb, indicative mood, present tense, third person singular, and agrees with its nominative "*to countenance persons who are guilty of bad actions.*" R. I. *Scarcely,* is an adverb of quality. *One,* is a numeral adjective, agreeing with its noun "*remove.*" R. XV. *Remove,* is an abstract noun, third person singular, nominative case. R. XXVI. *From,* is a preposition. *Actually,* is an adverb, qualifying the participle committing. *Committing,* is the present participle of the regular active verb "*to commit.*" *Them,* is a plural pronoun, third person, objective case, agreeing with the antecedent noun "*actions*" in number and person, and is governed by the participle "*committing.*" R. XXI.

RULE III.

Every verb, except in the infinitive mood, or the

*participle, ought to have a nominative case, ex-
pressed or understood.*

Ex. 7. SPEAK *modestly of thyself.*

Speak, is an irregular verb neuter, imperative mood,
second person singular, and agrees with its nominative " *thou,*"understood. R. III. *Modestly,* is an adverb, qualifying the verb " *speak.*" *Of,* is a preposition. *Thyself* is a compound pronoun, second
person singular, objective case, governed by the
preposition " *of.*" R. XXII.

Ex. 8. STUDY *your grammar daily.*

Study, is a regular verb neuter, imperative mood,
second person singular, and agrees with its nominative " *thou,*" understood. R. III. *Your,* is a
personal pronoun, second person singular, possessive case. *Grammar,* is a particular noun, singular number, objective case, governed by the
pronoun " *your.*" R. XVIII.

Ex. 9. GUARD *against passion.*

Guard, is a regular verb neuter, imperative
mood, second person singular, and agrees with its
nominative " *thou,*" understood. R. III. *Against,*
is a preposition. *Passion,* is an abstract noun,
singular number, objective case, governed by the
preposition " *against.*" R. XXII.

RULE IV.

*When the nominative case has no personal tense
of a verb, but is put before a participle indepen-*

dently on the rest of the sentence, it is called THE CASE ABSOLUTE.

Ex. 10. THAT HAVING BEEN DISCUSSED LONG AGO, *there is no occasion to resume the debate.*

That having been discussed long ago, being independent on the rest of the sentence, is put in the case absolute. R. IV. *There,* is an adverb of place. *Is,* is the neuter substantive verb, indicative mood, present tense, third person singular, and agrees with its nominative "*occasion.*" R. I. *No,* is an adjective, and belongs to the noun "*occasion.*" R. XV. *Occasion,* is an abstract noun, singular number, nominative case to the verb "*is.*" R. I. *To resume,* is a regular verb active, infinitive mood, present tense, governed by the verb "*is.*" R. XXVII. *The,* is the definite or particular article. *Debate,* is an abstract noun, singular number, objective case, governed by the verb "*resume.*" R. XX.

Ex. 11. *He intends,* PROVIDED HE CAN GET PERMISSION, *to accompany us.*

He, is a personal pronoun, sign of the third person singular, masculine gender, nominative case to the verb "*intends.*" R. I. *Intends,* is a regular verb active, indicative mood, present tense, third person singular, agreeing with its nominative "*he.*" R. I. *Provided he can get permission,* being independent on the rest of the sentence, is put in the case absolute. R. IV. *To accompany,* is a regular verb active, infinitive mood, present tense, governed by the verb "*intends.*" R. XXVII. *Us,* is a personal pronoun, first person plural, objective case, governed by the verb "*intends.*" R. XX.

Ex. 12. Shame being lost, *all virtue is lost.*

Shame being lost, being independent on the rest of the sentence, is put in the case absolute. R. IV. *All,* is an adjective, and belongs to its noun "*virtue.*" R. XV. *Virtue,* is an abstract noun, singular number, nominative case to the verb "*is lost.*" R. I. *Is lost,* is an irregular verb passive, indicative mood, present tense, third person singular, agreeing with its nominative "*virtue.*" R. I.

RULE V.

Two or more nouns or pronouns, in the singular number, joined by copulative conjunctions, expressed or implied, must have verbs, nouns, and pronouns, agreeing with them in the plural number.

Ex. 13. Truth and honesty *need not an oath.*

Truth, is an abstract noun, singular number, and nominative to the verb "*need.*" R. I. *And,* is a copulative conjunction, connecting the nouns "*truth* and *honesty.*" R. XXX. *Honesty,* is an abstract noun, singular number, nominative case. *Need,* is a regular verb active, indicative mood, present tense, third person plural, agreeing with its nominatives "*truth* and *honesty.*" R. V. *Not,* is an adverb of negation. *An,* is the indefinite article. *Oath,* is an abstract noun, singular number, objective case, governed by the verb "*need.*" R. XX.

Ex. 14. Milton and Shakspeare *were eminent writers.*

Milton, is a proper noun substantive, the name is " *Milton*," the substance "*animal*," singular number, masculine gender, nominative case to the verb "*were*." R. I. *And*, is a copulative conjunction, connecting the nouns " *Milton* and *Shakspeare*." R. xxx. *Shakspeare*, is a proper noun substantive, the name is " *Shakspeare*," the substance " *animal*," singular number, masculine gender, nominative case. *Were*, is an irregular verb neuter, indicative mood, imperfect tense, third person plural, agreeing with its nominatives " *Milton* and *Shakspeare*." R. v. *Eminent*, is an adjective, positive state, and belongs to its noun " *writers*." R. xv. *Writers*, is a common noun substantive, the name is "*writers*," the substance " *animal*," third person plural, masculine gender, nominative case. R. XXVI.

Ex. 15. WISDOM, VIRTUE, HONOUR, *dwell with the golden mediocrity*.

Wisdom, is an abstract noun, singular number, and nominative case to the verb " *dwell*." R. I. *Virtue*, is an abstract noun, singular number, nominative case. *Honour*, is an abstract noun, singular number, nominative case, and " *wisdom, virtue, honour*," are connected by the copulative conjunction " *and*," understood. R. xxx. *Dwell*, is an irregular verb neuter, indicative mood, present tense, third person plural, agreeing with its nominatives " *wisdom, virtue, honour*." R. v. *With*, is a preposition. *The*, is the definite article. *Golden*, is an adjective, and belongs to the noun " *mediocrity*." R. xv. *Mediocrity*, is an abstract noun, singular number, objective case, governed by the preposition " *with*." R. XXII.

RULE VI.

When a noun, or pronoun, of the singular number is separated by a disjunctive conjunction, it requires a singular verb.

Ex. 16. John or Mary *has taken the paper.*

John, is a proper noun substantive, the name is " *John*" the substance " *animal,*" singular number, masculine gender, nominative to " *has taken.*" R. I. *Or* is a disjunctive conjunction. *Mary,* is a proper noun substantive, the name is " *Mary,*" the substance " *animal,*" singular number, feminine gender, nominative case. *Has taken,* is an irregular verb active, indicative mood, present tense, third person singular, and agrees with its nominative, " *John* or *Mary.*" R. VI. *The* is the definite article. *Paper,* is a common noun substantive, the name is *paper,* the substance " *vegetable,*" singular number, objective case, governed by the verb " *has taken.*" R. XX.

Ex. 17. *Man's* HAPPINESS OR MISERY *is in a great measure put into his own hands.*

Man's, is a common noun substantive, the name is " *man's,*" the substance " *animal,*" singular number, masculine gender, possessive case, and is governed by the noun " *happiness.*" R. XVIII. *Happiness,* is an abstract noun, singular number, nominative case to the verb " *is put.*" R. I. *Or,* is a disjunctive conjunction. *Misery,* is an abstract noun, singular number, nominative case. R. XXX. *Is put,* is an irregular verb active, indicative mood, present tense, third person singular, agreeing with its nominative, " *happiness* or *misery.* R. VI. *In a great measure,* being independent on the rest of the sentence, may be put in the case absolute. R. IV. *Into,* is a preposition governing the noun " *hands.*" *His* is a pronominal adjective of the possessive kind, singular number, masculine gender, and belongs to the noun substantive " *hands.*" R. XV. *Own* is an adjective, and belongs to the noun " *hands.*" R. XV. *Hands,* is a common noun substantive, the name is " *hands,*" the substance " *animal,*" plural number, masculine gender, objective case, governed by the preposition " *into.*" R. XXII.

Ex. 18. HENRY OR CHARLES *intends to accompany me to-morrow.*

Henry is a proper noun substantive, the name is " *Henry,*" the substance " *animal,*" singular number, masculine gender, and nominative to the verb " *intends.*" R. I. *Or,* is a disjunctive conjunction. *Charles,* is a proper noun substantive, the name is " *Charles,*" the substance " *animal,*" singular number, masculine gender, nominative case. " *Intends,*" is a regular verb neuter, indicative mood, present tense, third person singular, and agrees with its nominative " *Henry or Charles.*" R. VI. *To accompany,* is a regular verb active, infinitive mood, present tense, governed by the verb " *intends.*" R. XXVII. *Me,* is a personal pronoun, first person singular, objective case, governed by the verb " *to accompany.*" R. XX. *To-morrow,* is an adverb of time.

RULE VII.

A noun of multitude may have a verb or pronoun agreeing with it either of the singular or plural number, unless it conveys the idea of plurality, in which case it must have a plural verb or pronoun.

Ex. 19. *My* PEOPLE DO *not* CONSIDER; *they have not known me.*

My, is a pronominal adjective, possessive kind, first person singular, and belongs to the noun " *people*." R. XV. *People,* is a noun of multitude, conveying plurality of idea, agreeing with the verb " *do consider*." R. VII. *Do consider,* is a regular verb neuter, indicative mood, present tense, third person plural, and agrees with its nominative " *people*." R. I. *Not,* is an adverb of negation. *They* is a personal pronoun, sign of the third person plural, and nominative case to the verb " *have known*." R. I. *Have known,* is an irregular verb active, indicative mood, perfect tense, third person plural, agreeing with its nominative " *they*." R. I. *Not,* is an adverb of negation. *Me,* is a personal pronoun, first person singular, objective case, agreeing with its antecedent " *my*" in gender, number, and person, R. VIII., and governed by the verb " *have known*." R. XX.

Ex. 20. *The* SCHOOL IS *dismissed.*

The, is the definite article, *school,* is a noun of multitude conveying unity of idea, agreeing with its singular verb " *is dismissed*." R. VII. *Is dismissed,* is a regular verb passive, indicative mood, present tense, third person singular, and agrees with its nominative " *school*." R. I.

Ex. 21. SEAMEN SHORTEN SAIL *as they near their port.*

Seamen, is a noun of multitude conveying plurality of idea, agreeing with the verb " *shorten sail*." R. VII. *Shorten sail,* is a regular verb active, indicative mood, present tense, third person

plural, agreeing with its nominative " *seamen.*"
As, is a conjunction. *They*, is a personal pronoun,
sign of the third person plural, agreeing with its
antecedent " *seamen*," in number, gender, and person, nominative case, being the same case as " *seamen,*" because it signifies the same thing. R. XIX.
Near, is a preposition. *Their*, is a pronominal
adjective, possessive kind, third person plural, masculine gender, and belongs to the noun " *port.*"
R. XV. *Port*, is a common noun substantive, singular number, objective case, governed by the preposition " *near.*" R. XXII.

RULE VIII.

*Personal pronouns must occupy the position,
which their antecedents would fill if repeated, agree
with them in gender, number, and person, and with
the pronouns governed in the objective case.*

Ex. 22. *He lives long enough,* WHO *lives well.*

He is a personal pronoun, sign of the third person singular, masculine gender, nominative case to
the verb " *lives.*" R. I. *Lives*, is a regular verb
neuter, indicative mood, present tense, third person
singular, agreeing with its nominative " *he.*" R. I.
Long enough, is an adjective positive state, referring
to the noun " *man*" understood. R. XV. *Who*, is
a relative pronoun, third person singular, masculine
gender, nominative case to the verb " *lives,*" agreeing with its antecedent " *he.*" R. VIII. *Lives*, is
a regular verb neuter, indicative mood, present
tense, third person singular, agreeing with its nominative "*who.*" R. I. *Well*, is an adverb of quality.

Ex. 23. *This is the* FRIEND WHOM *I greatly esteem.*

This, is a pronominal adjective of the demonstrative kind, singular number, agreeing with the noun " *man* or *woman*" understood. R. XV. *Is,* is the neuter substantive verb, indicative mood, present tense, third person singular, agreeing with its nominative " *man* or *woman*" understood. R. I. *The* is the definite or particular article. *Friend,* is a common noun substantive, the noun is " *friend,*" the substance " *animal,*" masculine or feminine gender, nominative case. R. XXVI. *Whom,* is a relative pronoun, objective case, agreeing with its antecedent " *friend,*" and governed by the verb " *esteem.*" R. VIII. and R. XX. *I,* is a personal pronoun, sign of the first person singular, nominative case to the verb " *esteem.*" R. I. *Greatly,* is an adverb of quality. *Esteem,* is a regular verb active, indicative mood, first person, present tense, agreeing with its nominative " *I.*" R. I.

Ex. 24. *Gaming is the* VICE WHICH *he repented of too late.*

Gaming, is a participle noun, singular number, nominative case to the verb " *is.*" R. I. *Is,* is the neuter substantive verb, indicative mood, present tense, third person singular, agreeing with its nominative " *gaming.*" R. I. *The,* is the definite article. *Vice,* is an abstract noun, singular number, nominative case. R. XXVI. *Which,* is a relative pronoun, third person, objective case, agreeing with its antecedent " *vice,*" and governed by the preposition " *of.*" R. VIII. and R. XXII. *He,* is a personal pronoun, sign of the third person singular, masculine gender, and nominative to the verb " *repented.*" R. I. *Repented,* is a regular verb neuter, indicative mood, imperfect tense, third person singular, agreeing with its nominative *" he."* R. I. *Of,* is a preposition governing the pronoun *" which." " Too late"* is an adverb of time.

RULE IX.

The relative pronoun being of the same person with its antecedent, should immediately follow it, and the verb agrees with it accordingly.

Ex. 25. *A* MAN WHO IS *truly religious.*

A, is the indefinite general article. *Man,* is a common noun substantive, the name is *" man,"* the substance *" animal,"* singular number, masculine gender, nominative case to the verb *" is."* R. I. *Who,* is a relative pronoun, third person singular, nominative case, agreeing with its antecedent *" man,"* in gender, number, and person, R. IX. *Is,* is the neuter substantive verb, indicative mood, present tense, third person singular, agreeing with its nominative *" man."* R. I. *Truly,* is an adverb of quality. *Religious,* is an adjective, positive state, and belongs to the noun *" man"* understood. R. XV.

Ex. 26. I WHO *teach from experience.*

I, is a personal pronoun, sign of the first person singular, nominative case to the verb *" teach."* R. I. *Who,* is a relative pronoun, first person singular, nominative case, agreeing with its antecedent *" I"* in gender, number, and person. R. IX. *Teach,* is an irregular verb active, indicative mood, present tense, first person singular, agreeing with its nominative *" I."* R. I. *From,* is a preposition. *Expe-*

rience, is an abstract noun, singular number, objective case, governed by the preposition *" from."* R. XXII.

Ex. 27. *The* HORSE THAT WON *the plate.*

The, is the particular article. *Horse* is a common substantive, the name is *" horse,"* the substance *" animal,"* singular number, masculine gender, nominative case to the verb *"won."* R. I. *That,* is a relative pronoun, third person singular, nominative case, and agrees with its antecedent *" horse."* R. IX. *Won,* is an irregular verb active, indicative mood, perfect tense, third person singular, agreeing with its nominative *" horse."* R. I. *The,* is the definite article. *" Plate "* is a common noun substantive, the name is *" plate,"* the substance *" fossil,"* singular number, objective case, governed by the verb *" won."* R. XX.

RULE X.

The relative is the nominative to the verb, when no nominative comes between it and the verb.

Ex. 28. *He will be rewarded,* WHO *attends to instruction.*

He, is a personal pronoun, sign of the third person singular number, masculine gender, nominative case to the verb *" will be rewarded."* R. I. *Will be rewarded,* is a regular verb active, composed of the auxiliaries *" will be "* and the perfect participle *" rewarded,"* indicative mood, first future tense, third person singular, agreeing with its nominative *" he."* R. I. *Who,* is a relative pronoun, third person singular, masculine gender, nominative case to the verb *" attends."* R. X. *Attends,* is a regular verb neuter, indicative mood, present tense, third person singular, and agrees with its nominative " *who*." R. I. *To*, is a preposition. *Instruction*, is an abstract noun, singular number, objective case, governed by the preposition " *to*." R. XXII.

Ex. 29. *They are truly wise,* WHO *do justice, love mercy, and walk humbly with their* GOD.

They, is a personal pronoun, sign of the third person plural, nominative case to the verb " *are*." R. I. *Are,* is the neuter substantive verb, indicative mood, present tense, third person plural, agreeing with its nominative " *they*." R. I. *Truly*, is an adverb of quality. *Wise,* is an adjective, positive state, and refers to the noun " *person* " understood. R. xv. *Who,* is a relative pronoun, third person plural, and nominative to the verb " *do*." R. x. *Do*, is an irregular verb active, indicative mood, present tense, third person plural, agreeing with its nominative " who." R. I. *Justice* is an abstract noun, singular number, objective case, governed by the active verb " *do*." R. xx. *Love,* is a regular verb active, indicative mood, present tense, third person plural, agreeing with its nominative " *who* " understood. R. I. *Mercy,* is an abstract noun, singular number, objective case, governed by the verb " *love*." R. xx. *And*, is a copulative conjunction, connecting " *do justice, love mercy, and walk humbly*." R. xxx. *Walk*, is a regular verb neuter, indicative mood, present tense, third person plural, agreeing with its nominative " *who*" understood. R. I. *Humbly,* is an adverb of quality. *With,* is a preposition. *Their*, is a pronominal adjective, of the possessive kind, and belongs to the noun " GOD." R. xv. GOD is a proper noun, the name is " *God,*" the substance, " *incomprehensible,*" singular number, objective

case, governed by the preposition " *with.*" R.
XXII.

Ex. 30. *He is happy* WHO *is obedient to the law.*

He, is a personal pronoun, sign of the third
person singular, masculine gender, nominative
case to the verb " *is.*" R. I. *Is,* is the neuter
substantive verb, indicative mood, present tense,
third person singular, agreeing with its nominative " he." R. I. *Happy,* is an adjective,
positive state, and belongs to the noun " *man*"
understood. R. XV. *Who,* is a relative pronoun, third person singular, masculine gender,
nominative case to the verb " *is.*" R. I and R. X.
Is, is the neuter substantive verb, indicative mood,
present tense, third person singular, agreeing with
its nominative " *who.*" R. I. *Obedient,* is an adjective, positive state, and belongs to the noun
" *laws.*" R. XV. *To,* is a preposition. *The,* is the
definite article. *Law,* is an abstract noun, singular
number, objective case, governed by the preposition " *to* " R. XXII.

RULE XI.

*When the nominative comes between the relative
and the verb, the relative is governed by some word
in its own member of the sentence.*

Ex. 31. *He* WHO *preserves me, to* WHOM *I owe
my being,* WHOSE *I am, and* WHOM *I serve is eternal.*

He, is a personal pronoun, sign of the third person singular, nominative case to the verb " *is.*" R. I.
Who, is a relative pronoun, third person, singular,
agreeing with its antecedent " *he,*" and nominative

to the verb " *preserves.*" R. I. and R. XI.   *Preserves*, is a regular verb active, indicative mood, present tense, third person singular, agreeing with its nominative " *who.*" R. I.   *Me*, is a personal pronoun, first person singular, objective case, governed by the verb " *preserves.*" R. XX.   *To*, is a preposition.   *Whom*, is a relative pronoun, third person singular, objective case, agreeing with its antecedent " *he,*" and governed by the preposition " *to.*" R. XXII. and R. XI.   *I* is a personal pronoun, first person singular, nominative case to the verb " *owe.*" R. I.   *Owe*, is a regular verb active, indicative mood, present tense, first person singular, and agrees with its nominative " *I.*" R. I.   *My*, is a pronominal adjective, possessive kind, and belongs to the noun " *being.*" R. XV.   *Being* is a common noun, the name is " *being,*" the substance " *animal,*" singular number, objective case, governed by the verb " *owe.*" R. XX.   *Whose*, is a relative pronoun, third person singular, possessive case, agreeing with its antecedent " *he,*" and governed by the noun " *being.*" R. XVIII. and R. XI.   *I*, is a personal pronoun, first person singular, nominative to the verb " *am.*" R. I.   *Am*, is the neuter substantive verb, indicative mood, present tense, first person singular, and agrees with its nominative " *I.*" R. I.   *And*, is a copulative conjunction. *Whom*, is a relative pronoun, third person singular, objective case, agreeing with its antecedent " *he,*" and governed by the verb " *serve.*" R. XX. and R. XI.   *I*, is a personal pronoun, first person singular, nominative case to the verb " *serve.*" R. I.   *Serve*, is a regular verb active, indicative mood, present tense, first person singular, agreeing with its nominative " *I.*" R. I.   *Is*, is the neuter substantive verb, indicative mood, present tense, first person singular, agreeing with its nominative " *he.*" R. I.

Eternal, is a proper noun, singular number, objective case, governed by the verb " *serve.*" R. XX.

Ex. 32. *Pestalozzi, by* WHOM *you were educated, lives comfortably at Yverdun.*

Pestalozzi, is a proper noun substantive; the name is " *Pestalozzi,*" the substance " *animal,*" singular number, masculine gender, nominative case to the verb " *lives.*" R. I. *By* is a preposition. *Whom,* is a relative pronoun, third person singular, masculine gender, objective case, agreeing with its antecedent master, and governed by the preposition " *by.*" R. XXII. and R. XI. *You* is a personal pronoun, second person plural, nominative case to the verb " *were educated.*" R. I. *Were educated,* is a regular verb passive, indicative mood, imperfect tense, second person plural, agreeing with its nominative " *you.*" R. I. *Lives,* is a regular verb neuter, indicative mood, present tense, third person singular, agreeing with its nominative " *Pestalozzi.*" R. I. *Comfortably* is an adverb of quality. *At,* is a preposition. *Yverdun* is a particular noun substantive, singular number, objective case, governed by the preposition " *at.*" R. XXII.

Ex. 33. *The officer has been disgraced,* WHO *ceded the garrison to the enemy.*

The, is the particular article, *officer* is a common noun substantive, the name is " *officer,*" the substance " *animal,*" singular number, masculine gender, and nominative to the verb " *has been disgraced.*" R. I. *Has been disgraced,* is a regular verb passive, perfect tense, third person singular, agreeing with its nominative " *officer.* R. I. *Who,* is a relative pronoun, third person singular, masculine gender, agreeing with its antecedent " *officer,*" and nominative to the verb " *ceded.*" R. I. and R. XI.

Ceded, is a regular verb active, indicative mood, imperfect tense, third person singular, and agrees with its nominative " *who.*" R. I. *The,* is the definite or particular article. *Garrison,* is a common noun substantive, the name is " *garrison,*" the substance " *various,*" singular number, objective case, governed by the verb " *ceded.*" R. xx. *To,* is a preposition, *the,* is the definite article. *Enemy* is a common noun substantive, the name is " *enemy,*" the substance " *animal,*" plural number, objective case, governed by the preposition " *to.*" R. XXII.

RULE XII.

When both the antecedent and the relative become nominatives, each to different verbs, the relative is the nominative to the former, and the antecedent to the latter verb.

Ex. 34. HE WHO *swims in sin, will sink in sorrow.*

He, is a personal pronoun, sign of the third person singular, masculine gender, nominative to the verb " *will sink.*" R. I. and R. XII. *Who,* is a relative pronoun, third person singular, masculine gender, agreeing with its antecedent " *he,*" and nominative to the verb " *swims.*" R. I. and R. XII. *Swims* is an irregular verb neuter, indicative mood, present tense, third person singular, agreeing with its nominative " *who.*" R. I. *In* is a preposition. *Sin* is an abstract noun, singular number, objective case, governed by the preposition " *in.*" R. XXII. *Will sink,* is an irregular verb neuter, indicative mood, first future tense, third person singular, agreeing with its nominative " *he.*" R. I. *In,* is a preposition. *Sorrow,* is an abstract noun, singular number, objective case, governed by the preposition " *in.*" R. XXII.

Ex. 35. HE WHO *is religious will find joy, peace and comfort at the day of retribution.*

He, is a personal pronoun, third person singular, masculine gender, nominative case to the verb " *will find.* R. I. and R. XII. *Who,* is a relative pronoun, third person singular, masculine gender, agreeing with its antecedent " *he,*" and nominative to the verb " *is.* R. I. and R. XXII. *Is,* is the neuter substantive verb, indicative mood, present tense, third person singular, agreeing with its nominative " *who.*" R. I. *Religious,* is an adjective, positive state, and belongs to the noun " *person*" understood. R. XV. *Will find,* is an irregular verb active, indicative mood, first future tense, third person singular, agreeing with its nominative, " *he.*" R. I. *Joy,* is an abstract noun, singular number, objective case, governed by the verb " *will find.*" R. XX. *Peace,* is an abstract noun, singular number, objective case, governed by the verb " *will find.*" R. XX. *And,* is a copulative conjunction, connecting " *joy, peace, comfort.*" R. XXX. *Comfort,* is an abstract noun, singular number, objective case, governed by the verb " *will find.*" R. XX. *At,* is a preposition. *The,* is the definite article. *Day,* is a common noun, singular number, objective case, governed by the preposition " *at.*" R. XXII. *Of,* is a preposition. *Retribution,* is a particular noun, singular number, objective case, governed by the preposition " *of.*" R. XXII.

Ex. 36. WELLINGTON, WHO *conquered Buonaparte, has been created a Duke.*

Wellington, is a proper noun substantive, the name is " *Wellington,*" the substance " *animal,*" singular number, masculine gender, nominative case to the verb " *hath been created.* R. I. *Who,* is a relative pronoun, third person singular, masculine gender, agreeing with its antecedent " *Wellington*," and nominative to the verb " *conquered*." R. I. and R. XII. *Conquered*, is a regular verb active, indicative mood, imperfect tense, third person singular, and agrees with its nominative " *who*." R. I. *Buonaparte*, is a proper noun substantive, the name is " *Buonaparte*," the substance " *animal*," singular number, masculine gender, objective case, governed by the verb " *conquered*." R. XX. *Hath been created*, is a regular verb passive, indicative mood, perfect tense, third person singular, agreeing with its nominative " *Wellington*." R. I. *A*, is the indefinite or general article. *Duke*, is a proper noun, singular number, objective case, and governed by the verb " *created*." R. XX.

RULE XIII.

When the relative is preceded by two nominatives of different persons, the relative and the verb may agree in person with either, according to the sense.

Ex. 37. *I am the* Lord, that *maketh all things; that stretcheth forth the heavens alone.*

I, is a personal pronoun, sign of the first person singular, nominative case to the verb " *am*." R. I. *Am*, is the neuter substantive verb, indicative mood, present tense, first person singular, agreeing with the nominative " *I*." R. I. *The*, is the definite article. *Lord*, is a proper name, singular number, nominative case. R. XXVI. *That*, is a relative pronoun, third person singular, agreeing with its antecedent " *Lord*," and nominative to the verb " *maketh*." R. XIII. R. IX. and R. I. *Maketh*, is an irregular verb active, indicative mood, present tense, third person singular, agreeing with its nominative "*that.*" R. I. *All,* is an adjective, belonging to the noun "*things.*" R. xv. *Things,* is a common noun substantive, the name is "*things,*" the substance "*animal, vegetable, fossil,* and *fluid,*" plural number, objective case, governed by the verb "*maketh.*" R. xx. *That,* is a relative pronoun, third person singular, agreeing with its antecedent "*Lord,*" and nominative to the verb "*stretcheth.*" R. XIII. R. IX. and R. I. *Stretcheth,* is a regular verb active, indicative mood, present tense, third person singular, agreeing with its nominative "*that.*" R. I. *Forth,* is an adverb. *The,* is the definite article. *Heavens,* is a particular noun, plural number, objective case, governed by the verb "*stretcheth.*" R. xx. *Alone,* is an adjective, and belongs to the noun "*Lord.*" R. xv.

Ex. 38. THOU *art the* MAN, *who swam across the river.*

Thou, is a personal pronoun, sign of the second person singular, nominative case to the verb "*art.*" R. I. *Art,* is the neuter substantive verb, indicative mood, present tense, second person singular, agreeing with its nominative "*thou.*" R. I. *The,* is the definite or particular article. *Man,* is a common noun substantive, the name is "*man,*" the substance "*animal,*" singular number, masculine gender, nominative case. R. XXVI. *Who,* is a relative pronoun, third person singular, agreeing with its antecedent "*man,*" and nominative to the verb "*swam.*" R. XIII. R. IX. R. I. *Swam,* is an irregular verb active, indicative mood, imperfect tense, third person singular, and agrees with its nominative "*who.*" R. I. *Across,* is an adverb. *The,* is the definite article. *River,* is a common noun substantive, the name is "*river,*" the substance *"fluid,"* singular number, objective case, governed by the verb *" swam."* R. XX.

Ex. 39. PRINCES *are* MEN, WHO *ought to be exemplary in their conduct.*

Princes, is a common noun substantive, the name is *" princes,"* the substance *" animal,"* plural number, masculine gender, and nominative to the verb *" are."* R. I. *Are* is the neuter substantive verb, indicative mood, present tense, third person plural, and agrees with its nominative *" princes."* R. I. *Men,* is a common noun substantive, the name is *" men,"* the substance *" animal,"* plural number, masculine gender, nominative case. R. XXVI. *Who,* is a relative pronoun, third person plural, agreeing with its antecedent, *" princes or men,"* nominative case to the verb *" ought."* R. XIII. R. IX. and R. I. *Ought* is an imperfect verb, indicative mood, present tense, third person plural, agreeing with its nominative *" who."* R. I. *To be,* is the primary auxiliary neuter verb, infinitive mood, present tense, and governed by the verb *" ought."* R. XXVII. *Exemplary,* is an adjective, positive state, and belongs to the noun *" conduct.."* R. XV. *In,* is a preposition. *Their,* is a pronominal adjective, of the possessive kind, and belongs to the noun *" conduct."* R. XV. *Conduct* is an abstract noun, singular number, objective case, governed by the preposition *" in."* R. XXII.

RULE XIV.

When the relative is of the interrogative kind, the noun or pronoun containing the answer must be in the same case, as that which contains the question.

Ex. 40. Whose *carriage is that?* My Father's.

Whose, is a relative pronoun of the interrogative kind, and relates to the answer *"my father's,"* singular number, possessive case, governed by the noun *"carriage."* R. XIV. and R. XVIII. *Carriage,* is a common noun substantive, the name is *" carriage,"* the substance *" various,"* singular number, nominative case to the verb *" is."* R. I. *Is,* is the neuter substantive verb, indicative mood, present tense, third person singular, and agrees with its nominative *" carriage."* R. I. *That,* is a pronominal adjective of the demonstrative kind, and belongs to the noun *" carriage."* R. XV. *My,* is a pronominal adjective of the possessive kind, and belongs to the noun *" father."* R. XV. *Father's,* is a common noun substantive, the name is *" father's,"* the substance *" animal,"* singular number, possessive case, governed by the noun *"carriage"* understood. R. XIV. and R. XVIII.

Ex. 41. Who *teaches us?*

Who, is a relative pronoun of the interrogative kind, singular number, nominative case to the verb *" teaches,"* R. I. the word to which it refers, its subsequent is the noun containing the answer to the question. R. XIV. *Teaches,* is an irregular verb active, indicative mood, present tense, third person singular, agreeing with its nominative *" who."* R. I. *Us,* is a personal pronoun, first person plural, objective case, governed by the verb *" teaches."* R. XX.

Ex. 42. When *did Charles go?* Yesterday.

When, is an adverb of time, used interrogatively, and relates to the answer *" yesterday."* R. XIV.

Did go, is an irregular verb neuter, indicative mood, imperfect tense, third person singular, agreeing with its nominative, " *Charles.*" R. I. *Charles,* is a common noun substantive, the name is " *Charles,*" the substance " *animal,*" singular number, masculine gender, nominative case to the verb " *did go.*" R. I. *Yesterday,* is an adverb of time past. R. XIV.

RULE XV.

Every adjective, and every pronominal adjective, belongs to a noun expressed or understood ; and must agree with it in number.

Ex. 43. PROUD *children are lightly esteemed.*

Proud, is an adjective, positive state, and belongs to the noun " *children.*" R. XV. *Children,* is a common noun substantive, the name is " *children,*" the substance " *animal,*" plural number, masculine or feminine gender, and nominative case to the verb " *are esteemed.*" R. I. *Are esteemed,* is a regular verb active, indicative mood, present tense, third person plural, agreeing with its nominative " *children.*" R. I. *Lightly,* is an adverb of quality.

Ex. 44. *A* WISE *man acts wisely.*

A, is the indefinite article. *Wise,* is an adjective, positive state, and belongs to the noun " *man.*" R. XV. *Man,* is a common noun substantive, the name is " *man,*" the substance " *animal,*" singular number, nominative case to the verb " *acts.*" R. I. *Acts* is a regular verb neuter, indicative mood, present tense, third person singular, agreeing with its nominative " *man.*" R. I. *Wisely*, is an adverb of quality.

Ex. 45. PRETTY *toys please* YOUNG *children.*

Pretty is an adjective, positive state, and belongs to the noun " *toys.*" R. xv. *Toys* is a common noun substantive, the name is " *toys,*" the substance " *various,*" plural number, nominative case to the verb " *please.*" R. I. *Please* is a regular verb active, indicative mood, present tense, third person plural, agreeing with its nominative " *toys.*" R. I. *Young*, is an adjective, positive state, and belongs to the noun " *children.*" R. xv. *Children*, is a common noun substantive, the name is " *children,*" the substance " *animal,*" plural number, masculine and feminine gender, objective case, and governed by the verb " *please.*" R. xx.

Ex. 46. THIS *book will please Maria.*

This, is a pronominal adjective of the demonstrative kind, singular, and belongs to the noun " *book.*" R. xv. *Book*, is a common noun substantive, the name is " *book,*" the substance " *vegetable,*" singular number, nominative case to the verb " *will please.*" R. I. *Will please*, is a regular verb active, indicative mood, first future tense, third person singular, agreeing with its nominative " *book.*" R. I. *Maria*, is a proper noun substantive, the name is " *Maria,*" the substance " *animal,*" singular number, feminine gender, objective case, governed by the verb " *will please.*" R. xx.

Ex. 47. ANOTHER *hat will suit me* BETTER.

Another, is a pronominal adjective of the inde-

K

finite kind, singular number, and belongs to the noun " *hat.*" R. XV.   *Hat,* is a common noun substantive, the name is " *hat,*" the substance " *animal* or *vegetable,*" singular number, nominative case to the verb " *will suit.*" R. I.   *Will suit,* is a regular verb active, indicative mood, first future tense, third person singular, agreeing with its nominative " *hat.*" R. I.   *Me,* is a personal pronoun, first person singular, objective case, governed by the verb " *will suit.*" R. XX.   *Better,* is an adjective in the comparative degree, and belongs to the noun " *head*" understood. R. XV.

Ex. 48. OTHER *studies occupy his attention.*

Other, is a pronominal adjective of the indefinite kind, plural, and belongs to the noun " *studies.*" R. XV.   *Studies,* is an abstract noun, plural number, nominative case to the verb " *occupy.*" R. I. *Occupy,* is a regular verb active, indicative mood, present tense, third person plural, agreeing with its nominative " *studies.*" R. I.   *His,* is a pronominal adjective of the possessive kind, third person singular number, and belongs to the noun " *attention.*" R. XV.   *Attention,* is an abstract noun singular, objective case, and is governed by the verb " *occupy.*" R. XX.

RULE XVI.

The distributive pronominal adjectives, each, every, either, *agree with nouns, pronouns, and verbs of the singular number only.*

Ex. 49. EACH *of them receives instruction.*

Each, is a pronominal adjective of the distributive kind, singular number, nominative case to the verb " *receives*" R. I. *Of,* is a preposition. *Them,* is a personal pronoun, third person plural, objective case, governed by the preposition " *of.*" R. XXII. *Receives,* is a regular verb active, indicative mood, present tense, third person singular, agreeing with its nominative case " *each.*" R. XVI. and R. I. *Instruction,* is an abstract noun, singular number, objective case, governed by the verb " *receives.*" R. XX. and R. XVI.

Ex. 50. EVERY *man must answer for himself.*

Every is a pronominal adjective of the distributive kind, and belongs to its noun " *man.*" R. XV. *Man,* is a common noun substantive, the name is " *man,*" the substance " *animal,*" singular number, masculine gender, nominative case to the verb " *must answer.*" R. I. *Must answer,* is a regular verb neuter, indicative mood, first future tense, third person singular, and agrees with its nominative " *man.*" R. I. *For,* is a preposition. *Himself,* is a pronominal adjective of the possessive kind, third person singular, masculine gender, agreeing with the distributive pronominal adjective " *every,*" and belongs to the noun " *deeds*" understood. R. XVI.

Ex. 51. EITHER *of these two slates may be taken home.*

Either, is a pronominal adjective of the distributive kind, singular, and nominative case to the verb " *may be taken.*" R. I. *Of,* is a preposition. *These,* is a pronominal adjective of the demonstrative kind, plural, and belongs to the noun " *slates.*" R. XV. *Two,* is an adjective, and belongs to the noun " *slates.*" R. XV. *Slates,* is a common noun substantive, the name is " *slates,*" the substance

K 2

" *fossil,*" plural number, objective case, governed by the preposition " *of.*" R. XXII. *May be taken,* is an irregular verb active, potential mood, present tense, third person singular, agreeing with its nominative " *either.*" R. XVI. *Home,* is a common noun, singular number, objective case, governed by the verb " *may be taken.*" R. XX.

RULE XVII.

When the adjective has a preposition before it, and the noun is understood, the adjective and preposition assume the nature of an adverb, and may be taken as such.

Ex. 52. *The master seemed to be* IN EARNEST.

The, is the definite article. *Master,* is a common noun substantive, the name is " *master,*" the substance " *animal,*" singular number, masculine gender, nominative case to the verb " *seemed.*" R. I. *Seemed,* is a regular verb neuter, indicative mood, imperfect tense, third person singular, and agrees with its nominative " *master.*" R. I. *To be,* is the primary auxiliary neuter verb, infinitive mood, present tense, governed by the verb " *seemed.*" R. XXVII. *In,* is a preposition, followed by the adjective " *earnest,*" and in this case are used as an adverb.

Ex. 53. *Ann sued* IN VAIN *for pardon.*

Ann, is a proper noun substantive, the name is " *Ann,*" the substance " *animal,*" singular number, feminine gender, nominative case to the verb " *sued.*" R. I. *Sued,* is a regular verb neuter, indicative mood, imperfect tense, third person singular, and agrees with its nominative "*Ann.*" R. I. *In,* is a preposition placed before the adjective *vain,* and used as an adverb, according to R. XVII. *For,* is a preposition. *Pardon,* is an abstract noun, singular number, objective case, governed by the preposition "*for.*" R. XXII.

Ex. 54. *He will not associate* WITH COMMON *children.*

He, is a personal pronoun, sign of the third person singular, masculine gender, nominative case to the verb "*will associate.*" R. I. *Will associate,* is a regular verb active, indicative mood, first future tense, third person singular, agreeing with its nominative "*he.*" R. I. *Not,* is an adverb of negation. *With,* is a preposition, *common,* is an adjective, and are taken adverbially. R. XVII. *Children,* is a common noun substantive, the name is "*children,*" the substance "*animal,*" plural number, masculine or feminine gender, objective case, and governed by the verb "*will associate.*' R. XX.

RULE XVIII.

One noun governs another signifying offspring, production, or property, in the possessive or genitive case.

Ex. 55. SLANDER'S TONGUE *is like a serpent's sting.*

Slander's is an abstract noun, singular number, possessive case, governed by the noun "*tongue.*" R. XVIII. *Tongue,* is a common noun substantive, the name is "*tongue,*" the substance "*animal,*" singular number, nominative case to the verb "*is.*"

R. I. *Is,* is the neuter substantive verb, indicative mood, present tense, third person singular, agreeing with its nominative, " *tongue.*" R. I. *Like,* is an adverb of comparison. *A,* is the indefinite article. *Serpent's,* is a common noun substantive, the name is " *serpent's,*" the substance " *animal,*" singular number, possessive case, governed by the noun " *sting.*" R. XVIII. *Sting,* is a common noun, singular number, nominative case. R. XXVI.

Ex. 56. *A just* MAN'S PATH *is a shining light.*

A, is the indefinite article. *Just,* is an adjective, positive state, and refers to the noun " *man's.*" R. XV. *Man's,* is a common noun substantive, the name is " *man's,*" the substance " *animal,*" singular number, masculine gender, possessive case, governed by the noun " *path.*" R. XVIII. *Path,* is a common noun, singular number, nominative case to the verb " *is.*" R. I. *Is,* is the neuter substantive verb, indicative mood, present tense, third person singular, agreeing with its nominative " *path.*" R. I. *A,* is the indefinite or general article. *Shining,* is a participle, used as an adjective to qualify the noun " *light.*" R. XV. and XXI. *Light,* is a common noun, singular, nominative case. R. XXVI.

Ex. 57. *Wisdom's precepts form the good man's interest and happiness.*

Wisdom's, is an abstract noun, singular number, possessive case, governed by the noun " *precepts.*" R. XVIII. *Precepts,* is an abstract noun, plural number, nominative case to the verb " *form.*" R. I. *Form,* is a regular verb active, indicative mood, present tense, third person singular, agreeing with its nominative " *precepts.*" R. I. *The,* is the definite or particular article. *Good,* is an adjective,

positive state, and belongs to the noun " *man's.*"
R. xv. *Man's,* is a common noun substantive, the
name is " *man's,*" the substance " *animal,*" singular
number, masculine gender, possessive case, governed by the nouns " *interest* and *happiness.*"
R. xviii. *Interest,* is an abstract noun, singular
number, objective case, governed by the verb
" *form.*" R. xx. *And,* is a copulative conjunction,
connecting " *interest* and *happiness.*" R. xxx. *Happiness,* is an abstract noun singular, objective case,
governed by the verb " *form.*" R. xx.

RULE XIX.

*When two nouns, signifying the same thing, come
together or are separated by a neuter verb, they are
put in the same case by* APPOSITION.

Ex. 58. IDLENESS *the* PARENT *of want should
be avoided by all mankind.*

Idleness, is an abstract noun, singular number,
nominative case to the verb " *should be avoided.*"
R. I. *The,* is the definite article. *Parent,* is a
common noun, singular number, nominative case,
signifying the same thing as " *idleness.*" R. xix.
Of, is a preposition. *Want,* is an abstract noun,
singular number, objective case, governed by the
preposition " *of.*" R. xxii. *Should be avoided,*
is a regular verb passive, potential mood, imperfect
tense, third person singular, agreeing with its nominative " *idleness* or *parent.*" R. I. *By,* is a preposition. *All,* is an adjective, and belongs to the
noun " *mankind.*" R. xv. *Mankind,* is a common
noun substantive, the name is " *mankind,*" the
substance " *animal,*" masculine and feminine gen-

K 4

der, because it includes men and women, objective case, governed by the preposition " *by*." R. XXII.

Ex. 59. ZADOK *the* PRIEST, *and* NATHAN *the* PROPHET, *anointed* SOLOMON KING *over Israel.*

Zadok, is a proper noun substantive, the name is " *Zadok,*" the substance " *animal,*" singular number, masculine gender, nominative case to the verb " *anointed.*" R. I.   *The,* is the definite article. *Priest,* is a common noun substantive, singular number, nominative case, signifying the same as " *Zadok.*" R. XIX.   *And,* is a conjunction. *Nathan,* is a proper noun substantive, the name is " *Nathan,*" the substance " *animal,*" singular number, masculine gender, nominative case, the copulative *and* connects " *Zadok the priest, and Nathan the prophet.*" R. V.   *The,* is the definite article.   *Prophet,* is a common noun substantive, singular number, nominative case, signifying the same as " *Nathan.*" R. XIX.   *Anointed,* is the perfect or passive participle of the verb " *to anoint,*" and agrees with its nominative, " *Zadok, &c.*" R. I.   *Solomon,* is a proper noun substantive, the name is " *Solomon,*" the substance " *animal,*" singular number, objective case, governed by the participle " *anointed.*" R. XXI.   *King,* is a common noun substantive, singular number, objective case, signifying the same as " *Solomon.*" R. XIX. *Over,* is a preposition.   *Israel,* is a particular noun, singular number, objective case, governed by the preposition " *over.*" R. XXII.

Ex. 60. *Buonaparte contended with* WELLINGTON, *who is the greatest* GENERAL *in Europe.*

Buonaparte, is a proper name, singular number, masculine gender, nominative case to the verb

" *contended.*" R. I.   *Contended,* is a regular verb neuter, indicative mood, imperfect tense, third person singular, agreeing with its nominative " *Buonaparte.*" R. I.   *With,* is a preposition. *Wellington,* is a proper name, singular number, masculine gender, objective case, governed by the preposition " *with.*" R. XXII.   *Who,* is a relative pronoun, third person singular, agreeing with its antecedent " *Wellington,*" and nominative to the verb " *is.*" R. VIII. and R. I.   *Is,* is the neuter substantive verb, indicative mood, present tense, third person singular, agreeing with its nominative " *who.*" R. I.   *The,* is the definite or particular article.   *Greatest,* is an adjective, superlative degree, and belongs to the noun " *general.*" R. XV. *General,* is a common noun substantive, the name is " *general,*" the substance " *animal,*" singular number, masculine gender, nominative case, R. XIX. and R. XXVI.   *In,* is a preposition.   *Europe,* is a particular noun, singular number, objective case, governed by the preposition " *in.*" R. XXII.

RULE XX.

Active verbs govern the objective Case.

Ex. 61. *We* WILL PRAISE *the Lord.*

We, is a personal pronoun, sign of the first person plural, nominative case to the verb " *will praise.*" R. I.   *Will praise,* is a regular verb active, indicative mood, first future tense, first person plural, agreeing with its nominative " *we.*" R. I.   *The,* is the definite article.   *Lord,* is a proper noun, the name is " *Lord,*" the substance " *incomprehensible,*" singular number, objective case, governed by the verb " *will praise.*" R. XX.

K 5

Ex. 62. *Religion* COMFORTS *us.*

Religion, is an abstract noun, singular number, and nominative to the verb " *comforts*." R. I. *Comforts,* is a regular verb active, indicative mood, present tense, third person singular, agreeing with its nominative, " *religion*" R. I. *Us,* is a personal pronoun, first person plural, objective case, governed by the verb " *comforts*."

Ex. 63. *Truth* ENNOBLES *us.*

Truth, is an an abstract noun, singular number, and nominative to the verb " *ennobles*." R. I. *Ennobles,* is a regular verb active, indicative mood, present tense, third person singular, agreeing with its nominative " *truth*." R. I. *Us,* is a personal pronoun, first person plural, objective case, governed by the verb " *ennobles*." R. XX.

RULE XXI.

Participles, like active verbs, govern the objective case.

Ex. 64. *I saw her* TEARING *the frock.*

I, is a personal pronoun, sign of the first person singular, and nominative to the verb " *saw*." R. I. *Saw,* is an irregular verb active, indicative mood, imperfect tense, first person singular, agreeing with its nominative " *I*." R. I. *Her,* is a pronominal adjective, possessive kind, third person singular, feminine gender, objective case, and governed by the verb " *saw*." R. XX. *Tearing,* is the present participle of the irregular active verb "*to tear,*" agreeing with the pronoun " *her*." *The,* is the definite article. *Frock,* is a common noun substantive, the name is " *frock,*" the substance " *vegetable,*" singular number, objective case, governed by the participle " *tearing.*" R. XXI.

Ex. 65. *I have no pleasure in* HEARING *wicked children.*

I, is a personal pronoun, sign of the first person singular, and nominative to the verb " *have.*" R. I. *Have,* is an irregular verb active, indicative mood, present tense, first person singular, agreeing with its nominative " *I.*" R. I.   *No,* is an adjective, and belongs to the noun " *pleasure.*" R. XV. *Pleasure,* is an abstract noun, singular number, objective case, governed by the verb " *have.*" R. XX.   *In,* is a preposition. *Hearing,* is the present participle of the irregular active verb " *to hear,*" governed by the preposition " *in.*"   *Wicked,* is an adjective, positive state, and belongs to the noun " *children.*" R. XV.   *Children,* is a common noun substantive, the name is " *children,*" the substance " *animal,*" plural number, objective case, governed by the participle " *hearing.*" R. XXI.

Ex. 66. *By* DEPRECIATING *others we expose ourselves.*

By, is a preposition. *Depreciating,* is the present participle of the regular active verb " *to depreciate,*" governed by the preposition " *by.*" *Others,* is a pronominal adjective, of the indefinite kind, plural number, objective case, governed by the participle " *depreciating.*" R. XXI. *We,* is a personal pronoun, sign of the first person plural, nominative case to the verb " *expose.*" R. I.   *Expose,* is a regular verb active, indicative mood, present tense, first person plural, agreeing with its nominative " *we.*" R. I.   *Ourselves,* is a compound pronoun, plural number, objective case, governed by the verb " *expose.*" R. XX.

RULE XXII.

Prepositions govern the objective Case.

Ex. 67. *I gave the ring* TO *Mary.*

I, is a personal pronoun, sign of the first person singular, and nominative to the verb " *gave.*" R. I. *Gave,* is an irregular verb active, indicative mood, imperfect tense, first person singular, agreeing with its nominative " *I.*" R. I.   *The,* is the definite article.   *Ring,* is a common noun substantive, the name is " *ring,*" the substance " *fossil,*" singular number, objective case, governed by the verb " *gave.*" R. XX.   *To,* is a preposition.   *Mary,* is a proper noun substantive, the noun is " *Mary,*" the substance " *animal,*" singular number, feminine gender, objective case, governed by the preposition " *to.*" R. XXII.

Ex. 68. FROM *whom did he receive that information.*

From, is a preposition.   *Whom,* is a relative pronoun, third person singular, objective case, governed by the preposition " *from.*" R. XXII.   *Did receive,* is a regular verb active, indicative mood, imperfect tense, third person singular, agreeing with its nominative " *he.*" R. I.   *He,* is a personal pronoun, sign of the third person singular, masculine gender, nominative case to the verb " *did receive.*" R. I.   *That,* is a pronominal adjective of the demonstrative kind, third person singular, and belongs to the noun "*information.*" R. XV. *Information*, is an abstract noun, singular number, objective case, governed by the verb "*did receive.*" R. XX.

Ex. 69. *We are all accountable creatures each* FOR *himself.*

We, is a personal pronoun, first person plural, nominative case to the verb "*are.*" R. I. *Are*, is an irregular verb neuter, indicative mood, present tense, first person plural, agreeing with its nominative "*we.*" R. I. *All*, is an adverb. *Accountable*, is an adjective, positive state, and belongs to the noun "*creatures.*" R. XV. *Creatures*, is a common noun substantive, the name is "*creatures*," the substance "*animal*," plural number, nominative case. R. XXVI. *Each*, is a pronominal adjective, of the distributive kind, and belongs to the noun "*person*" implied. R. XV. *For*, is a preposition. *Himself*, is a compound pronoun, third person singular, objective case, agreeing with the distributive pronominal adjective "*each*," and governed by the preposition "*for.*" R. XVI. and R. XXII.

RULE XXIII.

The governing prepositions to *and* for *are sometimes distinctly understood, especially after active verbs.*

Ex. 70. *I transmit you a copy of the resolution.*

I, is a personal pronoun, first person singular, and nominative to the verb "*transmit.*" R. I. *Transmit*, is a regular verb active, indicative mood, present tense, first person singular, agreeing with its nominative " *I.*" R. I. *You,* is a personal pronoun, second person singular, objective case, governed by the proposition " *to* " understood. R. XXIII. and R. XXII. *A,* is the indefinite article. *Copy,* is a common noun, singular number, objective case, governed by the verb "*transmit.*" R. XX. *Of,* is a preposition. *The,* is the definite article. *Resolution,* is a particular noun, singular number, objective case, governed by the preposition " *of.*" R. XXII.

Ex. 71. *We bought them some grapes.*

We, is a personal pronoun, first person plural, nominative case to the verb " *bought.*" R. I. *Bought,* is an irregular verb active, indicative mood, imperfect tense, first person plural, agreeing with its nominative " *we.*" R. I. *Them,* is a personal pronoun, third person plural, objective case, governed by the preposition " *for* " understood. R. XXIII. and R. XII. *Some,* is an adjective, and belongs to the noun " *grapes.*" R. XV. *Grapes,* is a common noun substantive, the name is "*grapes,*" the substance " *vegetable,*" plural number, objective case, governed by the verb " *bought.*" R. XX.

Ex. 72. *Send Jane the thimble.*

Send, is an irregular verb active, imperative mood, second person singular, and agrees with its nominative " *thou* " implied. R. III. *Jane,* is a proper noun substantive, the name is " *Jane,*" the substance " *animal,*" singular number, objective case, governed by the preposition " *to* " understood. R. XXIII. and R. XXII. *The,* is the definite article. *Thimble,* is a common noun substantive, the name is " *thimble,*" the substance " *fossil,*" singular number, objective case, governed by the verb " *send.*" R. XX.

RULE XXIV.

The preposition is frequently separated by the relative which it governs.

Ex. 73. *The lady whom Ann went to the concert* WITH *is a delightful singer.*

The, is the definite article. *Lady,* is a common noun substantive, singular number, feminine gender, and nominative case to the verb " *is.*" R. I. *Whom,* is a relative pronoun, third person singular, agreeing with its antecedent " *lady,*" objective case, governed by the preposition " *with.*" R. XXII. *Ann,* is a proper noun substantive, the name is " *Ann,*" the substance " *animal,*" singular number, nominative case to the verb " *went.*" R. I. *Went,* is an irregular verb neuter, indicative mood, imperfect tense, third person singular, agreeing with its nominative " *Ann.*" R. I. *To,* is a preposition. *The,* is the definite article. *Concert,* is a particular noun, singular number, objective case, governed by the preposition " *to.*" R. XXII. *With,* is a preposition, governing " *whom.*" R. XXIV. *Is,* is the neuter substantive verb, indicative mood, present tense, third person singular, agreeing with its nominative " *lady.*" R. I. *A,* is the indefinite article. *Delightful,* is an adjective, positive state, and belongs to the noun " *singer.*" R. XV. *Singer,* is a common noun substantive, the name is " *singer,*" the substance " *animal,*" singular number, nominative case, being the same as " *lady.*" R. XIX. and R. XXVI.

Ex. 74. *Whom wilt thou give it to?*

Whom, is a relative pronoun, of the interrogative kind, third person singular, objective case, governed

208 ENGLISH GRAMMAR.

by the proposition " *to.*" R. XXII. *Wilt give,* is an irregular verb active, indicative mood, first future tense, second person singular, and agrees with its nominative " *thou.*" R. I. *Thou,* is a personal pronoun, sign of the second person singular, nominative case to the verb " *wilt give.*" R. I. *It,* is a neuter pronoun, singular number, objective case, governed by the verb " *wilt give.*" R. XX. *To,* is a preposition, governing " *whom.* R. XXIV.

Ex. 75. *She is a reader whom I am much delighted* WITH.

She, is a personal pronoun, third person singular, feminine gender, nominative case to the verb " *is.*" R. I. *Is,* is the neuter substantive verb, indicative mood, present tense, third person singular, agreeing with its nominative " *she.*" R. I. *A,* is the indefinite article. *Reader,* is a common noun substantive, the name is " *reader,*" the substance " *animal,*" singular number, nominative case. R. XXVI. *Whom,* is a relative pronoun, third person singular, agreeing with its antecedent " *she,*" objective case, governed by the preposition " *with.*" R. XXII. *I,* is a personal pronoun, sign of the first person singular, and nominative to the verb " *am delighted.*" R. I. *Am delighted,* is a regular verb active, indicative mood, present tense, first person singular, agreeing with its nominative " *I.*" R. I. *Much,* is an adverb of quality. *With,* is a preposition, governing " *whom.*" R. XXIV.

RULE XXV.

Prepositions are sometimes allowed to conclude a sentence, because the relative who or which is thereby often superseded.

Ex. 76. *We seldom provide for the day, we must give an account* OF.

We, is a personal pronoun, sign of the first person plural, nominative to the verb "*provide.*" R. I. *Seldom,* is an adverb of quality. *Provide,* is a regular verb active, indicative mood, present tense, first person plural, agreeing with its nominative "*we.*" R. I. *For,* is a preposition. *The,* is the definite article. *Day,* is a particular noun, singular number, objective case, governed by the preposition "*for.*" R. XXII. *We,* is a personal pronoun, first person plural, nominative case to the verb "*must give.*" R. I. *Must give,* is an irregular verb active, indicative mood, present tense, first person plural, agreeing with its nominative "*we.*" R. I. *An,* is the indefinite article. *Account,* is an abstract noun, singular number, objective case, governed by the verb "*must give.*" R. XX. *Of,* is a preposition, governing the relative "*which*" understood. R. XXV.

Ex. 77. *That is the man I lent the horse* TO.

That, is a pronominal adjective of the demonstrative kind, and belongs to the noun "*man.*" R. XV. *Is,* is the neuter substantive verb, indicative mood, present tense, third person singular, agreeing with its nominative "*man.*" R. I. *The,* is the definite article. *Man,* is a common noun substantive, the name is "*man,*" the substance, "*animal,*" singular number, masculine gender, nominative case to the verb "*is,*" R. I. *I,* is a personal pronoun, first person singular, nominative case to the verb "*lent.*" R. I. *Lent,* is an irregular verb active, indicative mood, imperfect tense, first person singular, agreeing with its nominative "*I.*" R. I. *The,* is the definite article. *Horse,* is a common noun substantive, the name is "*horse*," the substance "*animal*," singular number, masculine gender, objective case, governed by the verb "*lent*." R. XX. *To*, is a preposition, governing the relative "*whom*" understood. R. XXV.

Ex. 78. *He is a boy I am very fond* OF.

He, is a personal pronoun, third person singular, and nominative to the verb "*is*." R. I. *Is*, is the neuter substantive verb, indicative mood, present tense, third person singular, agreeing with its nominative "*he*." R. I. *A*, is the indefinite article. *Boy*, is a common noun substantive, the name is "*boy*," the substance "*animal*," singular number, masculine gender, nominative case. R. XXVI. *I*, is a personal pronoun, first person singular, and nominative to the verb "*am*." R. I. *Am*, is the neuter substantive verb, indicative mood, present tense, first person singular, agreeing with its nominative "*I*." R. I. *Very*, is an adverb of quality. *Fond*, is an adjective, and belongs to the noun "*boy*." R. XXII. *Of*, is a preposition, governing the relative "*which*" understood. R. XXV.

RULE XXVI.

The primary verb TO BE *is always preceded and followed by a noun or pronoun in the same case.*

Ex. 79. *I* AM *he.*

I, is a personal pronoun, first person singular, and nominative to the verb "*am*." R. I. *Am*, is the neuter substantive verb, indicative mood, present tense, first person singular, agreeing with its nominative "*I*." R. I. *He*, is a personal pronoun, third person, singular, nominative case. R. XXVI.

Ex. 80. *It* WAS *she.*

It, is the neuter pronoun, third person singular, and nominative to the verb " *was.*" R. I. *Was,* is an irregular verb neuter, indicative mood, imperfect tense, third person singular, and agrees with its nominative " *it.*" R. I. *She,* is a personal pronoun, third person singular, feminine gender, nominative case. R. XXVI.

Ex. 81. *George* IS *a good boy.*

George, is a proper noun substantive, the name is " *George,*" the substance " *animal,*" singular number, masculine gender, nominative case to the verb " *is,*" R. I. *Is,* is the neuter substantive verb, indicative mood, present tense, third person singular, agreeing with the nominative " *George.*" R. I. *A,* is the indefinite article. *Good,* is an adjective, positive state, and belongs to the noun " *boy.*" R. XV. *Boy,* is a common noun substantive, the name is " *boy,*" the substance " *animal,*" singular number, masculine gender, nominative case. R. XXVI.

RULE XXVII.

One verb governs another that follows it or depends upon it, in the infinitive mood.

Ex. 82. *We intend* TO STUDY *Grammar.*

We, is a personal pronoun, first person plural, nominative case to the verb " *intend.*" R. I. *Intend,* is a regular verb active, indicative mood, present tense, first person plural, agreeing with its nominative " *we.*" R. I. *To study,* is a regular verb active, infinitive mood, present tense, governed by the verb " *intend.*" R. XXVII. *Grammar,* is a particular noun, singular number, objective case, governed by the verb " *intend.*" R. XX.

ENGLISH GRAMMAR.

Ex. 83. *We should be prepared* TO GIVE *an account of our actions.*

We, is a personal pronoun, first person plural, nominative case to the verb " *should be prepared.*" R. I. *Should be prepared,* is a regular verb active, potential mood, imperfect tense, first person plural, and agrees with its nominative " *we.*" R. I. *To render,* is a regular verb active, infinitive mood, present tense, governed by the verb *Should be prepared.*" R. XXVII. *An,* is the indefinite article. *Account,* is an abstract noun, singular number, objective case, governed by the verb " *to render.*" R. XX. *Of,* is a preposition. *Our,* is a pronominal adjective, possessive kind, plural, and belongs to the noun " *actions.*" R. XV. *Actions,* is an abstract noun, plural number, objective case, governed by the preposition " *of.*" R. XXII.

Ex. 84. *Learn* TO BE *obedient to your superiors.*

Learn, is an irregular verb active, imperative mood, second person singular, and agrees with the nominative " *thou*" implied. R. III *To be,* is the primary auxiliary neuter verb, infinitive mood, present tense, governed by the verb " *learn.*" R. XXVII. *Obedient,* is an adjective, positive state, and belongs to the noun " *superiors.*" R. XV. *To,* is a preposition. *Your,* is a pronominal adjective, possessive kind, singular, and belongs to the noun " *superiors.*" R. XV. *Superiors,* is a common noun substantive, the name is " *superiors,*" the substance " *animal,*" plural number, objective case, governed by the preposition " *to.*" R. XXII.

RULE XXVIII.

Participles have the same government as the verbs from which they are derived.

Ex. 85. *John takes pleasure in* TORMENTING *flies*.

John, is a proper noun substantive, the name is " *John*, the substance " *animal*," singular number, masculine gender, nominative case to the verb " *takes*." R. I. *Takes*, is an irregular verb active, indicative mood, present tense, third person singular, agreeing with its nominative " *John*." R. I. *Pleasure*, is an abstract noun, singular number, objective case, governed by the verb "*takes*." R. XX. *In*, is a preposition. *Tormenting*, is the present participle of the verb " *to torment*." *Flies*, is a common noun substantive, the name is "*flies*," the substance " *animal*," plural number, objective case, governed by the participle " *tormenting*." R. XXVIII.

Ex. 86. *I saw him* TEARING *the book*.

I, is a personal pronoun, first person singular, nominative case to the verb " *saw*." R. I. *Saw*, is an irregular verb active, indicative mood, imperfect tense, first person singular, and agrees with its nominative " *I*." R. I. *Him*, is a personal pronoun, third person singular, masculine gender, objective case, governed by the verb " *saw*." R. XX. *Tearing*, is the present participle of the verb " *to tear*." *The*, is the definite article. *Book*, is a common noun substantive, the name is " *book*," the substance " *vegetable*," singular number, objective case, governed by the participle " *tearing*," R. XXVIII.

Ex. 87. *He is* ADMONISHING *Robert*.

He, is a personal pronoun, third person, singular masculine gender, nominative case to the verb

" *is.*" R. I. *Is*, is the neuter substantive verb, indicative mood, present tense, third person singular, and agrees with its nominative " he." R. I. *Admonishing*, is the present participle of the verb " *to admonish.*" *Robert*, is a proper noun substantive, the name is " *Robert*," the substance " *animal*," singular number, masculine gender, objective case, governed by the participle " *admonishing.* R. XXVIII.

RULE XXIX.

The auxiliary in the third person singular of the present and imperfect tense of the indicative mood governs the principal verb, by requiring it to be of the plural number.

Ex. 88. *The ship* DID SAIL *down the river.*

The, is the definite article. *Ship*, is a common noun substantive, the name is " *ship*," the substance " *various*,"singular number, nominative case to the verb " *did sail*." R. I. *Did sail*, is a regular verb neuter, indicative mood, imperfect tense, third person singular, agreeing with its nominative " *ship*." R. XXIX. *Down*, is a preposition. *The*, is the definite article. *River*, is a common noun substantive, the name is " *river*," the substance " *fluid*," singular number, objective case, governed by the preposition " *down*." R. XXII.

Ex. 89. *He* DOES INSTRUCT *them.*

He, is a personal pronoun, third person singular, masculine gender, nominative case to the verb " *does instruct*." R. I. *Does instruct*, is a regular verb active, indicative mood, present tense, third person singular, and agrees with its nominative "*he.*"

R. XXIX. *Them,* is a personal pronoun, third person plural, objective case, governed by the verb " *instruct.*" R. XX.

Ex. 90. *She* DID EXCEL *her brother.*

She is a personal pronoun, third person singular, feminine gender, nominative case to the verb " *did, excel.*" R. I. *Did excel,* is a regular verb active indicative mood, imperfect tense, third person singular, and agrees with its nominative case " *she.*" R. XXIX. *Her,* is a pronominal adjective, possessive kind, third person singular, and belongs to the noun " *brother.*" R. XV. *Brother,* is a common noun substantive, the name is " *brother,*" the substance " *animal,*" singular number, objective case, governed by the verb " *did excel.*" R. XX.

RULE XXX

Conjunctions connect the same moods and tenses of verbs, and cases of nouns and pronouns.

Ex. 91. *My brother* AND *he are tolerable grammarians.*

My, is a pronominal adjective of the possessive kind, and belongs to the noun " *brother.*" R. XV. *Brother,* is a common noun substantive, the noun is " *brother,*" the substance, " *animal,*" singular number, masculine gender, and nominative to the verb " *are.*" R. I. *And,* is a copulative conjunction. *He,* is a personal pronoun, third person singular, masculine gender, nominative case, and " *and*" connects " *brother*" and " *he.*" R. XXX. *Are,* is an irregular verb neuter, indicative mood, present tense, third person plural, agreeing with its nominatives " *brother*" and " *he.*" R. V. and R. I.

Tolerable, is an adjective, positive state, and belongs to the noun " *grammarians.*" R. XV. *Grammarians,* is a common noun substantive, the name is " *grammarians,*" the substance " *animal,*" plural number, masculine gender, nominative case. R. XXVI.

Ex. 92. *Religion* AND *piety are to be observed* AND *admired.*

Religion is an abstract noun, singular number, nominative case to the verb " *are.*" R. I. *And,* is a copulative conjunction. *Piety,* is an abstract noun, singular number, nominative case, and " *and* " connects " *religion*" and *piety.* R. XXX. *Are,* is an irregular verb neuter, indicative mood, present tense, third person plural, agreeing with its nominatives " *religion*" and " *piety.*" R. V. and R. I. *To be observed,* is a regular verb passive, infinitive mood, present tense, governed by the verb " *are.*" R. XXVII. *And,* is a copulative conjunction. *Admired,* is a regular verb passive, infinitive mood, present tense, and " *and* " connects " *to be observed and admired.*" R. XXX.

Ex. 93. *He* AND *she are happily united.*

He, is a personal pronoun, third person singular, masculine gender, nominative case to the verb " *are.*" R. I. *And,* is a copulative conjunction. *She,* is a personal pronoun, third person singular, feminine gender, nominative case, and " *and*" connects " *he* " and " *she.*" R. XXX. *Are united,* is a regular verb active, indicative mood, present tense, third person plural, and agrees with its nominatives " *he*" and " *she.*" R. V. and R. I. *Happily,* is an adverb of quality.

RULE XXXI.

Some conjunctions require the indicative, some the subjunctive mood after them. It is a general rule, that when the conjunction is of a doubtful nature, the verb must be put in the subjunctive *mood; but when it is used to elucidate any member of the sentence, it will be in the* indicative *mood.*

Ex. 94. THOUGH HE IS *high, he hath respect to the lowly.*

Though, is a concessive conjunction. *He*, is a personal pronoun, sign of the third person singular, masculine gender, nominative case to the verb "*is.*" R. I. *Is*, is the neuter substantive verb, indicative mood, present tense, third person singular, and agrees with its nominative "*he.*" R. XXXI. and R. I. *High*, is an adjective, positive state, and belongs to the noun "PERSON" understood. R. XX. *He*, is a personal pronoun, sign of the third person singular, masculine gender, nominative case to the verb "*hath respect.*" R. I. *Hath respect*, is a regular verb active, indicative mood, perfect tense, third person singular, agreeing with its nominative "*he.*" R. I. *To*, is a preposition. *The*, is the definite article. *Lowly*, is an adjective, positive state, and belongs to the noun "*persons*" understood. R. XV.

Ex. 95. IF FLATTERY BE *nectar to the ear, it is too often poison to the soul.*

If, is a conditional conjunction. *Flattery*, is an abstract noun, singular number, nominative case to the verb "*be.*" *Be*, is the neuter substantive verb, subjunctive mood, because something doubtful is

L

implied, present tense, third person singular, agreeing with its nominative " *flattery.*" R. XXXI. *Nectar,* is a particular noun, singular number, nominative case. R. XXVI. *To,* is a preposition. *The,* is the definite article. *Ear,* is a common noun substantive, the name is " *ear,*" the substance " *animal,*" singular number, objective case, governed by the preposition " *to.*" R. XXII. *It,* is the neuter pronoun, third person singular, and nominative to the verb " *is.*" R. I. *Is,* is the neuter substantive verb, indicative mood, present tense, third person singular, agreeing with its nominative " *it.*" R. I. *Too often,* is an adverb of indefinite time. *Poison,* is a common noun substantive, singular number, and nominative case. R. XXVI. *To,* is a preposition. *The,* is the definite article. *Soul,* is a common noun substantive, the name is " *soul,*" the substance " *animal,*" singular number, objective case, governed by the preposition " *to.*" R. XXII.

Ex. 96. WERE SHE AMIABLE, *he would be a happy man.*

Were, is an irregular verb neuter, subjunctive mood, something doubtful being understood, imperfect tense, third person singular, agreeing with its nominative case " *she.*" R. XXXI. *She,* is a personal pronoun, third person singular, feminine gender, nominative case to the verb " *were.*" R. I. *Amiable* is an adjective, positive state, and belongs to the noun " *woman,*" understood, R. XV. *He,* is a personal pronoun, third person singular, nominative case to the verb " *would be.*" R. I. *Would be,* is an irregular verb neuter, potential mood, imperfect tense, third person singular, agreeing with its nominative " *he.*" R. I. *A,* is the indefinite article. *Happy,* is an adjective, positive state, and belongs to the noun " *man.*" R. XV. *Man,* is a common noun substantive, the name is " *man*," the substance " *animal*," singular number, nominative case. R. XXVI.

Ex. 97. *He improves*, BECAUSE *he pays attention.*

He, is a personal pronoun, sign of the third person singular, masculine gender, nominative case to the verb " *improves*." R. I. *Improves*, is a regular verb neuter, indicative mood, present tense, third person singular, agreeing with its nominative " *he*." R. I. *Because*, is a conditional conjunction. *He*, is a personal pronoun, third person singular, masculine gender, and nominative to the verb " *pays*." R. I. *Pays* is an irregular verb active, indicative mood, present tense, third person singular, agreeing with its nominative " *he*." R. XXXI. *Attention*, is an abstract noun, singular number, objective case, governed by the verb " *pays*." R. XX.

Ex. 98. As *the master was absent, the children were unruly.*

As, is a conjunction. *The*, is the definite or particular article. *Master*, is a common noun substantive, the name is " *master*," the substance " *animal*," singular number, masculine gender, and nominative to the verb " *was absent*." R. I. *Was absent*, is a regular verb active, indicative mood, imperfect tense, third person singular, agreeing with its nominative " *master*." R. XXXI. and R. I. *The*, is the definite article. *Children*, is a common noun substantive, the name is " *children*," the substance " *animal*," plural number, and nominative to the verb " *were*." R. I. *Were*, is an irregular verb neuter, indicative mood, imperfect tense, third person plural, agreeing with its nomi native " *children.*" R. I.   *Unruly,* is an adjective, positive state, and belongs to the noun " *children.*" R. XV.

Ex. 99. IF HE COMMAND *I will obey.*

If is a conditional conjunction.   *He,* is a personal pronoun, sign of the third person singular, masculine gender, and nominative to the verb " *command.*" R. I.   *Command,* is a regular verb active, subjunctive mood, present tense, third person singular, agreeing with its nominative " *he.*" R. XXXI. and R. I.   *I,* is a personal pronoun, sign of the first person singular, and nominative to the verb " *will obey.*" R. I.   *Will obey,* is a regular verb active, indicative mood, first future tense, first person singular, agreeing with its nominative " *I.*" R. I.

RULE XXXII.

The interjections O! Oh! *and* Ah! *require the objective case of a pronoun in the first person after them :—but the nominative in the second person.*

Ex. 100. AH ME! *where shall I seek for comfort.*

Ah, is an interjection.   *Me,* is a personal pronoun, first person singular, objective case, governed by the interjection " *ah!*" or the preposition " *to*" implied ; as, " Ah ! woe is ' *to*' me." R. XXXII.   *Where,* is an interrogative adverb of place.   *Shall seek,* is an irregular verb active, indicative mood, first future tense, first person singular, agreeing with its nominative " *I.*" R. I.   *I,* is a personal pronoun, representing the noun or person who speaks, nominative case to the verb

" shall seek." R. I. *For,* is a preposition. *Comfort,* is an abstract noun, singular number, objective case, governed by the preposition *" for."* R. XXII.

Ex. 101. OH! *happy* US *surrounded with so many blessings.*

Oh, is an interjection. *Happy,* is an adjective, positive state, and belongs to the noun *" persons"* understood. R. XV. *Us,* is a personal pronoun, first person plural, objective case, governed by the interjection *" Oh!"* or the preposition *"to"* implied, as, *"Oh! happiness to us who are surrounded."* R. XXXII. *Surrounded,* is a regular verb active, indicative mood, present tense, first person plural, agreeing with its nominative *" who"* understood, R. I. *With,* is a preposition. *So,* is an adverb of quantity. *Many,* is an adjective, positive state, qualifying the noun *" blessings."* R. XV. *Blessings,* is an abstract noun, plural number, objective case, governed by the preposition *" with."* R. XXII.

Ex. 102. OH THOU! *who dwellest in heaven.*

Oh, is an interjection. *Thou,* is a personal pronoun, sign of the second person or noun spoken to, singular number, and nominative case, governed by the interjection *" oh,"* or the preposition *" to"* understood; as, *" Oh! glory, honour, praise, power, might, majesty, and dominion be to Thou, who dwellest in heaven, preserve my soul."* R. XXXII. *Who,* is a relative pronoun, second person singular, agreeing with its antecedent *" thou,"* and nominative to the verb *" dwellest."* R. I. *In,* is a preposition. *Heaven,* is a particular noun, singular number, objective case, governed by the preposition *" in."* R. XXII.

PART IV.

OF COMPOSITION.

§ 1. *Essays.*

THE first and most effectual step in training young persons to write in an easy manner is to accustom them, *after one reading,* to write the leading events of the narrative or story, by way of note or outline on their slates; directing them to notice the *agent,* the *action,* and the *subject,* as the principal parts in all members, sentences, and periods, then fill up the blanks and compare it with the original.

Ex. 1. *Beware of pride, it is the most dangerous of all sins.*

You that are young in years and in grace, are in danger of being puffed up with pride. Beware of this as of a quicksand, in which you would be in danger of being swallowed up. It is the counsel of the blessed Spirit, that young men be exhorted " to be sober-minded." And Solomon, under his inspiration, hath told us, " that pride goeth before destruction, and a haughty spirit before a fall." Therefore let no man think more highly of himself than he ought to think.

SKETCH. Young in years, grace, danger, puffed, pride, beware, quicksand, danger, swallowed up, counsel, spirit, sober-minded, Solomon, inspiration, pride, destruction, haughty spirit, fall, man, think, highly.

When they are perfectly acquainted with exercises of this kind, the sketch or outline may be

considerably shortened as in the following example :—

Ex. II.   *Chastity is an additional ornament to*
                Beauty.

There is no charm in the female sex, that can
supply the place of virtue. Without innocence,
beauty is unlovely, and quality contemptible; good-
breeding degenerates into wantonness, and wit into
impudence.   It is observed, that all the virtues are
represented by painters and statuaries under female
shapes; but if any one of them has a more particular title to that sex, it is modesty.

OUTLINE.   Charm, sex, virtue, innocence, unlovely, contemptible, wantonness, impudence, virtues, painters, female shapes, particular title, modesty.

They should next be directed to divide the discourse into detached sentences ; and after the
second reading to write it on their slates in its
original form.

Ex. III.   *The pleasures resulting from a prudent*
                use of our faculties.

Happy that man, who, unembarrassed by vulgar
cares, master of himself, his time, and fortune,
spends his time in making himself wiser, and his
fortune in making others, and therefore himself,
happier; who, as the will and understanding are
the two ennobling faculties of the soul, thinks
himself not complete, till his mind be embel-
lished with a valuable portion of knowledge, as
well as his will enriched with every virtue; who
has furnished himself with all the advantages to
relish solitude, and enliven conversation; when
serious, not sullen; and when cheerful, not indis-

creetly gay; his ambition, not to be admired for a false glare of greatness, but beloved for the gentle and sober lustre of his wisdom and goodness. The greatest minister of state has not more business to do in a public capacity, than he, and indeed every man else may find in the retired and still scenes of life. Even in his private walks, every thing that is visible convinceth him there is present a BEING invisible. Aided by divine revelation, he reads plain legible traces of the DIVINITY in every thing he meets: he sees the DEITY in every tree, as Moses did in the burning bush, though not in so glaring a manner; and when he sees HIM, he adores HIM with the tribute of a grateful heart.

Detached Sentences.

Happy is the man, who, master of himself, spends his time and fortune to make himself and others happy.

Enriching the reasoning faculties of his soul, the will and understanding, with knowledge and virtue.

He is cheerful in solitude, and discreet in conversation; admired for his humility, and beloved for his goodness.

In all his walks through life, he relies on *God*, whose Providence shines conspicuous in every object; and he adores his Creator with a grateful heart.

In the third step they should write the whole from memory, without the aid of a sketch, as in the first and second examples; or detached sentences as in the third. Here a portion of history should be distinctly read to the pupils, the substance of which must be repeated by the whole class, and after a second reading direct them to write it on their slates.

To exercise the reasoning faculties and cultivate

a taste for composition, some familiar subject should be named, for them to write on, and to enlarge the discourse to such extent as the parent or teacher may be pleased to direct; as in the following example; which may be given for that purpose.

Ex. IV. *On the improvement of time.*

The power of looking forward into futurity, though it is the distinguishing mark of reason, yet, if misapplied, will serve only to flatter the imagination, mislead the mind, and imbitter the comforts of life.

If, instead of indulging vain and uncertain expectations, every man were to employ his thoughts, " *how to improve the present hour,*" he would find solid advantages resulting from his conduct, and be enabled to cast a retrospective eye, upon past life, with pleasure and approbation.

Ex. V. *Extended.*

The power of looking forward into futurity, though it is the distinguishing mark of reason, yet, if misapplied, or misused will only serve to flatter the imagination, mislead the mind into a mazy track of errors, and imbitter the comforts of life. It is a misfortune incident to all men, more especially to people of volatile dispositions, that they know not how to enjoy the present hour. The mind is perpetually planning new schemes of future happiness, and contemplating distant prospects of pleasure, which he flatters himself he is one day to possess, and when his expectation is realized, he looks upon it with indifference.

This disposition in the human mind, to leave what it has, or the things which are behind, to press forward to what is before, has, no doubt, its use in

L 5

the constitution of man ; and was, as every thing else, ordained with wisdom by the GREAT CREATOR, to lead him on to further improvement in the search of greater perfection and happiness.

It is our interest as well as our duty to seize on the present opportunity of improving our time to the best advantage, while it is yet in our power, considering that it flies from us every moment, and is never to return for a second trial of our obedience.

Ex. VI. *This subject more enlarged.*

The power of looking forward into futurity, though it is the distinguishing mark of reason, yet, if misapplied, or misused, will serve only to flatter the imagination, mislead the mind into a mazy tract of errors, and imbitter the comforts of life. It is a misfortune, incident to all men, more especially to people of volatile dispositions, that, they know not how to enjoy the present hour. The mind is perpetually planning schemes of future happiness, and contemplating distant prospects of pleasure, which he flatters himself he is one day to possess, instead of endeavouring to enjoy the present with solid satisfaction.

This disposition of mind makes us live in a continual state of expectation ; for, when we have gained any thing which we have long wished for, when the tardy revolution of time has brought to us what we long impatiently expected, we soon grow cool with possession, and look with indifference upon that which so lately engaged our attention, and was the sole object of our hopes. Like children, we long for a bauble :—no sooner have we got it,— but we are tired,—and wish for another.

One would be inclined to imagine, that so many fruitless endeavours and repeated disappointments, would effectually cure us of indulging our minds in the fond expectation of future felicity : yet such is our nature, that notwithstanding the most convincing demonstrations of the folly of building upon futurity, though we see people unexpectedly sink into the grave, who were engaged in the same eager pursuits with ourselves, we still continue to persevere in the delusion.

This disposition in the human mind, to leave what it has, or the things which are behind, to press forward to what is before, has, no doubt, its use in the constitution of man ; and was, as every thing else, ordained with wisdom by the GREAT CREATOR, to lead him into further improvement in the search of greater perfection and happiness. But this, like all our faculties or dispositions, must be regulated and guided by reason, to produce the intended effects.

Would every man, instead of indulging vain and uncertain expectations, instead of forming romantic schemes of visionary happiness, employ his thoughts and the faculties of his mind in studying how he may best improve the present hour, he would find solid advantages resulting from his conduct, and be enabled to cast a retrospective eye upon past life, with pleasure and approbation.

It is our interest, as well as our duty, to seize on the present opportunity of improving our time to the best advantage, while it is yet in our power, considering that it flies from us every moment, and is never to return for a second trial of our obedience. When we stand on the brink of the grave, we see things as they really are, without any mask of false colouring. At that awful period, power will have lost its strength to protect—riches their value to relieve,—knowledge its voice to instruct,—pleasures their charms to allure; so that the power which was not before exerted to defend the helpless, the wealth which never fed the poor, the knowledge

which never persuaded to virtue, and the time
spent in vicious pleasures, were most wretchedly
employed, and, at the gloomy hour of death, can
neither give hope, peace, nor comfort.

Ex. VII. *The same subject further extended and
concluded.*

The power of looking forward into futurity,
though it is the distinguishing mark of reason, yet,
if misapplied, or misused, will serve only to flatter
the imagination, mislead the mind into a mazy track
of errors, and imbitter the comforts of life. It is a
misfortune incident to all men, more especially to
people of volatile dispositions, that they know not
how to enjoy the present hour. The mind is perpetually planning new schemes of future happiness,
and contemplating distant prospects of pleasure,
which he flatters himself he is one day to possess,
instead of endeavouring to enjoy the present with
solid satisfaction.

This disposition of mind makes us live in a continual state of expectation; for, when we have
gained any thing which we have long wished for,
when the tardy revolution of time has brought to
us what we long impatiently expected, we soon
grow cool with possession, and look with indifference upon that which so lately engaged our attention, and was the sole object of our hopes.—
Like children we long for the bauble:—no sooner
have we got it,—but we are tired,—and wish for
another. More pleased with the gratification of our
wayward humours than with the possession of the
thing we wanted, new objects, new pleasures, then
strike our imaginations: these we pursue with the
same earnestness; these we long for with the same

impatience, and possess with the same disappointment and dissatisfaction.

One would be inclined to imagine, that so many
fruitless endeavours and repeated disappointments,
would effectually cure us of indulging our minds in
the fond expectation of future fel city; that we
should at least be prevailed upon to sit down contented in our respective stations, to enjoy the
blessings that are set before us, and to make the
most of that only portion of time which we can
with any certainty call our own: yet such is our
nature, that, notwithstanding the most convincing
demonstrations of the folly of building upon futurity, though we see people unexpectedly sink into
the grave, who were engaged in the same eager
pursuits with ourselves, we still continue to persevere in the delusion.

This disposition of the human mind, to leave
what it has, or the things which are behind, as the
apostle phrases it, to press forward to what is
before, has no doubt its use in the constitution of
man; and was, as every thing else, ordained with
wisdom by the GREAT CREATOR, to lead him on
to further improvement in the search of greater
perfection and happiness. But this, like all our
faculties or dispositions, must be regulated and
guided by reason, to produce the intended effects.
Were this to be the case, he would learn, from
thence, that he is designed for higher improvement
and happiness, and beyond what he can attain to in
this world, and consequently direct his thoughts to,
some future state of being.

Would every man, instead of indulging vain and
uncertain expectations, instead of forming romantic
schemes of visionary happiness, employ his thoughts
and the faculties of his mind in studying how he
may best improve the present hour, he would find

solid advantage resulting from his conduct, and be enabled to cast a retrospective eye upon past life, with pleasure and self-approbation.

Happiness, as much as our nature can admit of, is in every man's power to obtain : it does not require a great genius, or eminent abilities, to render life agreeable; on the contrary, we often see great wits more miserable and unhappy than even those of meaner abilities. This must be ascribed as well to their negligence of, and inattention to, the duties of religion and christianity, as to the volatility of their dispositions, and uncommon vigour of imagination, which makes them constantly languish after novelties, and as constantly leave their wishes unsatisfied and disappointed. But it is our interest, as well as our duty, to seize on the present opportunity of improving our time to the best advantage, while it is yet in our power, considering that it flies from us every moment, and is never to return for a second trial of our obedience. When we stand on the brink of the grave, we see things as they really are, without any mask of colouring. At that awful period, power will have lost its strength to protect, —riches their value to relieve,—knowledge its voice to instruct,—pleasures their charms to allure ; so that the power which was not before exerted to defend the helpless, the wealth which never fed the poor, the knowledge which never persuaded to virtue, and the time spent in vicious pleasures, were most wretchedly employed, and, at the gloomy hour of death, can neither give hope, peace, nor comfort. How sweet, on the other hand, the reflections of those whose time has been employed to good purposes, according to their capacities and stations in the world ! How happy are the prospects of the great, whose power defended the oppressed ;—of the rich, whose wealth relieved the indigent, and raised merit from distress ;—of the learned, whose knowledge diffused a love of virtue and piety ; and of every person who did all the good, and prevented all the evil, in their power! Their time and their talents were wisely employed, and the reflection on it will give them pleasure at that awful period, and their *Hopes* will ascend to a happy immortality beyond the grave.

This mode of cultivating the reasoning faculties in composition should, in the first instance, commence with simple stories, progressively unfolding fresh beauties, like the flower in the bud, opening more and more to the view until the full blown flower appears. In this manner the parent or teacher must lead children on, constantly furnishing them with hints to awaken the understanding, and by interrogatories lead them on from simple narrative to the most sublime and dignified moral subjects. The example here given is designed for the concluding part of this section—they may commence with the following story :—

Ex. VIII. *The two Bees.*

Two bees went to gather honey, one wise, the other careless,—arriving at an extensive garden, the wise bee feasted on delicious flowers, and gained a profusion of honey for his hive,—while the careless bee seeing a bottle full of honey, rushed headlong into it, and becoming intoxicated with sensual pleasures, lost his life.

Ex. IX. *Enlarged.*

On a fine morning in summer, two bees set forth in quest of honey ; the one wise and temperate, the other careless and extravagant. They soon arrived at an extensive garden enriched with aromatic herbs, the most fragrant flowers, and delicious fruits. Here they found a phial filled with honey, into which the thoughtless epicure plunged headlong with a view to indulge himself in all the pleasures of sensuality. After the wise bee had regaled himself on the riches and bounties of Providence, and gained a profusion of honey for his hive, he called upon his friend to return; but found him so intoxicated with pleasures, and so unable to extricate himself from the bottle, that his life was sacrificed to his imprudence.

Ex. X. *The same story further extended and concluded.*

On a fine morning in summer, two bees set forth in quest of honey; the one wise and temperate, the other careless and extravagant. They soon arrived at an extensive garden enriched with a profusion of aromatic herbs, the most fragrant flowers, and delicious fruits. They regaled themselves for a time on the various dainties that were spread before them, the one loading his thigh at intervals with provisions for the hive against the distant winter; the other revelling in sweets without regard to any thing but his present gratification. At length they found a wide-mouthed phial, suspended to a peach-tree, filled with honey and exposed to their taste in the most alluring manner. The thoughtless epicure, regardless of all his friend's remonstrances, plunged headlong into the phial, resolving to indulge himself in all the pleasures of sensuality. The philosopher on the other hand, sipped a little with caution: but, being suspicious of danger, flew off to fruits and flowers; where, by the moderation of his meals, he improved his relish for the true enjoyment of them. In the evening he called upon his friend, to inquire whether he would return to the hive; but found him surfeited in sweets, which he was as unable to leave, as to enjoy. Clogged in his wings, enfeebled in his feet, and his whole frame totally enervated, he was just able to bid his friend adieu, and to lament with his latest breath, that, though a taste of pleasure may quicken the relish of life, an unrestrained indulgence is inevitable destruction.

§ 2. OF THEMES.

A theme is a short dissertation on any general head or subject; in which the reasoning powers of children are brought into action, their judgment formed, and their taste for composition discovered, from the manner they are led to prove the truth of the Theme; that is, by a close and demonstrative mode of reasoning agreeable to the following rules :—

I. The PROPOSITION, in which the truth of the theme is affirmed.

II. The REASON, where the pupil produces arguments to prove the truth of the proposition.

III. The CONFIRMATION; here he establishes the truth of the former by additional proofs.

IV. The COMPARISON, or SIMILE, in which he evinces the truth of the proposition, by its resemblance to something in nature or art.

V. The EXAMPLE, here instances are produced from history by way of application to confirm the truth of the proposition.

VI. The TESTIMONY, or QUOTATION, where some passage is brought forward from other authors in evidence or illustration of what has been already produced.

VII. And *lastly*, the CONCLUSION, where he sums up the whole, and proves the practical use of the theme.

Ex.   *On filial duty and affection.*

I. Proposition.   Honour thy father and thy mother, is an express commandment; and the only one to which a promise is annexed.

II. Reason.   Nothing can be more just or reasonable than that we should love, honour, and succour those who are the very authors of our being, and to whose tender cares, under heaven, we owe the continuance of it during the helpless state of infancy.

III. Confirmation.   If the kindness of the parent be not such as to work upon the affections of the child, yet still the parent has a title to respect and obedience, on the principle of duty; a principle which the voice of nature dictates; which reason inculcates; which human laws, and human customs all join to enforce; and which the word of GOD strictly commands.

IV. Comparison or *Simile.*   It is reported of storks that they live to an advanced age, or if we may use the expression " to second childhood;" during that period they are attended and carefully supported by their young, who supply them with food, carry them from place to place, and cover them with their wings to keep them warm;—thus returning, as much as lies in their power, the care which was bestowed on them in their helpless state. A striking example of filial piety inspired by instinct; which reason itself need not be ashamed to imitate.

V. Example.   Among the Israelites, the slightest offence against a parent was punished in the most exemplary manner.

VI. Testimony, or *Quotation.*   " Honour thy father and thy mother, as the Lord thy GOD hath commanded thee; that thy days may be prolonged, and that it may go well with thee." Deut. v. 16. Ex. xx. 12. Matt. xv. 4. Ephes. vi. 2.

" Have I no tears for thee, my father?
Can I forget thy cares, from helpless years,
Thy tenderness for me? An eye still beam'd
With love! A brow that never knew a frown!
Nor a harsh word thy tongue! Shall I for these
Repay thy stooping venerable age
With shame, disquiet, anguish, and dishonour?
It must not be!—Thou first of angels! come,
Sweet filial Piety! and firm my breast;
Yes, let one daughter to her fate submit,
Be nobly wretched, but her father happy."

VII. *Conclusion.* Love, charity, and an intercourse of good offices, are what, undoubtedly, we owe to mankind: and he who omits them is guilty of such a crime as generally carries its punishment with it;—but to our parents much more than all this is due; and when we are serving them we ought to reflect, that whatever difficulties we go through for their sakes, we cannot do more for them than they have done for us; and that there is no danger of overpaying the vast debt of gratitude they have laid us under.

In fine, we should consider that it is a duty most peculiarly insisted on by Heaven itself; and, if we obey the command, there is no doubt but we shall also receive the reward annexed to it.

§ 3.   OF REGULAR SUBJECTS.

In accustoming young persons to write on any subject, the parent or teacher should question them on such points of the discourse proposed for their consideration as will furnish them with a general view of the whole, and lead them on, step by step, from one part to another, till they perfectly comprehend it, and are enabled to write on any subject, similar to the following form.

I. The DEFINITION, or explanatory introduction.

II. The CAUSE, motive, or reason of the discourse.

III. The ANTIQUITY, or NOVELTY of the subject.

IV. The UNIVERSALITY, or LOCALITY, of the point discussed.

V. And *lastly*, the CONCLUSION, in which the advantage or disadvantage of the whole should be clearly proved.

Ex. *On the importance of daily studying the Bible.*

I. DEFINITION. The word BIBLE means *book*, and the Holy Scripture is so called because it is the BOOK of *books*—the best book. The word SCRIPTURE signifies *writings*. The Bible is divided into two Testaments or Covenants—the old and the new. As a *Testament*, the Bible is the will of our gracious REDEEMER, full of noble gifts and legacies, confirmed to us by the death of the Testator. As a *Covenant* or agreement between GOD and *Man*, the old covenant, *the Law*, is holy, just, and good, and the new covenant, *the Gospel*, is full of grace and truth, "the power of GOD unto salvation to every one that believeth."

II. CAUSE, *a motive for studying the* BIBLE.— The Bible, with the help of the Holy Spirit, affords a sure direction to GOD, to heaven, to everlasting bliss; "the testimony of the LORD is sure, making wise the simple." By means of the Bible GOD himself condescends to "direct your paths." In all important points it is so plain "that he who runs may read." Read your Bible, therefore, with a heart devoted to GOD; have a fixed determination to give up every thing the Bible condemns, and to do the whole will of GOD. Keep in mind our Lord's direction, and depend upon His promise. " If any man will do His will, he shall know of the doctrine, whether it be of GOD."

III. ANTIQUITY. The first five books of the OLD TESTAMENT, were written by Moses, more than 3,000 years ago, and are the most ancient writings in the world.

IV. UNIVERSALITY. It is expressly declared that " they shall teach no more every man his neighbour, and every man his brother, saying, Know the LORD; for they shall all know Me, from the least of them unto the greatest of them, saith the Lord."

It is observable, that in all ages and in every country, where the word of GOD hath been revealed, however various and opposite in their characters, inclinations, and manners, the people were, yet, all have united in one essential point; namely, that the Bible is not only true, but that it contains a revelation to man of the mind and will of GOD.

LOCALITY. By the blessing of GOD, and the operation of the Holy Spirit upon the people of the British empire, since the year 1804, through the instrumentality of the British and Foreign Bible Society, that Divine Book hath been printed in one hundred and twenty-six languages or dialects, and 426,320 Bibles, with 393,000 Testaments have been circulated in various parts of Europe, Asia, Africa, and America: proving this grand truth, that " Christ came to be a light to lighten the Gentiles, and the glory of His people Israel."

V. ADVANTAGE. The grand secret in the study of the Scripture, is therein to discover Him, who is the way, the truth, and the life. " The light of the knowledge of the glory of GOD will then shine

into your heart, in the face of JESUS CHRIST."
Read the Bible with a view to guide you to the
knowledge of Him. " The knowledge of CHRIST,"
says Cecil, " is a wonderful mystery. To understand and enter into His various offices and characters, the glories of His person and work—His
relation to us, and ours to Him, and to GOD the
Father and the Spirit through Him—this is the
knowledge of CHRIST. To know JESUS CHRIST
for ourselves is to make Him our consolation, delight, strength, righteousness, companion, and end."
" Let this also," says Archbishop Leighton, " com-
mend the Scriptures much to our diligence and
affection, that their great theme is our REDEEMER,
and Salvation wrought by Him—that they contain
the display of His excellencies, and are the lively
picture of His matchless beauty. Were we more
engaged in reading them, we should daily see more
of Him in them, and so of necessity love Him more.
But we must look into them carefully: the letter is
but the case; the spiritual sense is what we should
desire to see. If we dig deep into these golden
mines, we shall find treasures of comfort that cannot
be spent, a fountain of mercies that cannot be
exhausted. STUDY THE BIBLE, it will illuminate
your mind; its precepts will guide you through
every difficulty; its doctrines will support you
under every trial; its promises will console you in
many sorrows, and will enable you even " to pass
through the valley of the shadow of death, and fear
no evil."

§ 4. OF ORATIONS.

On whatever subject any one intends to discourse,
he will most commonly begin with some introduction, in order to prepare the minds of his hearers;
then state his subject, and explain the facts con-

nected with it; he will employ arguments for establishing his own opinion, and overthrowing that of his antagonist: he may, perhaps, if there be room for it, endeavour to touch the passions of his audience; and after having said all he thinks proper, will bring his discourse to a close, by some peroration or conclusion.

This being the natural train of speaking, the parts that compose the regular formal ORATION, are the six following:

I. The EXORDIUM, or INTRODUCTION.

II. The STATEMENT and the division of the subject.

III. The NARRATION, or EXPLICATION.

IV. The REASONING, or ARGUMENTS.

V. The PATHETIC parts;

VI. And LASTLY, the CONCLUSION.

The exordium, or introduction, is manifestly common to all kinds of public speaking. It is not a rhetorical invention. It is founded upon nature and suggested by common sense.

I. The introduction should be easy and natural; correct expressions and a modest deportment are always favourable and prepossessing.

II. After the introduction, comes the proposition or enunciation of the subject; this should be as clear and distinct as possible, and expressed in a few plain words, without the least affectation.

To this, generally, succeeds the division, or the laying down the method of the discourse. In a sermon, a pleading, or any discourse where division is proper to be used, the most material rules are,

1st. That the several parts into which the subject is divided, be really distinct from one another; that is, that no one mingle with another.

2dly. We must take care to follow the order of nature, and divide the subject into those parts into which it is most easily and naturally resolved.

3dly. The several members of a division ought to exhaust the subject ; otherwise, we do not make a complete division.

4thly. The terms in which our partitions are expressed, should be as concise as possible ; precision is to be studied, above all things, in laying down your method.

And 5thly. Avoid an unnecessary multiplication of heads.

III. The next constituent part of a discourse, is the narration or explication : to be clear and distinct, to be probable, and to be concise, are the qualities which critics chiefly require in narration ; each of which carries, sufficiently, the evidence of its importance.

IV. The argumentative or reasoning part of a discourse, is of vast importance ; because the great end for which men speak on any serious occasion, is to convince their hearers of something being either true, or right, or good ; and, by means of this conviction, to influence their practice. Reason and argument are the foundation of all manly and persuasive eloquence.

In argument we must attend, *first*, to the invention of them ; *2dly*, the proper disposition and arrangement of them ; and *3dly*, the expressing of them in such a style and manner, as to give them their full force.

Two different methods may be used by orators in the conduct of their reasoning ; namely, the *analytic* and the *synthetic*.

The *analytic* is that in which the orator conceals his intention concerning the point he is to prove, till he has gradually brought his hearers to the designed conclusion. But the mode of reasoning most generally used, and most suited to the train of popular speaking, is the *synthetic* ; when the point to be proved is fairly laid down, and one argument after another is made to bear upon it, till the hearers be fully convinced.

V. In the *pathetic* part, the following directions may be found useful :

First, consider carefully, whether the subject admit the pathetic, and render it proper : and if it does, what part of the discourse is the most proper for attempting it.

2dly. Never set apart a head of your discourse in form, for raising any passion ; never give warning that you are about to be pathetic.

3dly. There is a great difference between shewing the hearers that they ought to be moved, and actually moving them ; therefore,

4thly. The only effectual method is, to be moved yourselves. There are a thousand interesting circumstances suggested by real passion, which no art can imitate, and no refinement can supply.

5thly. It is necessary to attend to the proper language of the passions. The internal emotion of the speaker adds pathos to his words, his looks, his gestures, and his whole manner, which exerts a power almost irresistible over those who hear him.

6thly. Avoid interweaving any thing of a foreign nature with the pathetic part of a discourse ; sacrifice all beauties however bright and showy, which would divert the mind from the principal object, and which would amuse the imagination rather than touch the heart.

Lastly, Never attempt prolonging the pathetic too much. Warm emotions are too violent to be lasting. Study the proper time of making a retreat ; of making a transition from the passionate to the calm tone ; in such a manner, however, as to descend without falling, by keeping up the same strain of sentiment that was carried on before, though now expressing it with more moderation.

VI. The *Peroration,* or *Conclusion.* In every

M

discourse, it is a matter of consequence to hit the precise time of concluding so as to bring our subject just to a point; neither ending abruptly and unexpectedly; nor disappointing the expectation of the hearers, when they look for the close; and continuing to hover round and round the conclusion, till they become heartily tired of us. We should endeavour to go off with a good grace; not to end with a languishing and drawling sentence; but to close with dignity and spirit, that we may leave the minds of the hearers warm; and dismiss them with a favourable impression of the subject and of the speaker.

Ex. *On the duty to our teachers and instructors, arising from the great importance of knowledge and religion.*

I. INTRODUCTION. Teachers and instructors include all those who have the care of our education, and of our instruction in religion; whom we are to obey and listen to, with humility and attention, as the means of our advancement in knowledge and religion.

II. PROPOSITION, *or* ENUNCIATION *of the* SUBJECT. The duty which young people owe to their instructors, cannot be shewn better, than in the effect which the instructions they receive produce upon them. They would do well, therefore, to consider the advantages of an early attention to these two things, both of great importance, KNOWLEDGE and RELIGION.

III. NARRATION, or EXPLICATION. The great use of knowledge in all its various branches, is to free the mind from the prejudices of ignorance; and to give it higher, and more enlarged conceptions, than are the mere growth of rude nature. By reading, you add the experience of others to your own; it is the improvement of the mind, that makes the difference between man and man; and gives one man a real superiority over another. The mind must be employed, and what can fill up its vacancies more rationally than the acquisition of knowledge? Let us, therefore, thank GOD for the opportunities He hath afforded us; and not turn into a curse those means of leisure, which might become so great a blessing. Yet, however necessary to us *Knowledge* may be, *Religion* we know is infinitely more so. The one adorns a man, and gives him true superiority and rank in life; but the other is absolutely essential to his eternal happiness.

IV. ARGUMENT. In the midst of youth, health, and abundance, the world is apt to appear a very gay and pleasing scene; it engages our desires; and in a degree satisfies them also. But it is wisdom to consider, that a time will come, when youth, health, and fortune will all fail us; and if disappointment and vexation do not sour our taste for pleasure, at least sickness and infirmity will destroy it. In these gloomy seasons, and above all, at the approach of death, what will become of us without religion? When this world fails, where shall we fly, if we expect no refuge in another? Without holy hope in GOD, and resignation to His will, and trust in Him for deliverance, what is there that can secure us against the evils of life. The great utility therefore of *Knowledge* and *Religion* being thus apparent, it is highly incumbent upon us to pay a studious attention to them in our youth. If we do not, it is more than probable that we shall never do it: that we shall grow old in ignorance, by neglecting the one; and old in vice by neglecting the other.

V. PATHETIC. Youth is the season of warm and generous emotions. The heart should then spontaneously rise into the admiration of what is

great; glow with the love of what is fair and excellent; and melt at the discovery of tenderness
and goodness. Where can any object be found, so
proper to kindle those affections, as the Father of
the universe, and the Author of all felicity! Un-
moved by veneration, can you contemplate that
grandeur and majesty which His works every where
display? Untouched by gratitude, can you view
that profusion of good, which, in this pleasing
season of life, His beneficent hand pours around
you? Happy in the love and affection of those with
whom you are connected, look up to the SUPREME
BEING, as the inspirer of all the friendship which
has ever been shewn you by others; Himself your
best and your first friend; formerly, the supporter
of your infancy, and the guide of your childhood;
now, the guardian of your youth, and the hope of
your coming years. View religious homage as a
natural expression of gratitude to Him for all His
goodness. Consider it as the service of the GOD
of your fathers; of Him to whom your parents
devoted you; of Him whom in former ages your
ancestors honoured; and by whom they are now
rewarded and blessed in heaven. Connected with
so many tender sensibilities of soul, let religion be
with you, not the cold and barren offspring of spe-
culation, but the warm and vigorous dictate of the
heart.

VI. *Conclusion.* Youth bears the same proportion to our more advanced life, as this world bears
to the next. In this life we must form and cultivate
those habits of virtue, which must qualify us for a
better state. In manhood we bear the fruit, which
has in youth been planted. If we have sauntered
away our youth, we must expect to be ignorant
men. If indolence and inattention have taken an
early possession of us, they will probably increase
as we advance in life; and make us a burden to

ourselves, and useless to society. If again, we suffer ourselves to be misled by vicious inclinations, they will daily get new strength, and end in dissolute lives. But if we cultivate our minds in our youth, acquire habits of attention and industry, of virtue and sobriety, we shall find ourselves well prepared to act our future parts in life ; and what above all things ought to be our care, by gaining this command over ourselves, we shall be more able, as we get forward in the world, to resist every new temptation as it arises. Let each of us therefore do his duty in that station which Providence hath assigned; ever remembering, that the next world will soon destroy all earthly distinctions. *One distinction* only will remain among the sons of men at that time—the distinction between good and bad; and this distinction it is worth all our pains and all our ambition to acquire.

§ 5. OF THE GENERAL CHARACTERS OF STYLE OR COMPOSITION.

Of Figures.

Figures, in general, may be described to be that language, which is prompted either by the imagination, or by the passions.

Rhetoricians commonly divide them into two great classes ; *figures of words* and *figures of thought*.

Figures of words are commonly called TROPES. A trope consists in a word's being employed to signify something that is different from its original and primitive meaning, so that if you alter the word, you destroy the figure.

Thus in the following sentence: " Light ariseth to the upright in darkness," the *trope* consists in " light and darkness," being not meant literally, but substituted for *comfort* and *adversity*, on account of some resemblance or analogy which light and darkness are supposed to bear to these conditions of life.

Figures of thought, suppose the words to be used in their proper and literal meaning, and the figure to consist in the turn of the thought. They appear in *exclamations, interrogations, apostrophes,* and *comparisons;* where, though you vary the words that are used, or translate them from one language into another, you may, nevertheless, still preserve the same figure in the thought. These figures may be considered under the following heads :

First. Tropes or figures, enrich language, and render it more copious. By this means, words and phrases are multiplied for expressing all sorts of ideas : for describing even the minutest differences ; the nicest shades and colours of thought ; which no language could possibly do by proper words alone, without assistance from tropes.

Secondly. They bestow dignity upon style. The familiarity of common words, to which our ears are much accustomed, tends to degrade style. When we want to adapt our language to the tone of an elevated subject, we should be greatly at a loss, if we could not borrow assistance from figures ; which properly employed, have a similar effect on language, with what is produced by the rich and splendid dress of a person of rank ; to create respect, and to give an air of magnificence to him who wears it. Assistance of this kind is often needed in prose compositions ; but poetry could not subsist without it. Hence figures form the constant language of poetry.

To say, that " the sun rises," is trite and common, but it becomes a magnificent image when expressed, as Thomson has done : —

" But yonder comes the powerful king of day
Rejoicing in the east."

To say that " All men are subject alike to death."
presents only a simple idea; but it rises and fills
the imagination when painted thus by Horace :—

> " With equal pace impartial fate
> Knocks at the palace, as the cottage gate."

In the *third* place, figures give us the pleasure of
enjoying two objects presented together without
confusion, to our view; the principal idea, that is
the subject of the discourse, along with its accessory, which gives it the figurative dress. We
see one thing in another, as Aristotle expresses it;
which is always agreeable to the mind. For there
is nothing with which the fancy is more delighted,
than with comparisons, and resemblances of objects; and all tropes are founded upon some relation
or analogy between one thing and another.

When, for example, in place of " youth," we
say, the " morning of life," the fancy is immediately
entertained with all the resembling circumstances
which presently occur between these two objects.
At one moment, we have before us a certain period
of human life, and a certain time of the day, so
related to each other, that the imagination plays
between them with pleasure, and contemplates two
similar objects, in one view, without embarrassment
or confusion. Not only so, but,

In the *fourth* place, figures are attended with
this farther advantage, of giving us frequently a much
clearer and more striking view of the principal
object, than we could have if it were expressed in
simple terms, and divested of its accessory ideas.

This is, indeed, their principal advantage; they
exhibit the object on which they are employed in a
picturesque form; they can render an abstract conception in some degree, an object of sense; they
surround it with such circumstances as enable the

mind to lay hold of it steadily, and to contemplate it fully.

This effect of figures is happily touched in the following lines of Dr. Akenside, and illustrated by a very sublime figure :—

> " Then the inexpressive strain
> Diffuses its enchantment. Fancy dreams
> Of sacred fountains and Elysian groves,
> And vales of bliss, the intellectual Power
> Bends from his awful throne a wond'ring ear
> And smiles."——

§ 6. METAPHOR.

Metaphor is a figure founded entirely on the resemblance which one subject bears to another. Thence, it is much allied to simile, or comparison; and is indeed no other than a comparison, expressed in an abridged form.

The following beautiful metaphor fully illustrates this figure; at the conclusion of Lord Boling-broke's remarks on the History of England, speaking of the conduct of Charles I. to his last parliament; he says, " About a month after their meeting, he dissolved them; and, as soon as he had dissolved them, he repented; but he repented too late of his rashness. Well might he repent, for the vessel was now full, and this last drop made the waters of bitterness overflow."

Here, the metaphor is continued through several expressions. The *vessel* is put for the state or temper of the nation already *full,* that is, provoked to the highest by former oppressions and wrongs; this *last drop,* stands for the provocation recently received by the abrupt dissolution of parliament, and the *overflowing of the waters of bitterness,* beautifully expresses all the effects of resentment let loose by an exasperated people.

In the use of metaphors the following rules ought to be attended to.

First, that they are suited to the nature of the subject of which we treat: neither too many, nor too gay, nor too elevated for it; that we neither attempt to force the subject, by means of them, into a degree of elevation which is not congruous to it; nor, on the other hand, allow it to sink below its proper dignity.

One of the greatest secrets in composition is, to know when to be simple. This always gives a heightening to ornament, in its proper place. The right disposition of the shade makes the light and colouring strike the more. " He is truly eloquent who can discourse of humble subjects in a plain style, who can treat important ones with dignity, and speak of things which are of a middle nature, in a temperate strain. For one who, upon no occasion, can express himself in a calm, orderly, distinct manner, when he begins to be on fire before his reade are prepared to kindle along with him, has the ap-pearance of raving like a madman among persons who are in their senses, or of reeling like a drunkard, in the midst of sober company." This admonition should be strictly attended to by young practiti-oners in the art of writing, who are apt to be carried away by an undistinguishing admiration of what is showy and florid, whether in its place or not.

The *second* rule, respects the choice of objects, from whence metaphors, and other figures are to be drawn.

The field for figurative language is very wide. All nature, to speak in the style of figures, opens its stores to us, and admits us to gather, from all sensible objects, whatever can illustrate intellectual or moral ideas. Not only the gay and splendid objects of sense, but the grave, the terrifying and

even the gloomy and dismal, may, on different occasions, be introduced into figures with propriety.

In the *third* place as metaphors should be drawn
from objects of some dignity, so particular care
should be taken that the resemblance, which is the
foundation of the metaphor, be clear and perspicuous, not far-fetched, nor difficult to discover.
Metaphors, like other ornaments, lose their whole
grace, when they do not seem natural and easy.

In the *fourth* place, it must be carefully attended
to, in the conduct of metaphors, never to jumble
metaphorical and plain language together; never to
contrast a period so, that part of it must be understood metaphorically, part literally; this always
produces a disagreeable confusion.

> " Long to my joys my dearest Lord is lost
> His country's buckler, and the Grecian boast;
> Now from my fond embrace by tempests torn,
> Our other column of the state is borne,
> Nor took a kind adieu, nor sought consent."

Here, in one line of the Odyssey, her son is figured
as a column; and in the next, he returns to be a
person, to whom it belongs to take adieu and ask
consent. This is inconsistent.

The works of Ossian abound with beautiful and
correct metaphors; such as that on a *hero:* " In
peace, thou art the gale of spring; in war, the
mountain storm." Or this, on a woman: " She
was covered with the light of beauty; but her heart
was the house of pride."

In the *fifth* place, never make two different metaphors meet on one subject. This is what is
called mixed metaphor, and is indeed one of the
grossest abuses of this figure, such as Shakspeare's
expression, " to take arms against a sea of troubles."
This makes a most unnatural medley, and con-
founds the imagination entirely.

Quinctilian has sufficiently guarded us against it.

" We must be particularly attentive to end with the same kind of metaphor with which we have begun. Some, when they begin the figure with a tempest, conclude it with a conflagration, which forms a shameful inconsistency."

Addison's rule is a good one for examining the propriety of metaphors, when we doubt whether or not they be of the mixed kind: namely, that we should try to form a picture upon them, and consider how the parts would agree, and what sort of figure the whole would present, when delineated with a pencil.

As metaphors ought never to be mixed, so in the *sixth* place, we should avoid crowding them together on the same object. Supposing each of the metaphors to be preserved distinct, yet, if they be heaped on one another, they produce a confusion somewhat of the same kind with the mixed metaphor.

Ex. " There is a time, when factions, by the vehemence of their fermentation, stun, and disable one another."

Here, Lord Bolingbroke represents factions, first as discordant fluids, the mixture of which produces violent fermentation : but he quickly relinquishes this view of them, and imputes to them operations and effects, consequent only on the supposition of their being solid bodies in motion. They maim and dismember one another by forcible collisions.

The only *other rule* concerning metaphors, which we shall add, is, that they be not too far pursued. If the resemblance on which the figure is founded, be long dwelt upon, and carried into all its minute circumstances, we make an allegory instead of a metaphor; we tire the reader, who soon becomes weary of this play of fancy: and we render our discourse obscure. This is called straining a metaphor.

§7.   COMPARISONS OR SIMILIES.

Comparisons or similies differ chiefly from metaphors in the vigour of imagination with which they are conceived.   In the use of *metaphors*, we suppose the primary object transformed into the resembling one.   In the use of *comparisons* we soar not so high, but content ourselves with remarking *similitude* merely.

If, for instance, I discover a resemblance between a man and a horse in swiftness, between a man and an oak in strength, or between a man and a rock in steadiness, such resemblances, being new, and generally unobserved, excite surprise and pleasure, and improve my conceptions of the swiftness, strength, and steadiness of the man.

Hence results the first general principle concerning good comparisons of resemblance; they must be drawn from one species of things to another, and never instituted between things of the same species.

Shakspeare compares " adversity to a toad,— and slander to the bite of a crocodile."

The following comparisons from Ossian are successfully formed.   " Often, like the evening sun, comes the memory of former times on my soul."

" Pleasant are the words of the song, and lovely are the tales of other times.   They are like the dew of the morning on the hill of roses, when the sun is faint on its side, and the lake is settled and blue in the vale."

All comparisons may be reduced to the following heads.

I. Those which improve our conceptions of the objects they are brought to illustrate, we call *explaining comparisons*.

II. Those which augment the pleasure of imagination by a splendid assemblage of other adjacent and agreeable objects,—we call *embellishing comparisons*.

III. And, finally, those which elevate or depress the principal object, an operation often requisite in writing, but more particularly in speaking,—we call *comparisons* of *advantage*, or of *disadvantage*.

All manner of subjects admit of *explaining comparisons*. Let an author be reasoning ever so strictly, or treating the most abstruse point in philosophy, he may very properly introduce a comparison with a view to make his subject better understood.

Of this nature is the following in Harris's Hermes, employed to explain a very abstract point, the distinction between the powers of sense and imagination in the human mind. " As wax," says he, " would not be adequate to the purpose of signature, if it had not the power to retain as well as to receive the impression, the same holds of the soul with respect to sense and imagination. Sense is its receptive power; imagination its retentive. Had it sense without imagination, it would not be as wax, but as water, where though all impressions be instantly made, yet as soon as they are made they are instantly lost."

The most vigorous imagination can scarcely be supposed to have conceived more striking comparisons, or better adapted to improve our conceptions of the principal object, than the following ones of Shakspeare. Describing the effects of concealed love, he makes this happy comparison :

" She never told her love,
But let concealment, like a worm in the bud,
Feed on her damask cheek. She pin'd in thought,
And with a green and yellow melancholy,
She sat, like patience on a monument,
Smiling at grief."

Embellishing comparisons, are introduced not so much with a view to inform and instruct, as to adorn the subject of which we treat.

To describe the nature of soft and melancholy music, Ossian says, " The music of Carryl was, like the memory of joys that are past, pleasant and mournful to the soul.

The *third* sort of *comparisons* are employed to elevate or depress the principal object.

The following example must aggrandize our conceptions of the valour of Hector, however great we can suppose it to have been in reality.

> " Girt in surrounding flames, he seems to fall
> Like fire from Jove, and bursts upon them all;
> Bursts as a wave, that from the clouds impends,
> And swell'd with tempest o'er the ship descends.
> White are the decks with foam; the winds aloud
> Howl o'er the masts, and ring through every shroud.
> Pale, trembling, tired, the sailors freeze with fears,
> And instant death in every wave appears,
> So pale the Greeks the eyes of Hector meet,
> The chief so thunders, and so shakes the fleet."

§ 8. PERSONIFICATION.

Personification, or *Prosopopeia,* is a figure which consists in ascribing life and action to inanimate objects. It has its origin in the influence that imagination and passion have upon our perceptions and opinions.

Antony in Shakspeare, thus addresses the dead body of Cæsar:

> " O pardon me, thou bleeding piece of earth."

Not only the inanimate parts of nature are personified, but the qualities and members of the body; even abstract ideas have some times conferred upon them the same important prerogative.

Thus, hope and fear, love and hatred, the head,

the hands, the feet, prosperity and adversity, are often addressed as independent living agents.

Personification may be divided into two classes; the *first* called *descriptive*, which is addressed chiefly to the imagination; the *second*, *passionate*, the object of which is to afford gratification to the passions.

A descriptive personification is derived from the disposition of the imagination to indulge in such views of nature and art, as tend most to gratify itself; so life and motion are capital sources of pleasure, in the contemplation of the objects with which we are surrounded.

Strip the Seasons of Thomson, and the Georgics of Virgil, of this sprightly ornament, and you will reduce the two most beautiful didactic poems the world ever saw, to dry, uninteresting, uninstructive details of natural history.

Passionate personification results from the momentary conviction which the violence of passion is qualified to inspire, —that the inanimate objects which engage its attention are endowed with sensibility and intelligence.

Fear prompts this figure; Milton, speaking of the eating of the forbidden fruit, thus sings:

" Earth trembled from her entrails, as again
In pangs, and nature gave a second groan :
Sky low'r'd, and, muttering thunder, some sad drops
Wept, at completing of the mortal sin."

§ 9. ALLEGORY.

Allegory is a species of writing, in which one thing is expressed, and another thing is understood. They are employed chiefly when a writer desires to communicate some important intelligence or advice, but is not permitted to deliver it in plain terms. It is also used for ornament, or to convey instruction so as to interest the imagination, and flatter the understanding, by giving the reader the appearance of instructing himself.

A finer and more correct allegory is not to be found than in the 80th Psalm, 6 to 16 verses, where a vineyard is made to represent GOD's people the Jews.

Allegories may be divided into three kinds; *first*, those calculated for ornament: *secondly*, those designed for instruction; and *thirdly*, those intended both to adorn and instruct.

Akenside employs a beautiful allegory, of the ornamental kind, to communicate a very familiar sentiment, that industry is necessary to acquire reputation in every line of life, though some men are more susceptible of culture than others.

> " In vain,
> Without fair Culture's kind paternal aid,
> Without enliv'ning suns and genial show'rs,
> And shelter from the blast,—in vain we hope
> The tender plant should raise its blooming head,
> Or yield the harvest promis'd in its spring.
> Nor yet will every soil with equal stores
> Repay the tiller's labour, or attend
> His will obsequious, whether to produce
> The olive or the laurel."

The principal purpose of the *second* sort of allegories, is to communicate instruction.

The *third* sort of allegories are calculated both for ornament and instruction; and of this species may be accounted the allegorical personifications which are often introduced into epic poetry, and sometimes into tragedy.

No picture can more forcibly impress the imagination, no reasoning can so effectually excite the aversion of the heart, as the allegories of *Sin* and *Death*, in Paradise Lost. The poet paints, first Sin, and then Death, guarding the gates of hell at the FALL of Adam and Eve.

"Before the gates there sat,
On either side, a formidable shape.
The one seem'd woman to the waist, and fair,
But ended foul in many a scaly fold,
Voluminous and vast, a serpent arm'd
With mortal sting; about her middle round
A cry of hell-hounds, never ceasing bark'd
With wide Cerberean mouths, full loud, and rung
A hideous peal; yet when they list would creep,
If aught disturb'd their noise, into her womb,
And kennel there; yet there still bark'd and howl'd
Within, unseen."

"The other shape,
If shape it might be call'd that shape had none,
Or substance might be call'd that shadow seem'd,
For each seem'd either; black it stood as night,
Fierce as ten furies, terrible as hell,
And shook a dreadful dart; what seem'd his head
The likeness of a kingly crown had on."

The following picture of Slander, drawn by Shakspeare, has much allegorical merit.

"No, 'tis Slander,
Whose edge is sharper than the sword, whose tongue
Outvenoms all the worms of Nile, whose breath
Rides on the posting winds, and doth belie
All corners of the world, kings, queens, and states,
Maids, matrons, nay, the secrets of the grave."

§ 10. APOSTROPHE.

Apostrophe is a turning off from the regular course of the subject, to address some person or thing.

Apostophes are divided into two classes; the *first* are of considerable length, in which the pleasure of the imagination is consulted: and *secondly*, short ones expressive of the violence of passion.

Ossian gives us many examples of the first class. His address to the moon, is one of the most pleasant pictures of this sort, which, perhaps, any language can supply.

"Daughter of Heaven, fair art thou! the silence

of thy face is pleasant : thou comest forth in love-
liness ; the stars attend thy blue steps in the east.
The clouds rejoice in thy presence, O Moon ! and
brighten their dark-brown sides. Who is like thee
in heaven, daughter of the night ? The stars are
ashamed in thy presence, and turn aside their
sparkling eyes. Whither dost thou retire from
thy course, when the darkness of thy countenance
grows ? Hast thou thy hall like Ossian ? Dwellest
thou in the shadow of grief ? Have thy sisters
fallen from heaven ? and are they who rejoiced with
thee at night no more ?—Yes, they have fallen, fair
light ! and often dost thou retire to mourn.—But
thou thyself shall one night fail, and leave thy blue
path in heaven. The stars will then lift their heads;
they who in thy presence were astonished will
rejoice."

The apostrophes of the second class are the
offspring of deep agitation : and the subsequent
example will illustrate the nature of their influence
and operation. In the tragedy of Douglas, Lady
Randolph thus accounts for the loss of her son :

" That very night in which my son was born,
My nurse, the only confidant I had,
Set out with him to reach her sister's house ;
But nurse nor infant have I ever seen,
Nor heard of Anna, since that fatal hour.
My murder'd child ! had thy fond mother fear'd
The loss of thee, she had loud fame defied,
Despised her father's rage, her father's grief,
And wander'd with thee through the scorning world."

§ 11. HYPERBOLE.

Hyperbole is also the offspring of the influence
of imagination and passion over our opinions, and
its purpose is to exalt our conceptions of an object
beyond its natural bounds.

All discourse and writing admit hyperbole. Though the offspring of the most violent passion, it is also consistent with composure of mind. It sometimes affords high enjoyments to the imagination, and indulges this faculty with the most magnificent exhibitions of nature and art. It shines, however, with most conspicuous lustre in the higher kinds of poetry and oratory. It appears chiefly in tragedy during the first transports of passion; and in all these cases, it may be employed to diminish as well as to magnify.

The fear of an enemy augments the conceptions of the size and prowess of their leader. As in the following example from Ossian:

" I saw their chief, tall as a rock of ice; his spear, the blasted fir; his shield, the rising moon; he sat on the shore, like a cloud of mist on the hill."

§ 12. CLIMAX OR AMPLIFICATION.

Climax, or Amplification, is nearly related to hyperbole, and differs from it chiefly in degree. The purpose of *hyperbole* is to exalt our conceptions beyond the truth; of *climax*, to elevate our ideas of the truth itself, by a series of circumstances, ascending one above another in respect of importance, and all pointing toward the same object.

The effect of this figure is peculiarly pleasant, when the gradation of the sentiment is denoted by members, which rise with an analogous swell in point of sound; as in the following example:

" Hear and learn to be silent; be silent and learn to understand; understand and learn to remember; remember and learn to act accordingly."

§ 13. ANTITHESIS.

As the design of a climax is to improve our conceptions of an object, by placing it at the head of a rising series; so the business of *Antithesis* is to produce a similar effect, by placing one object in opposition to another of the same kind.

The same rule must be observed in the use of antithesis which was found necessary in good comparisons resulting from contrast. They must take place between things of the same species. Substantives, attributes, qualities, faculties of the same kind must be set in opposition. To constitute an antithesis between a man and a lion, virtue and hunger, a figure and a colour, would be to form a contrast where there was no opposition. But to contrast one man with another, virtues with virtues, figures with figures, is pertinent and proper, because in these cases there may be striking opposition.

Lord Bolingbroke furnishes the following beautiful example : " If Cato may be censured, severely indeed, but justly, for abandoning the cause of liberty, which he would not, however, survive ; what shall we say of those, who embrace it faintly, pursue it irresolutely, grow tired of it when they have much to hope, and give it up when they have nothing to fear."

The beauty of genuine antithesis is so considerable, that we cannot wonder that many unsuccessful attempts have been made to acquire it.

A climax and antithesis are sometimes conjoined and carried on through several sentences.

Thus Pope, in the Essay on Man :

" Pride still is aiming at the blest abodes,
    MEN would be ANGELS,—ANGELS would be gods ;
    Aspiring to be GODS,—if ANGELS fell,
    Aspiring to be ANGELS,—MEN rebel.

§ 19. INTERROGATION, REPETITION, EXCLAMATION, IRONY AND VISION.

Interrogation. The unfeigned and literal use of interrogation is to ask a question; but when men are strongly moved, whatever they would affirm or deny, with great earnestness, they naturally put in the form of a question. The strongest confidence is thereby expressed of their own sentiment, by appealing to their hearers for the impossibility of the contrary.

Thus Balaam expressed himself to Balak: "The Lord is not a man that he should lie, neither the son of man that he should repent. Hath he said it? and shall he not do it? Hath he spoken it? and shall he not make it good?"

Repetition seizes some emphatical word or phrase, and to mark its importance, makes it recur frequently in the same sentence. It is significant of contrast and energy.

Dryden gives a most beautiful example of this figure, in Alexander's Feast; where he paints the sad reverse of fortune suffered by Darius in the following manner,

> " Deserted, at his greatest need,
>   By those his former bounty fed,
> He sung Darius, great and good,
>   By too severe a fate,
> Fallen, fallen, fallen, fallen,
> Fallen from his high estate, and welt'ring in his blood."

Exclamations are the effect of strong emotions of the mind; such as surprise, admiration, joy, grief.

I shall take the liberty to give an example, which is known to all, and well calculated to illustrate the figure now under consideration. "Turn with me, reader, turn thy mind back to the morning on which we heard it announced that her Royal Highness

Princess Charlotte of Saxe Coburg was no more! Have ye heard the news? said every Briton to his friend. News? what news? The Princess Charlotte's dead! Dead! the Princess Charlotte dead! did ye say? Yes! and her infant son too!! Good God! both mother and son! Such was the language of our heart, such the species of interrogation, repetition and exclamation which we used that doleful morn.

Vision, another figure of speech, proper only in animated and warm compositions, is produced, when, instead of relating something that is past, we use the present tense of the verb, and describe an action or event as actually passing before our eyes.

Thus Cicero, in his fourth oration against Cati line, pictures to his mind the execution of the conspiracy: " I seem to myself to behold this city, the ornament of the earth, and the capital of all nations, suddenly involved in one conflagration. I see before me the slaughtered heaps of citizens, lying unburied in the midst of their ruined country. The furious countenance of Cethegus rises to my view, while with a savage joy, he is triumphing in your miseries."

Irony. When we express ourselves in a manner contrary to our thoughts, not with a view to deceive, but to add force to our observations, we are then said to speak ironically.

The subjects of irony, are vices and follies of all kinds; and this mode of exposing them is often more effectual than serious reasoning.

Elijah used this figure when he challenged the priests of Baal to prove the truth of their deity. " Cry aloud, for he is a god: either he is talking, or he is pursuing, or he is in a journey, or peradventure he sleepeth, and must be awaked."

Exclamations and *irony* are sometimes united;

as in Cicero's oration for Balbus, where the orator derides his accuser, by saying, " O excellent interpreter of the law! master of antiquity! correcter and amender of our constitution."

Remember that the first law of good writing, is to attend principally and closely to the matter; and that even the highest ornament is of much inferior consideration.

§ 15. OF THE GENERAL CHARACTERS OF STYLE.

Words being the copies of our ideas there must always be a very intimate connexion between the manner in which we employ words, and our manner of thinking. From the peculiarity of thought and expression which belongs to every writer, there is a certain character imprinted on his style.

One of the first and most obvious distinctions of the different kinds of style, is what arises from an author's spreading out his thoughts more or less. This distinction forms, what are called the diffuse and the concise styles.

A CONCISE writer compresses his thoughts into the fewest possible words; he seeks to employ none but such as are most expressive.

A DIFFUSE writer unfolds his thought fully. He places it in a variety of lights, and gives the reader every possible assistance for understanding it completely.

The style of different authors seems to rise in the following gradation; a *dry*, a *plain*, a *neat*, an *elegant*, and a *flowing* manner.

Aristotle is the most complete example of a *dry style*. Never perhaps, was there any author who adhered so rigidly to the strictness of a didactic manner throughout all his writings, and conveyed so much instruction, without the least approach to ornament.

A PLAIN STYLE rises one degree above a dry style; a writer of this character employs very little ornament of any kind, and rests almost entirely upon his sense.

A NEAT STYLE comes next in order; and here we have arrived in the region of ornament; but that ornament not of the highest or most sparkling kind.

This style may be attained by a writer who has no great powers of fancy or genius: merely by industry, and careful attention to the rules of writing, and it is a style always agreeable.

It imprints a character of moderate elevation on our composition, and carries a decent degree of ornament, which is not unsuitable to any subject whatever.

A familiar letter, or a law paper, or the driest subject may be written with neatness; and a sermon, or a philosophical treatise, in a neat style, will be read with pleasure.

An ELEGANT STYLE is a character expressing a higher degree of ornament than a neat one; and, indeed is the term usually applied to style, when possessing all the virtues of ornament, without any of its excesses or defects.

When the ornaments, applied to a style, are too rich and gaudy in proportion to the subject; when they return upon us too fast, and strike us either with a dazzling lustre, or a false brilliancy, this forms what is called a FLORID STYLE; a term commonly used to signify the excess of ornament.

§ 16. DIRECTIONS FOR FORMING STYLE.

The *first* thing to be attended to, is, to study clear ideas on the subject concerning which you are to write or speak. This is a direction which may at first appear to have small relation to style. Its relation to it, however, is extremely close. The foundation of all good style, is good sense, accompanied with a lively imagination.

In the *second* place, in order to form a good style, the frequent practice of composing is indispensably necessary. By hasty and careless composition, we shall certainly acquire a very bad style; we ought, therefore to write slowly and with great care. " I enjoin," says Quinctilian, " that such as are beginning the practice of composition, write slowly, and with anxious deliberation. Their great object at first should be, to write as well as possible; practice will enable them to write speedily. By degrees, matter will offer itself still more readily; words will be at hand; composition will flow; every thing, as in the arrangement of a well-ordered family, will present itself in its proper place. The sum of the whole is this: by hasty composition, we shall never acquire the art of composing well; by writing well, we shall come to write speedily."

In the *third* place, with respect to the assistance that is to be gained from the writings of others, it is obvious, that we ought to render ourselves well acquainted with the style of the best authors. This is requisite, both in order to form a just taste in style, and to supply us with a full stock of words on every subject.

In the *fourth* place, guard yourself, at the same time, against a servile imitation of any author whatever. This is always dangerous. It hampers genius; it is likely to produce a stiff manner; and those who are given to close imitation, generally imitate an author's faults, as well as his beauties. No man will ever become a good writer or speaker, who has not some degree of confidence to follow his own genius.

In the *last* place, carry along with you this admonition, that, in any case, and on any occasion, attention to style must not engross you so much, as to detract from a higher degree of attention to the thoughts; " to your expression be attentive; but about your matter be solicitous."

THE END.

INDEX.

FINIS.

ERRATA.

Page Line
   5.   5. from bottom, *for* maaner *read* manner.
  26.   3. from bottom, *for* triangles *read* triangle.
  96. last, *for* oaded *read* loaded.
 118. 17. *for* comforts *read* comfort.
 128.   6. omit the word *the* at the end of the line.
 175.   4. from bottom, omit R. xxx.
 185. 1, 2. *for* objective case governed by the verb serve,
            R. xx. *read* nominative case R. xxvi.
 187.   5. from bottom *for* has *read* hath.
 196. Ex. 52. last line, after the word case *read* in earnest.
 197. Ex. 54. line 8, after and *read* with common.
 214.   3. *for* he *read* he.

LONDON:
PRINTED BY WILLIAM CLOWES,
Northumberland-court.

THE

YOUTH'S MEMORITER,

AND

ENGLISH EXERCISE BOOK,

IN TWO PARTS;

CONTAINING A RATIONAL

GRAMMAR OF THE ENGLISH LANGUAGE,

IN WHICH CASES, MOODS, COMPOUND TENSES, AND THE NUMBERS
AND PERSONS OF OUR VERBS HAVE BEEN RÉJECTED;

A VERBAL ANALYSIS,

OR A METHOD OF ACQUIRING THE SIGNIFICATIONS OF WORDS BY
A KNOWLEDGE OF THEIR COMPONENT
PARTS OR ELEMENTS;

AND

ORTHOGRAPHICAL EXERCISES,

UPON A PLAN ENTIRELY NEW,

COMPRISING IN ONE VOLUME ALL THAT IS NECESSARY FOR AN ENGLISH
SCHOLAR TO COMMIT TO MEMORY,
AND ALL THE EXERCISES USUALLY PUT INTO HIS HANDS.

Intended for the Use of Schools and private Tuition.

BY HENRY YOUNG.

LONDON:

WHITTAKER, TREACHER, AND CO. AVE-MARIA-LANE.

TO BE HAD OF ALL BOOKSELLERS.

1832.